INTERRUPTING DERRIDA

Whether he is elucidating tricky passages in Derrida's texts, confronting large issues such as the relation of deconstruction to politics and ethics, or gently correcting the misreadings of other commentators, Geoffrey Bennington is always a highly reliable and often an extremely entertaining guide. There are few readers of Derrida who achieve such fidelity to the windings of his thought.

Derek Attridge, University of York

Jacques Derrida's work continues to attract heated commentary and debate among philosophers, literary critics, social and cultural theorists, architects and artists. *Interrupting Derrida*, a major new book by Geoffrey Bennington, renowned Derrida scholar and translator of Derrida's work, presents incisive new readings of both Derrida and interpretations of Derrida's work.

Part I lays out Derrida's work as a whole, and examines its relevance to, and 'interruption' of, the traditional domains of ethics, politics and literature. The second part of the book provides compelling insights into some important motifs in Derrida's work, such as death, friendship, psychoanalysis, time and endings. The final section presents some trenchant appraisals of other influential accounts of Derrida's work.

Throughout, *Interrupting Derrida* is marked by a commitment to clarity and accuracy, but also by a refusal to simplify Derrida's often difficult thought.

Interrupting Derrida will be of great interest to all readers of Derrida, continental philosophy, and literary and cultural theory.

Geoffrey Bennington is Professor of French at the University of Sussex. His previous publications include *Legislations: The Politics of Deconstruction* and *Jacques Derrida*.

WARWICK STUDIES IN EUROPEAN PHILOSOPHY

Edited by Andrew Benjamin

Professor of Philosophy, University of Warwick

This series presents the best and most original work being done within the European philosophical tradition. The books included in the series seek not merely to reflect what is taking place within European philosophy but also to contribute to the growth and development of that plural tradition. Works written in the English language as well as translations into English are included, engaging the tradition at all levels – whether by introductions that show the contemporary philosophical force of certain works, collections that explore an important thinker or topic, or significant contributions that call for their own critical evaluations.

Also available:

INTERRUPTING
DERRIDA

Geoffrey Bennington

London and New York

First published 2000
by Routledge
11 New Fetter Lane, London EC4P 4EE

Simultaneously published in the USA and Canada
by Routledge
29 West 35th Street, New York, NY 10001

Routledge is an imprint of the Taylor & Francis Group

© 2000 Geoffrey Bennington

Typeset in Perpetua by Taylor & Francis Books Ltd
Printed and bound in Great Britain by Clays Ltd, St Ives plc

British Library Cataloguing in Publication Data
A catalogue record for this book is available from the British Library

Library of Congress Cataloging in Publication Data
Bennington, Geoffrey.
Interrupting Derrida / Geoffrey Bennington.
p. cm. – (Warwick studies in European philosophy)
Includes bibliographical references and index.
1. Derrida, Jacques. I. Title. II. Series.
B2430.D484 B457 2000
194–dc21   99–056919

ISBN 0–415–22426–8 (hbk)
ISBN 0–415–22427–6 (pbk)

FOR ALICE

CONTENTS

ACKNOWLEDGEMENTS

Several chapters of this book have been published elsewhere: details are given in the first footnote to each chapter. Acknowledgements are due to the following: Blackwell Publishers for Chapter 1; Cambridge University Press for Chapter 2; Macmillan for Chapters 3 and 6; Exeter University Press for Chapter 4; Stanford University Press for Chapter 5; *Imprimatur* for Chapter 11; and *The Oxford Literary Review* for Chapter 12.

Colleagues and friends too numerous to mention have helped me in many ways in the completion of this book. My thanks go especially to a succession of graduate students at the University of Sussex with whom I have developed and refined many of the points that appear in these essays. Special thanks to Benjamin Roberts for his invaluable bibliographical assistance in the preparation of the final typescript.

St Gervais des Sablons
August 1999

ABBREVIATIONS

The following abbreviations to works by Jacques Derrida are used throughout the book. Only works referred to in the book are included in this list. For a full bibliography, see Bennington and Derrida, *Jacques Derrida*, 2nd edn (Chicago: University of Chicago Press, 1999). Published translations have occasionally been altered in the interests of consistency and accuracy.

AC   *L'autre cap, suivi de la démocratie ajournée* (Paris: Minuit, 1991); tr. Pascale-Anne Brault and Michael Naas, *The Other Heading* (Bloomington: Indiana University Press, 1992)

AD   *Adieu à Emmanuel Lévinas* (Paris: Galilée, 1997); partial tr. Pascale-Anne Brault and Michael Naas, *Critical Inquiry* 23/1 (1996), 1–10

AF   *L'Archéologie du frivole: Lire Condillac* (Paris: Gonthier/Denoël, 1976); tr. John P. Leavey, Jr, *The Archeology of the Frivolous: Reading Condillac* (Pittsburgh: Duquesne University Press, 1980)

AL   *Acts of Literature*, ed. Derek Attridge (London and New York: Routledge, 1992)

AP   *Apories* (Paris: Galilée, 1996); tr. Thomas Dutoit, *Aporias* (Stanford: Stanford University Press, 1993)

CP   *La carte postale de Socrate à Freud et au-delà* (Paris: Aubier-Flammarion, 1980); tr. Alan Bass, *The Post Card* (Chicago: University of Chicago Press, 1987)

D   *La Dissémination* (Paris: Seuil, 1972); tr. Barbara Johnson, *Dissemination* (Chicago: University of Chicago Press, 1982)

DEM *Demeure: Maurice Blanchot* (Paris: Galilée, 1998)

DM   *Donner la mort* (Paris: Galilée, 1999). Adds a new final section to 'Donner la mort' (in Derrida et al., *L'éthique du don* (Paris: Métailié-Transition, 1992), 11–108 [tr. David Wills as *The Gift of Death* (Chicago: University of Chicago Press, 1995)])

ABBREVIATIONS

DP   *Du droit à la philosophie* (Paris: Galilée, 1990); partial translations: 'Punctuations: The Time of a Thesis', tr. K. McLaughlin, in Alan Montefiore (ed.), *Philosophy in France Today* (Cambridge: Cambridge University Press, 1983), 34–50; 'Mochlos, or the conflict of the faculties', tr. Richard Rand and Amy Wigant, in Richard Rand (ed.), *Logomachia: The Conflict of the Faculties* (Lincoln and London: University of Nebraska Press, 1992), 3–34

ED   *L'Ecriture et la différence* (Paris: Seuil, 1967); tr. Alan Bass, *Writing and Difference* (London: Routledge, 1978)

ESP *De l'esprit: Heidegger et la question* (Paris: Galilée, 1987); tr. Geoffrey Bennington and Rachel Bowlby, *Of Spirit: Heidegger and the Question* (Chicago: University of Chicago Press, 1989)

FL   *Force de loi* (Paris: Galilée, 1994); tr. Mary Quaintance, 'Force of Law: The "Mystical Foundation" of Authority', with original French text, *Cardozo Law Review*, 11/5–6 (1990), 920–1045

FS   'Foi et Savoir', in Derrida and Vattimo (eds), *La religion* (Paris: Seuil, 1996), 9–86

GEN *Le problème de la genèse dans la philosophie de Husserl* (Paris: PUF, 1990)

GL   *Glas* (Paris: Galilée, 1974; [repr. Denoël/Gonthier, 1981, 2 vols]); tr. John P. Leavey, Jr, and Richard Rand, *Glas* (University of Nebraska Press, 1986)

GR   *De la grammatologie* (Paris: Minuit, 1967); tr. Gayatri Spivak, *Of Grammatology* (Baltimore: Johns Hopkins University Press, 1976)

HOS *De l'hospitalité* (Paris: Calmann-Lévy, 1997)

JD   *Jacques Derrida* (in collaboration with Geoffrey Bennington) (Paris: Seuil, 1991); tr. Geoffrey Bennington, *Jacques Derrida* (Chicago: University of Chicago Press, 1993), 2nd edn 1999

K   *Khôra* (Paris: Galilée, 1993); tr. Ian McLeod, in *On the Name*, ed. T. Dutoit (Stanford: Stanford University Press, 1995)

LI   *Limited Inc.*, ed. Gerald Graff, tr. Samuel Weber and Jeffrey Mehlman (Evanston: Northwestern University Press, 1988)

M   *Marges de la philosophie* (Paris: Minuit, 1972); tr. Alan Bass, *Margins of Philosophy* (Chicago: University of Chicago Press, 1984)

MA   *Mal d'Archive* (Paris: Galilée, 1995); tr. Eric Prenowitz, *Archive Fever* (Chicago: University of Chicago Press, 1996)

MC   'Mes chances: Au rendez-vous de quelques stéréophonies épicuriennes' (*Tijdschrift voor Filosofie* 45/1 (1983), 3–40; tr. Harvey and Ronell, in J. H. Smith and W. Kerrigan (eds), *Taking Chances: Derrida, Psychoanalysis and Literature* (Baltimore: Johns Hopkins University Press, 1984), 1–32

MEM *Mémoires: For Paul de Man*, tr. Cecile Lindsay, Jonathan Culler, and Eduardo Cadava (Columbia University Press, 1986 [2nd enlarged edn 1989])

MON   *Le monolinguisme de l'autre* (Paris: Galilée, 1996); tr. Patrick Mensah, *Monolingualism of the Other or the Prosthesis of Origin* (Stanford: Stanford University Press, 1998)

OA   *L'Oreille de l'autre: Otobiographies, transferts, traductions: Textes et débats avec Jacques Derrida (Sous la direction de Claude Levesque et Christie Vance McDonald)* (Montréal: VLB, 1982); tr. Peggy Kamuf et al., *The Ear of the Other* (New York: Schocken, 1985 [2nd edn, University of Nebraska Press, 1988])

OG   *L'origine de la géométrie*, Edmund Husserl. Translated with an introduction (Paris: Presses Universitaires de France, 1962); tr. John P. Leavey, Jr (Brighton: Harvester, 1978)

OTO   *Otobiographies: L'enseignement de Nietzsche et la politique du nom propre* (Paris: Galilée, 1984); translations: 'Declarations of Independence', tr. Thomas Keenan and Thomas Pepper, *New Political Science* 15 (1986), 7–15; 'Otobiographies," tr. Avital Ronell, in *The Ear of the Other* (see *L'Oreille de l'autre*, OA above)

PA   *Politiques de l'amitié* (Paris: Galilée, 1994); tr. George Collins, *Politics of Friendship* (London: Verso, 1997)

PAR   *Parages* (Paris: Galilée, 1986); partial translations: 'Living On: Border Lines', tr. James Hulbert, in Bloom et al., *Deconstruction and Criticism* (New York: Seabury, 1979), 75–175; 'The Law of Genre', tr. Avital Ronell, *Glyph* 7 (1980), 202–29; 'Title (to be specified)', tr. Tom Conley, *Sub-stance* 31 (1981), 5–22

PAS   *Passions: l'offrande oblique* (Paris: Galilée, 1993), tr. D. Wood, in D. Wood (ed.), *Derrida: A Critical Reader* (Oxford: Blackwell, 1992), 5–35

POS   *Positions* (Paris: Minuit, 1972); tr. Alan Bass, *Positions* (Chicago: University of Chicago Press, 1981)

PRE   'Préjugés: devant la loi', in Lyotard et al., *La faculté de juger* (Paris: Minuit, 1985)

PS   *Point de suspension ...* Paris: Galilée, 1992); tr. Peggy Kamuf et al. as *Points ... (Interviews 1974–1994)* (Stanford: Stanford University Press, 1995)

PSY   *Psyché: Inventions de l'autre* (Paris: Galilée, 1987); partial translations: ATM, 'At This Very Moment in This Work Here I Am', tr. Ruben Berezdivin, in Robert Bernasconi and Simon Critchley (eds), *Re-Reading Lévinas* (London: Routledge, 1990), 11–48; HAS, 'How to Avoid Speaking: Denials', tr. Ken Frieden, in Sanford Budick and Wolfgang Iser (eds), *Languages of the Unsayable: The Play of Negativity in Literature and Literary Theory* (New York: Columbia University Press, 1989), 3–70; LJF, 'Letter to a Japanese Friend', tr. David Wood and Andrew Benjamin, in Peggy Kamuf (ed.), *A Derrida Reader: Between the Blinds* (New York: Columbia University Press, 1991), 269–276; NA, 'No Apocalypse, Not Now (full speed ahead, seven missives, seven missiles)', tr. Catherine Porter and

Philip Lewis, *Diacritics* 14/2 (1984), 20–31; NM, 'The Laws of Reflection: Nelson Mandela, In Admiration', tr. Mary Ann Caws and Isabelle Lorenz, in *For Nelson Mandela* (New York: Seaver Books, 1987), 13–42; NY, 'A Number of Yes', tr. Brian Holmes, in *Qui Parle* 2/2 (1988), 120–33; RLW, 'Racism's Last Word', tr. Peggy Kamuf, *Critical Inquiry* 12 (1985), 290–9

RES   *Résistances de la psychanalyse* (Paris: Galilée, 1996); tr. Peggy Kamuf, Pascale-Anne Braffit, and Michael Naas as *Resistances of Psychoanalysis* (Stanford: Stanford University Press, 1998)

SCH   *Schibboleth: pour Paul Celan* (Paris: Galilée, 1986); earlier version in English in G. Hartman and S. Budick (eds), *Midrash and Literature* (New Haven: Yale University Press, 1986), 307–47

SM   *Spectres de Marx. L'Etat de la dette, le travail du deuil et la nouvelle Internationale* (Paris: Galilée, 1993); tr. Peggy Kamuf as *Spectres of Marx: The State of the Debt, the Work of Mourning and the New International*, intro. by B. Magnus and S. Cullenberg (London: Routledge, 1994)

SN   *Sauf le nom* (Paris: Galilée, 1993); tr. Thomas Dutoit, in T. Dutoit (ed.), *On the Name* (Stanford: Stanford University Press, 1995)

SP   *Signéponge*, with parallel translation by Richard Rand (Chicago: University of Chicago Press, 1983); also French text only (Paris: Seuil, 1988)

TA   *D'un ton apocalyptique adopté naguère en philosophie* (Paris: Galilée, 1983); tr. John P. Leavey, Jr, 'Of an Apocalyptic Tone Recently Adopted in Philosophy', *The Oxford Literary Review* 6/2 (1984)

UG   *Ulysse gramophone: Deux mots pour Joyce* (Paris: Galilée, 1987); translations: 'Two Words for Joyce', tr. Geoff Bennington, in Derek Attridge and Daniel Ferrer (eds), *Post-Structuralist Joyce: Essays from the French* (Cambridge: Cambridge University Press, 1984), 145–59; 'Ulysses Gramophone: Hear Say Yes in Joyce', tr. Tina Kendall, in D. Attridge (ed.), *Acts of Literature* (London: Routledge, 1992), 256–309

VEP   *La Vérité en peinture* (Paris: Flammarion, 1978); tr. Geoff Bennington and Ian McLeod, *The Truth in Painting* (Chicago: University of Chicago Press, 1987)

VP   *La Voix et le phénomène* (Paris: Presses Universitaires de France, 1967); tr. David Allison, *Speech and Phenomena* (Evanston: Northwestern University Press, 1973)

VS   'Un ver à soie (points de vue piqués sur l'autre voile)', *Le contretemps* 2–3 (1997), repr. in Derrida and Hélène Cixous, *Voiles* (Paris: Galilée, 1998); tr. Geoffrey Bennington, 'A Silkworm of One's Own', *Oxford Literary Review* 18 (1996), 3–63

INTRODUCTION

Circumstances – of interruption

Circumstances are everything and nothing. Circumstance is both 'the total complex of essential attributes and attendant adjuncts of a fact or action', and 'a subordinate detail: an adventitious non-essential fact or detail' (Webster). Circumstances *stand around*, binding events into their contexts, determining them exhaustively, the completed circle of conditions[1] – and yet circumstances *just* stand around, adventitiously, doing nothing, merely contingent accessories to a fact or event to which they are not essential, always perhaps *interrupting* or breaking open the circle, leading astray. Circumstance, like contingency more generally, has no good intellectual standing: circumstantial writing is taken to be inferior in principle to writing generated by a supposed inner necessity of thought. Circumstances tend to inflect what is imagined to be a good directionality of thinking, to divert the writer from his or her brave forward-thrusting *project*, deflect him or her from the trajectory that the thought is supposed naturally to have, and to want to follow. Circumstantial writing takes on the negative values of journalism, or more generally of servile paid labour; and to that extent is not the noble product of pure thinking for its own sake. Philosophical writing, especially, should above all not be circumstantial.

This evaluation of the circumstantial is of course metaphysical through and through. One of the most insistent features of Derrida's thought is that it affirms the necessary inscription of thought and writing: where do we begin?, asks *Of Grammatology*, and replies, '*wherever we are:* in a text already where we believe ourselves to be',[2] that is, inscribed already in a complex network involving the language in which we write, with all the sedimentations that language brings with it, and all the differential and semi-independent histories that intersect at this point, on this occasion, this circumstance in which I now find myself reading and writing, singularly constituted by everything that tends to compromise my singularity just as soon as it makes it possible.

All the texts gathered in this volume are *essentially circumstantial*, attempting to answer, not always very reverentially or even very politely, to requests or

1

demands of one sort or another. All are circumstantial, but the type of circumstance varies, and the sections of the book reflect that variation. The first section includes pieces written for publications with an essentially pedagogic vocation: encyclopedias, 'readers' or 'handbooks': trying to encompass or concentrate *all* or at least *some* of Derrida into a reduced or at least time-saving, point-scoring, exam-answering or *pense-bête* form, or to elucidate one, supposedly limited, 'aspect' of his work, positioning a paradoxical reader who is supposed not to know anything about Derrida but who is yet imagined able to pick up Derrida's thought in condensed form. These pieces struggle to convey the perception that Derrida's work can be presented through recognisably rational arguments, although it cannot in fact strictly be described in terms of such (metaphysical) 'aspects', so that, without wishing to evacuate all meaning from terms such as 'politics', 'ethics', 'literature', we can show that Derrida's thinking can be said to be both *entirely* political, ethical or literary, and *not at all* political, ethical or literary, that 'both … and' structure also entailing a 'neither … nor', and thereby questioning the relation between a 'both … and' and/or a 'neither/nor' in general.[3] These pieces share a respect for pedagogical imperatives which also tries to respect the paradoxical imperative of all pedagogy, namely to work in view of its own redundancy: read these pieces *so that* you will need them no longer.

'Allographics' gathers more straightforwardly circumstantial pieces written for conferences and guided by the organisers' chosen themes, and on occasion reflecting on those circumstances and themes. In each case, Derrida's work is explicitly brought into contact with other writings, and often with writings *other* than the other writings with which his own work is always concerned. Derrida's work is allographic through and through, as some of the pieces in the earlier sections affirm, and in this section that allography is taken as the principle of a more general contamination or proliferation, in the hope of achieving, at least on occasion, in the circumstances, an 'other than' *other than* the 'other than' that inhabits Derrida's writing already.

In 'Philopolemics' I include, still explicitly under the sign of a Derridean thought,[4] a number of pieces explicitly examining and often contesting other readings of Derrida. In the wake of my 1988 pieces 'Deconstruction and the Philosophers' and 'L'Arroseur arrosé(e)'[5] I take up some really quite friendly differences and disagreements with some recent philosophical discussions of Derrida. 'Friendly' here itself refers to the suggestions I make in 'Forever friends' in the previous section, and means that the very friendly proximity of some of these discussions generates the need, always in admiration, for occasionally quite trenchant examination of differences, so that it becomes important to probe in detail Bernard Stiegler's provocatively mistaken view of the conceptual status of *différance*, Rodolphe Gasché's unrepentant re-philosophizing of Derrida, or Marian Hobson's interesting version of teleology and Kantian Idea in Derrida's early thought. These discussions do not simply aim to record a difference of opinion or belief about Derrida, but really do try to refute and demonstrate. Those refutations and demonstrations depend often enough on drawing attention to circumstance and context, or perhaps simply on differing appreciations of the *speed* with which events depart from circumstances.

These diversely circumstantial pieces naturally, and quite happily, fail to answer adequately or completely to the diverse circumstances for which they were written. None is *quite* appropriate for its circumstance, and to that extent each stands a chance of being readable outside that circumstance, for example in this volume. A new circumstance binds the old together, a little loosely, but not so loosely that 'Derrida' would be the only common thread running through them. It is not that these pieces have a secret and cunning 'agenda' or 'project' animating them in view of the gathering they now, still circumstantially, find here, and that it would be the purpose of this introduction to bring out and exhibit. No planned aim or goal guided these pieces towards their gathering in this volume. But weary fatality, as much as active necessity, still gives these pieces some claim to a signature other than Derrida's, and also writes them rather relentlessly into a history of the signatory and of other texts I have signed before. However diverse the circumstances to which they respond, these pieces were all also written, sometimes rather dispiritedly, in recognisably *similar* circumstances, each one, on re-reading, seeming to the author to arrive rather more at the sober and resigned recognition of the morning mirror than at the intoxication of the excitingly new. The moment of signature is always affirmative, but it cannot ever quite affirm as triumphantly as it might wish: I may write in order to monumentalise or even immortalise my signature, but my signature also haunts everything I write as the weight of a past I would like to escape. And this means that the signature, far from just escaping or redeeming circumstance, or simply saving texts from their circumstances, *itself* functions circumstantially up to a point. Here it seems to have moved slightly away from what I have repeatedly called elsewhere the paradox of the legislator[6] to a preoccupation with sense as constitutively bound up with a peculiar quasi-teleological or self-interrupting structure whereby the irreducible promise of meaning is the promise that it *is* only to the extent that meaning *never will* arrive to make it good. It is this structure, gathered round the figure of the frontier, which has determined the more sustained work that has been the more persistent circumstance underlying the more ephemeral occasions of the essays gathered here.[7]

'Interrupting Derrida': because Derrida himself practises an art of interruption with (all due) respect to metaphysics, so that he is the interruptor, and 'Interrupting' becomes his honorific title, as I argue for 'Applied' in the chapter here called simply 'X'; but also because these essays diversely interrupt Derrida, cut into the flow of his work, politely pause here and there to look more closely or to bring other interruptions into play. Such interruptions do not attempt to silence or drown out the master's voice, far from it, but to bring out further its own choral vanishings into other voices from the tradition. This can amount on occasion almost to suggesting that Derrida *just is* Kant or Plato, for example. This type of claim of quasi-identity entails a rethink of what *reading* is, and is complex and paradoxical enough to deserve fuller treatment elsewhere, in other circumstances.[8]

Part I

PEDAGOGICS

1

'JACQUES DERRIDA'

It is at least plausibly arguable that Derrida's will have been the most important philosophical contribution (in French, at least) of the last thirty years, in spite of the impassioned argument his work has provoked and still arouses (concretised in 1992 in the argument over Cambridge University's proposal to award him an honorary degree, but also in a series of other 'affairs' and polemics).[1] It is entirely proper that an account of his work should appear in a volume such as this, and yet the philosophically most striking thing about Derrida's work is probably that it is *not* philosophy in any straightforward sense, but its permanent traversal, excess or outflanking. Derrida has not so much re-defined philosophy (the traditional task of philosophy) as rendered it permanently in-definite. This difficult situation has been the cause of many misunderstandings of Derrida, by both philosophers and non-philosophers, and demands a delicacy of reading which is all but unmanageable, but which goes some way towards explaining the attraction Derrida's work has held for students of literature. It is unhelpful to view Derrida as belonging to any particular philosophical lineage, because his work upsets *all* the concepts that allow us to posit philosophical lineages (he is thus arguably as 'close' to Plato or Kant as to Heidegger or Nietzsche), and it is also difficult to discern any obvious lines of development or change in his thinking, which seems to have remained remarkably consistent – though constantly surprising and unpredictable – since the 1960s. But in spite of its undeniable difficulty, Derrida's work is in fact quite susceptible of reasoned exposition *up to a point*, beyond which something 'undecidable' begins to happen, as we shall see.

Derrida made his spectacular entry into the field of published philosophy in 1967, bringing out three major books (*De la grammatologie*, *L'Ecriture et la différence*, and *La Voix et le phénomène* – he had earlier published a long, prize-winning introduction to his own translation of Husserl's 'Origin of Geometry' appendix to the *Crisis* in 1962), and these books lay out most of the premises for Derrida's subsequent vast output (some 40 books to date, and thousands of pages of unpublished seminar material), although careful study of that subsequent output is necessary for this to be readily perceived (see too Derrida's own comments on the 1990 publication of his Master's dissertation from 1953, in which he is surprised to find already much of what was to come over the next forty years).[2] Derrida is concerned to argue something like this: the self-identifying tradition of Western philosophy ('Western metaphysics', 'onto-theology') is, as Heidegger argued, dominated by the value of *presence*. Whatever its perception of the complexities involved, and whatever its doctrinal inclination, metaphysics seeks out some supreme value which is inseparable from this value of presence, whatever particular content it may otherwise be supposed to exhibit. Establishing the excellence of this presence (which can be modulated across a huge variety of inflexions, including – perhaps even most commonly – those of more or less radical absence, of a presence now lost or always yet to come, *arkhe* and/or *telos* in the stories philosophy habitually tells) commits metaphysics to a thinking which makes privileged use of binary, oppositional structures, whereby a positively marked term is defined against a negatively marked one (presence as against absence, the inside as against the outside, the soul as against the body, meaning as against its sign, the spirit as against the letter, the clear as against the obscure, the literal as against the figural, the rational as against the irrational, the serious as against the non-serious, and so on, indefinitely). Even in cases where such oppositions are presented as neutral and descriptive, Derrida argues, they are in fact violently (i.e. dogmatically) hierarchical, the result of an 'ethico-theoretical decision', so that, for example, it is assumed without question that meaning is logically prior, and ontologically superior, to its linguistic expression, or that serious literal speech is logically prior, and ontologically superior, to jokes or fiction. What has become famous as 'deconstruction' involves less an *operation on* than a *demonstration about* such hierarchised binaries in the history of Western thought, and Derrida has found occasion in that demonstration to examine in some detail most of the established masters of the tradition.

It would have been difficult to predict that Derrida would find an entry point into this immense field by concentrating on the question of *writing*, led there perhaps by his – abandoned – doctoral project on 'The Ideality of the Literary Work'. Writing, since Plato's *Phaedrus* (the object of a long and brilliant reading ('Plato's Pharmacy'), in *La dissémination* (1972)) has had a bad press in the philosophical tradition. If meaning requires expression, says the philosopher, let this be essentially vocal: the spoken word coincides with its sense, disappears as it delivers up its meaning (especially, as Husserl will insist, in my monologue with myself, where the meaningful word need not even depart from my consciousness into the facticity of the world), and attests to the animating presence of the intending, meaning-giving consciousness of the speaker; whereas writing, mere mechanical adjunct to speech, extends the spatial and temporal range of linguistic communication but at the cost of producing a worrying material, worldly *remainder* in the form of *script* or *text* which invite repeated but repeatedly different readings without further corrective ('paternal') intervention from the intentional source (for, as Derrida shows without difficulty, the fact of writing analytically entails – as a 'necessary possibility' – the death of the writer (and of any particular reader, for writing generates a potentially endless series of different contexts in which it can be read)). Massively, for a tradition that does not begin with Plato and does not end with Austin or Lacan, the voice is 'naturally' privileged over writing as the place where, to use the terminology of Saussure, the signifier seems most transparent or subservient to its signified, which it exists only to relay. Husserl, on whom Derrida spends a great deal of time in these early texts, pursues the essence of what he calls the 'expressive' sign into the inner monologue of the transcendental subject, while writing is placed on the side of the merely indicative, the material and empirical, the contingent.

Nowhere does Derrida suggest that this tradition of thinking about writing and its relation to the ideality of meaning is simply *false* (if only because the values of true and false are complicit with what is here under analysis). The interpretative operation carried out on Husserl, Saussure or Plato (but we shall see that this is not interpretation *stricto sensu* – because interpretation cannot but share the presuppositions about sign and meaning that are here in question – and nor is it an operation, because this is not something that Derrida *does to* the texts he reads) consists, rather, through a constant and grateful, commemorative, recognition of their depth and rigour, in a demonstration ('deconstruction') that first unravels the hierarchisation of the speech/writing opposition (and with it that of the oppositions it brings along with it, for one of Derrida's constant claims about metaphysics will have been that pulling at a bit of it brings it all along too, that its concepts are organised in a network of mutually defining elements in dynamic solidarity, so that this construal of meaning is inseparable from a complex of positions about truth, *mimesis*, but also, say, life, death, sexual difference), and then questions not just the *hierarchy* of the opposition, but its very *oppositionality*. So, for example, Husserl is suspicious of writing because its availability for repeated access in a futurally open series of different contexts, away from the animating intention of its author, separates it from the transcendental 'life' the ideality of whose meaning it is supposed (teleologically) to express, but which it is more likely to betray or mortify: but the most ideal idealities, such as those of geometry, cannot but rest for their ideality (their repeatability as the same in an infinite series of actualisations) on the very graphic inscription that is elsewhere so suspect. But if writing is thus something like the condition of possibility of the very ideality it is also thought to bring low (so that, according to a logic constant in Derrida's thinking, the condition of possibility is simultaneously the condition of impossibility of the purity of the phenomenon made possible), then the valorisations implicit in the metaphysical description are radically disturbed, and it is shown to rest on something like a grounding incoherence.

Derrida pursues the deconstruction of speech and writing into its second stage by arguing, that not only is writing not simply a secondary adjunct to speech, but that all linguistic signs are, in a certain sense, radically written. The argument goes as follows: the metaphysical description of writing is that it is the (graphic) signifier of a (phonic) signifier, which is the signifier of an (ideal) signified; but it can be shown that all signifiers refer for their meaning only to other signifiers (this part of the argument drawing on the Saussure of the linguistic 'system of differences' as against the more traditional Saussure of the sign); if metaphysics wants to call 'signifier of signifier' by the name 'writing', it had therefore better call all language writing if it wants to be consistent. But this it does not want, for to call all language 'writing' in this way upsets its basic axiology, whereby writing *must* take a secondary place with respect to speech. Using the term 'writing' (or 'archi-writing') in this displaced (and apparently provocative) sense, then, both brings out a certain (repressed) truth of the metaphysical tradition (it is committed in spite of itself to the view that all meaning exhibits the features it nonetheless tries to limit to writing), and confronts it with its own foundational dogmatism (it flatly denies that this is the case). Metaphysics is thus redescribed as the variable economy of this contradiction.

My present, intended meaning is possible only because language as a system of differences allows its differential identification in terms of a system I inherit and do not dominate (I cannot simply choose the language I speak nor the concepts it provides me with); and its expression is possible only in the perspective of the necessary possibility of its repetition in the absence of my supposedly animating (or at least sub-scribing) intention. Whether actually written or spoken, my utterance functions only insofar as it always might be repeated in my absence (if necessary by mechanical means, but the *possibility* of these is built into language from the start, language has always been such that its mechanical repetition is possible): 'in my absence', radicalised, after my death. As you read this, you do not know (and this is an essential ignorance, not merely an empirical one, it is entailed by the structure of writing) whether I am alive or dead, nor, by extension, whether I am serious or not, whether I mean it or not, whether I really wrote it or not. Insofar as you are inclined to attribute intentions to me (or to someone) in this respect, you construct them retroactively on the basis of the text read, and the text read functions 'mechanically', independently of the intentions you attribute in fact, after the fact, to its supposed author. (This also suggests why subjectivity is an inscribed rather than foundational concept.)

Further, the fact that this text cannot *exhaustively* control the reading you give it (no text can *read itself without remainder*, although philosophy may be the discourse which has tried hardest to do just that, and the Hegelian system the most consistent try) implies that there is no end to reading, no conceivable horizon of interpretation. Deconstruction is not a form of hermeneutics, however supposedly radical, for just this reason: hermeneutics always proposes a convergent movement towards a unitary meaning (however much it may wish to respect ambiguity on the way), the word of God; deconstruction discerns a dispersive perspective in which there is no (one) meaning. Many readers of Derrida have lost their nerve at this point, fearing a nihilistic consequence which does not in fact follow (others have imagined that Derrida, who spends a lot of time justifying his readings, must here be caught in contradiction). The absence of a unitary horizon of meaning for the process of reading does not commit Derrida to the *recommendation* of meaninglessness, nor does it entail the equivalence in value of all different readings (rather the singularity of each), and indeed demands the most rigorous textual evidence for readings proposed: but it does argue that no one reading will ever be able to claim to have exhausted the textual resources available in the text being read.

This description still suggests too clear a separation between writing and reading: texts (of sufficient complexity – the memory of Gödel's theorem here is not fortuitous) *already* tend to read themselves, to offer up a preferred or 'official' reading (often the one assumed by subsequent readers to coincide with the author's intention): so Plato, Rousseau, Husserl, Saussure and many others (demonstrably) *declare* their preference for speech over writing; but they also manage (demonstrably) to *say* the very opposite too. Derrida's work consists essentially in bringing out the textual resources that question the 'official' version. These resources are demonstrably put forward, however discreetly, by the texts being read, and are not imported by Derrida, whose place in this process is thereby rendered problematical: it is not that Derrida (actively) deconstructs anything at all, but rather that he shows *metaphysics in deconstruction*. This is not the expression of a preference, but a bolder claim, namely that the deconstructive operation of apparent oppositions is the only possible 'ground' upon which metaphysics could ever claim to identify itself in the first place.

Derrida can thus be said to *repeat metaphysics differently*. All of his work consists in readings of (usually philosophical) texts carried by the tradition, then shown to upset traditionality as much as they respect it. (Another important strand of readings examines texts which look as though they might escape from metaphysics, only to show points of unthought complicity.) This can look like a problem merely for historians of philosophy (in fact it poses insuperable problems to any history of philosophy, because it renders unanswerable the question 'when?' posed of a text), but also involves consequences for 'doing' philosophy in general. Effects of identity *in general* (as much in, say, a perceptual field as in a linguistic system, though questions of language and meaning remain paramount in that metaphysics is *logocentric*) are now understood to be generated on the basis of *difference*. Derrida spends a good deal of effort establishing that this differential condition of identity need not give rise to a dialectic in the Hegelian sense: Hegel's famous demonstration in the *Greater Logic* that difference collapses dialectically into identity depends on an *absolutisation* of difference which Derrida is at pains to show is unthinkable (difference is intrinsically non-absolutisable, intrinsically finite) and on a prejudgement that difference is answerable to opposition (Hegel is, for example, *already* thinking difference as opposition when arguing that what is different from difference is identity). Difference (radicalised by Derrida's neologism *différance* to bring out both spatial and temporal resonances, identity being an effect of differences from other elements *and* between events of repetition) is the *milieu* in which identities are sketched but never quite achieved (any element being defined only in terms of all the others and all its repetitions, the *trace* of which remains as a sort of constitutive contamination), but never quite lost (*différance* can be thought of as a dispersion, but never an *absolute* dispersion). Identities depend on traces of other identities: but the trace 'itself', now the logically prior term, is not answerable to any metaphysical characterisation (it is, for example, neither present nor absent, and, as the condition of identity in general, is not itself *identifiable*).

Différance is one attempt to name this complex 'origin' of space and time and meaning, but there are many other attempts too: dissemination, *pharmakon*, trace, supplement, and many more, drawn from the apparent contingency of the texts of the tradition. A consistent argument for the non-originarity of identity can hardly propose a single name for the 'origin' of that non-originarity, whence the open series of names proposed. A consequence of this that has troubled many readers of Derrida is that the apparently transcendental privilege of *différance* (or the trace) cannot be maintained, insofar as differentially defined 'identities' can never achieve the stability required of a transcendental realm. In fact, the conjoined thinking of difference and repetition entails that anything like the transcendental is generated as a more or less provisional and unstable effect by a series of partially contingent and essentially singular events, whereby a given text tries to *put up* a transcendental term, and the deconstructive reading registers its inevitable fall back into its contingent textuality. For example, Descartes generates an immortal thinking substance on the back of the finitude of a mortal individual, and looks down on mortality as a contingency from the height thus achieved: but the deconstructive reading shows that that 'contingency' is the positive condition of the supposedly transcendental position, its 'transcendental' condition. For Derrida, the transcendental position itself has a transcendental in what the transcendental calls the empirical or the contingent. This does not mean that the transcendental can simply be debunked in a positivist or empiricist spirit (the gesture of the human sciences), because such a gesture, which would correspond to the *reversal* stage of deconstruction, cannot fail to generate a new transcendental term it is unable to deal with ('experience', 'history', 'society', 'material conditions', and so on, or even 'writing'), but that it must be thought as a *movement*, variously described in the texts of the tradition of philosophy, which there is no question of *doing without* (in some fantasy of a purely immanent materiality). This irreducible inscription of 'contingency' *in* the transcendental entails, among other things, that philosophical 'arguments' cannot be neatly separated from their 'expression', for example in a given natural language, or a given more or less idiosyncratic idiom (philosophical texts bear a singular *signature*), nor from the tradition which they bear and contest (the singularity of that signature is constitutively compromised by its intelligibility). In this sense, all philosophy is radically historical (and 'geographical'), and there is no doing philosophy that does not engage (even if in the mode of denial) with the history (and geography, including the social and political geography) of philosophy – but philosophy, which cannot help but attempt to reduce that history, can never quite understand this remainder of contingency, this spatio-temporal dispersion, which makes it possible. This configuration has often been called, by Derrida and others, 'quasi-transcendental', but this name, and the Kantian reference it involves, has at best a heuristic privilege with respect to many others in the open series of deconstructive events. There is no proper name for deconstruction or its 'results', whence the philosophical unease it cannot fail to generate.

This argument, which *limits* the pretensions of philosophy with respect to other disciplines (insofar as it posits the inability of philosophy ever to establish itself successfully as uniquely *philosophical*, and therefore opens it to scrutiny by non-philosophical agencies – especially perhaps psychoanalysis), simultaneously *extends* the philosophical domain beyond all definable limits (for these non-philosophical agencies are themselves both shot through with metaphysical values and assumptions and the bearers of a contingency metaphysics cannot quite manage). Many early receptions of Derrida by non-philosophers enthusiastically embraced what could look simply like a critique of philosophical pretension: Derrida seemed to some to make philosophy look like *no more than* a kind of writing, a particular use of language, a literary *genre*, a rhetoric, maybe even a set of essentially psychical operations. But Derrida has also spent a good deal of energy (especially perhaps in *L'Ecriture et la différence* (1967) and the 1972 collection *Marges de la philosophie*) showing how attempts to *reduce* philosophy in this way (anthropologically (Lévi-Strauss), historically (Foucault), poetically (Valéry), linguistically (Benveniste), psychoanalytically (Lacan), sociologically (Bourdieu)) rely on often naively unquestioned philosophical assumptions. For example, the attempt to reduce philosophy to a set of rhetorical tropes (and essentially metaphors) which have simply forgotten their metaphorical status and which can then be debunked in the name of something like 'literature' founders on its need to hold clear of this operation, to place in a transcendental position, just that concept (the concept of metaphor, a *philosophical* concept) which is supposed to achieve the reduction of *all* concepts. Similarly, linguistic reductions of philosophy transcendentalise a (philosophical) concept of language, historical reductions a (philosophical) concept of history, according to a mechanism we can follow Derrida in calling 'transcendental contraband'. The general form of this argument is that any attempt to claim an *escape* from metaphysics necessarily involves the blind appeal to at least one metaphysical concept which compromises the escape the moment it is claimed.

This situation has led some commentators to assume on Derrida's part, far from an iconoclastic desire to destroy philosophy in the name of 'play' (the object of much indignation from philosophers convinced of how very serious they are), a culpable and perhaps reactionary complicity with a metaphysics he is supposed to be denouncing: but Derrida's argument establishes that 'complicity with meta-physics' is both unavoidable (traditionality as the positive condition of thinking) and infinitely negotiable once the twin blindnesses of simple subservience and heroic oppositional revolt have been pointed out. The unease that this situation generates is, however, real. It looks as though Derrida has established, through recognisably rational argument, that metaphysical values (grounded in the *Ur*-value of presence) are untenable because of the prior necessity of *différance*; but also as though there is no simple alternative to those values (trying to make *différance* into an alternative value means thinking it in terms of a potential presence again: this is the 'libertarian' reception of Derrida). The relationship with metaphysics is endlessly negotiable, as Derrida shows through a series of similar but non-iden-tical encounters with the texts of the tradition, but it is still unclear what motivates these encounters or what dictates the strategy adopted in them. If we know *a priori* that metaphysics can be neither established nor overcome, what are we trying to achieve in our dealings with it?

This question, which has driven a number of commentators to identify what might appear to be a new stress in Derrida on ethical and political issues (although these questions are raised from his very earliest work in fact) can be given, if only provisionally, a negative and a positive characterisation. Negatively, in a spirit of critique which deconstruction never rejects but which cannot in principle exhaust it, deconstruction warns against metaphysical purifications, essentialisations, totalisations and transcendentalisations of all sorts. Thus, to take a dramatic example, Heidegger's engagement with Nazism (often thought to be an object of embarrassment to Derrida, whereas his writings on this matter are among his most uncompromisingly critical) can be shown to be related to Heidegger's unthought appeal to a metaphysical value ('spirit'). That this value is shared with eminent opponents of Nazism (Husserl, Valéry) points to deeper grounds of complicity to be considered with the utmost vigilance of thought (rather than quick assurances that Nazism is adequately thought by the values of humanism), and some of Heidegger's later thinking can help with that considera-tion. Although this demonstration has been greeted with a certain degree of confusion and bad faith, it suggests that deconstruction gives in principle some ethico-political guidance ('avoid uncritical appeals to metaphysical values') without, however, proposing any replacement metaphysical values.

This characterisation of deconstruction is, however, still a little misleading. We seem to have reached a position which states that on the one hand complicity with metaphysics is unavoidable, but that complicity with metaphysics is to be avoided as far as possible, without any guidance being given as to that 'as far as possible'. Some degree of confusion here is itself an object of affirmation for Derrida: deconstruction cannot provide rules for avoiding metaphysics, and never suggests that talk about contingency, writing, undecidability or dissemination will produce results which are necessarily 'better' than talk about necessity, speech, decidability or univocality (it is quite possible to talk logocentrically about, for example, dissemination, as some enthusiastic followers of Derrida have discovered to their cost). If deconstruction maintains that we are always in a *tension* between the metaphysical and its undoing, it cannot predict *a priori* what the best adjustment of that tension might be in a given case: although something like equivocality is affirmed as the 'ground' of any meaning whatsoever, Derrida nowhere suggests that *more* equivocality is necessarily better than *less*, for example.

What deconstruction can say more 'positively' about ethical and political issues does, however, depend on a certain affirmation of the undecidable. The argument goes as follows: for a decision to be worthy of the name, it must be more than the simple determinative subsumption of a case under a rule. Looking up the rule for the case and applying the rule is a matter for administration rather than ethics. Ethics begins where the case does not entirely correspond to any rule, and where the decision has to be taken without subsumption. A decision worthy of its name thus takes place in a situation of radical *indecision* or of undecidability of the case in question in terms of any rules for judging it. The decision must therefore involve a measure of *invention*, and that invention entails both an uncertainty and the affirmative projection of a future. A decision is like a performative which has both to perform and to invent the rules according to which it might, after the event of its performance, be received as 'happy'. This essential undecidability of the event as it arrives and calls for decision flows from the deconstructive analyses of language and time that we have already summarised. Already in *Of Grammatology*, Derrida announced that a thought of the trace bound together the possibility of meaning, the opening of temporality, and the relation to the other in general. This possibility of ethics in undecidability and inventivity is not itself (yet) ethical or political, but is, beyond good and evil (as Derrida said of writing in 1967) also the impossibility of any ethics's *being* ethical. But if this opening is not yet itself ethical, it gives both a principle for judging (any ethical or political judgement that closes off this condition of undecidability is *ipso facto* suspect) and a principle for the infinitisation of ethics and politics. This infinitisation, which takes place each time finitely, is also called justice. For all metaphysical doctrines of ethics and politics close off the undecidable at some point: political and moral philosophies of all colours project teleologies whereby politics and morals are oriented towards their end (in social justice, virtue, transparency, etc.), whereas the deconstructive construal cannot but suspend this teleological thrust (this has made it suspect to many commentators) with its radical appeal to a future (the coming of the undecidable singular event) which will never be a present (this future that is not a future present determining the claim from the earliest work that the future is necessarily monstrous, i.e. formless), although it always happens *now*. This appeal to an irreducibly futural future (the interminably *à-venir* or to-come) suspends deconstruction always this side of any ethical or political *doctrine* or *programme*. But Derrida is prepared to link this thinking to that of a democracy which is the ethico-political figure of the never-absolute, never-present dispersion of *différance*. Far from preventing ethico-political decisions of the most concrete and pressing kind, this democracy to-come would be the condition of possibility of all such decisions, and simultaneously the condition of impossibility of any self-righteousness about them.

Deconstruction thus, quite consistently, gives no grounds for any doctrinal ontology, epistemology or ethics. It is perhaps, then, not surprising that to date no remotely convincing philosophical critique of deconstruction has been forthcoming (the attempts by Searle and Habermas are risibly ill-informed, and other critics have carefully avoided all normal philosophical precautions before issuing unargued condemnations), perhaps because it is simply not susceptible to such a critique. Derrida's work seems to have managed the exploit of being intensely philosophical and yet impervious to any imaginable philosophical refutation. But it is also a mistake (made most notably by Rorty) to assume that Derrida is to be praised insofar as he is doing something simply non-philosophical (story-telling, literary invention), and criticised to the extent that he cannot help himself sometimes getting involved in philosophical argumentation. Derrida's work stands or falls on the rigour of its philosophical argumentation (it claims to pass *right through* philosophy), and demands the most philosophical reading it can be given: that this philosophical reading leads into uncertain zones inaccessible to philosophy as such is part of deconstruction's claim, and the source of the endless irritation it causes philosophers. But if Derrida is right, this irritation cannot be simply attached to the work of one philosopher or his followers: it must be ('always already') inscribed in all the texts of the tradition as the very possibility of philosophy itself. Writing, in Derrida's sense (which is not then different from Plato's sense), is already 'in' the *Phaedrus*, the quasi-transcendental is already 'in' Kant. In putting his name to his inimitable *oeuvre*, Derrida has also done no more than add a counter-signature to all the others who have given philosophy their ambivalent guarantee. This situation, which Derrida has not invented, is already deconstruction, which is thus unavoidable, however much it may continue to be denied.

2

DERRIDA AND POLITICS

Which means that, too political for some, [deconstruction] can appear to be demobilising to those who only recognise the political by means of pre-war signposts.[1]

I believe in the necessity of a certain tradition, in particular for political reasons.[2]

Derrida has never written a work of political philosophy. But given how radical his work appears, how far-reaching in its claims about metaphysics, it is not surprising that the reception of that work, at least in the English-speaking countries, has always involved an expectation or even a demand that it *should* give rise to a politics or a political philosophy. And although Derrida has been rather more chary than the traditional French Intellectual about taking up political positions, it has always seemed obvious that his work must have, at the very least, 'political implications', but less obvious what those implications might be – and it is probably true that Derrida has never been embraced unequivocally by any particular political persuasion, although the political centre of gravity of debate (rather than just denunciation or diatribe[3]) around his work has undoubtedly been the Left. Derrida is, obviously and self-proclaimedly, on the Left. But on the Left, there has always been a desire for Derrida to 'come clean'[4] about politics, and a lurking suspicion that his (at least apparent) failure to do so was in principle a reason for dissatisfaction. According to a very common mechanism, Derrida's apparent reticence about some forms of political statement and argument led to charges (from the self-appointed guardians of the 'Left' tradition in academic politics) of liberalism or even conservatism written into his most general philosophical arguments,[5] while his more obviously 'political' texts have given rise to objections on the grounds that they supposedly show no more than a decently liberal attitude, and not the sort of genuine recognisable radicality we might otherwise think it reasonable to expect.[6] Since the late 1980s, the Heidegger and De Man 'affairs',[7] in which Derrida's interest in thinkers seen as tainted by involvement with Nazism was taken by many as a sign of political culpability, have exacerbated a sense of political trouble around Derrida, and it is perhaps not coincidental that most of Derrida's more explicit political reflections have appeared since that time.[8]

There are, however, good reasons for thinking that this configuration of hope, expectation, demand or suspicion subsequently disappointed or confirmed is a poor and naive way of responding to the challenge and radicality of Derrida's work. The reasons for this can be formulated rapidly: it is misguided to expect Derrida's work to answer to the concepts of 'politics' or 'political philosophy' just because these are metaphysical concepts – and insofar as Derrida's constant concern has been to comprehend and exceed metaphysics, he can hardly be expected to rely simply on metaphysical means so to do.

In this way, the 'political' demand on Derrida would fall foul of a structure it is probably easiest to formulate in the context of his discussions, in the 1960s and '70s, of the then triumphalist discourses of the 'human sciences'. A number of these discourses (linguistics, poetics, rhetoric, anthropology, sociology, history, even psychoanalysis) appeared to offer powerful ways of *reducing* traditional philosophical problems to various positive conditions, so that metaphysics might plausibly be seen as *no more than* a particular use of language, a particular human activity or a conditioned historical practice, always to be finally explained by *something else* (language, metaphors, human nature, society, relations of production, etc.), that something else being the positive province of the 'human science' in question. Derrida's patient interrogation of these discourses involves demonstrating that in every case the very concepts supposed to operate the reduction of philosophy were *themselves* philosophical (metaphysical). According to a mechanism he would later describe as 'transcendental contraband', the very concept supposed to reduce the transcendental claims of philosophy itself comes to occupy a transcendental position which the discourse in question has no further means of understanding, just because it is premised on the claim to reduce the transcendental claims of philosophy to more positive 'realities' of whatever order.[9] Derrida's thinking, it now seems reasonably clear, follows a rhythm (now customarily called 'quasi-transcendental') which shuttles between what would be traditionally distinguished as transcendental and empirical planes, asserting the priority of neither and the subordination of both to a wider movement neither is in a position to understand.[10]

Although none of Derrida's texts most obviously devoted to exploring this configuration explicitly addresses the attempt at a *political* reduction of philosophy, it seems clear that similar objections obtain. The political demand made of Derrida by a variety of commentators is the demand for the concept 'politics' to be placed in the very transcendental position it is self-righteously supposed to reduce and explain, but to which it remains blind, and this, in conjunction with a similar analysis of the role of history, enables convincing refutations to be made of objections to Derrida from authors such as Fredric Jameson, Frank Lentricchia or Terry Eagleton. In many of these cases, the objections were driven at least in part by indignation at what was seen as a perverse or suspect silence on Derrida's part about Marx and Marxism, a silence that *Spectres of Marx* can always be thought not to have really or convincingly broken.[11]

The position of transcendental contraband in all of these cases is occupied by a concept or network of concepts that the discourse in question (marked by just this fact as essentially positivistic) cannot understand, which means that those concepts are in fact blindly and helplessly inherited from the metaphysical tradition. In the absence of critical analysis of this mechanism in general, the human sciences remain in thrall to the very metaphysical concepts they think they are reducing, and this affirmation is a constant from some of Derrida's earliest texts. For example, Lévi-Strauss cannot but use traditional concepts:

> This necessity is irreducible, it is not a historical contingency; we should carefully consider all its implications. But if no-one can escape it, if no-one is therefore responsible for giving in to it, however little, this does not mean that all ways of giving in to it are equally pertinent. The quality and fecundity of a discourse are perhaps to be measured by the critical rigour with which this relation to the history of metaphysics and inherited concepts is thought through. This is about a critical relation to the language of the human sciences and a critical responsibility of discourse. About posing expressly and systematically the problem of the status of a discourse borrowing from a heritage the resources necessary for the deconstruction of that heritage itself. A problem of *economy* and *strategy*.
>
> (ED, 414 [282])

Of economy and strategy, and therefore, we might want to say, of political calculation. Again, more ambivalently perhaps, the opening of 'Freud and the Scene of Writing':

> Freudian concepts ... all belong, without any exception, to the history of metaphysics ... . No doubt Freud's discourse − its syntax or, if you will, its work − is not to be confused with these necessarily metaphysical and traditional concepts. No doubt it is not exhausted by this belonging. Immediate witnesses to this are the precautions and the 'nominalism' with which Freud handles what he calls conceptual conventions and hypotheses. And a thought of difference is less attached to concepts than

to discourses. But the historical and theoretical meaning of these precautions was never reflected by Freud.

(*ibid.*, 294 [197–8])[12]

In *Spectres de Marx* the idea is taken further, in a context which cannot but be perceived as political, and which separates Derrida's understanding of a 'politics of memory' from the pieties it often involves:

Let us consider first the radical and necessary *heterogeneity* of an inheritance, the difference without opposition that must mark it, a 'disparateness' and a quasi-juxtaposition without dialectic (the very plural of what further on we shall call Marx's spirit*s*). An inheritance is never gathered, it is never one with itself. Its presumed unity, if there is one, can only consist in the *injunction* to *reaffirm by choosing*. *You must* [il faut] means you must filter, select, criticise, you must sort out among several of the possibilities which inhabit the same injunction. And inhabit it in contradictory fashion around a secret. If the legibility of a legacy were given, natural, transparent, univocal, if it did not simultaneously call for and defy interpretation, one would never have to inherit from it. One would be affected by it as by a cause – natural or genetic. One always inherits a secret, which says 'Read me, will you ever be up to it?'

(SM, 40 [16])

And, a little later:

Inheritance is never a given, it is always a task. It remains before us, as incontestably as the fact that, before even wanting it or refusing it, we are inheritors, and inheritors in mourning, like all inheritors. In particular for what is called Marxism. *To be* ... means ... *to inherit*. All questions about being or what one is to be (or not to be) are questions of inheritance. There is no backward-looking fervour involved in recalling this fact, no traditionalist flavour. Reaction, reactionary or reactive are only interpretations of the structure of inheritance. We *are* inheritors, which does not mean that we *have* or that we *receive* this or that, that a given inheritance enriches us one day with this or that, but that the *being* we are *is* first of all inheritance, like it or not, know it or not.

(SM, 94 [54])

The *explicit* political implications of this situation are, however, most clearly drawn in Derrida's text on Nelson Mandela: having pointed out Mandela's admiration for the European tradition of parliamentary democracy, Derrida goes on:

But if he admires this tradition, does that mean he is its inheritor, simply its inheritor? Yes and no, according to what one understands here by inheritance. One can recognise an authentic inheritor in he who conserves and reproduces, but also in he who respects the *logic* of the legacy to the point of turning it back on occasion against those who claim to be its holders, to the point of showing up against the usurpers the very thing that in the inheritance, has never yet been seen: to the point of bringing to light, by the unheard-of *act* of a reflection, what had never seen the light.

> (PSY, 456 [NM, 17]; cf. too PSY, 471–2 [NM, 34–5],
> and DP, 82 and 449)[13]

The point of these gestures seems to be that 'politics', so often invoked as though it were *eo ipso* something 'radical', remains in just the same position of passive inheritance until its metaphysical genealogy is interrogated, and is to that extent no more promising a candidate for 'radicality' than anything else. Political responsibility, on this view, would begin in the *active, critical* memory or reception of an inheritance or a tradition which will remember us if we do not remember it. And this means that Derrida's work will not provide satisfying answers within readily identifiable disciplinary boundaries, nor even (but perhaps this comes down to the same thing) within the domains of philosophy traditionally distinguished.[14] There is no easy way to distinguish logical concerns from epistemological ones in Derrida, nor these from ethical or political ones, simply because Derrida is working at a level that precedes the establishment of such demarcations. Even *Politiques de l'amitié*, Derrida's most sustained analysis of political themes, is focused on the apparently marginal motif of friendship, and is in no easy or obvious sense a work of political philosophy.

* * *

On the other hand, the insistence of this political worry or concern is not neutral or accidental, and it is certainly not in itself illegitimate or foolish to approach Derrida with political preoccupations, nor even to suspect that the *polemical* reactions we have mentioned are not *simply* unfortunate or misguided. The reason for this appears to be a fundamental ambiguity in the inherited philosophical concept of politics, or in the position philosophy can traditionally accord to politics and the thinking of politics. This ambiguity, which might be thought of as an uneasy complicity or a pacified antagonism between metaphysics and politics, can rapidly be illustrated in Aristotle. On the one hand, the *Metaphysics* duly claims that the supreme science of philosophy is the 'theoretical science of first principles and first causes' (982b, 9). But that statement is immediately preceded by the idea that 'The highest science, which is superior to every subordinate science, is the one that knows in view of what end each thing must be done. And this end is the good of each being and, in a general manner, the supreme good in nature as a whole' (982b, 3–7), and this slight indeterminacy, between 'principles' and 'causes' on the one hand, and 'ends' and 'goods' on the other, between archaeo-logy and teleo-logy, between what will later be clearly demarcated as the 'theoretical' and the 'practical' (no doubt linked here by the value of *freedom*) allows an apparently contradictory claim in the *Nicomachean Ethics*, at the begin-ning of which an apparently identical reasoning leads to a different conclusion:

> If, then, there is some end of the things we do, which we desire for its own sake (everything else being desired for the sake of this), and if we do not choose everything for the sake of something else (for at that rate the process would go on to infinity, so that our desire would be empty and vain), clearly this must be the good and the chief good. Will not the knowledge of it, then, have a great influence on life? Shall we not, like archers who have a mark to aim at, be more likely to hit upon what is right? If so, we must try, in outline at least, to determine what it is, and of which of the sciences or capacities it is the object. It would seem to belong to the most authoritative art and that which is most truly the master art. And politics appears to be of this nature; for it is this that ordains which of the sciences should be studied in a state, and which each class of citizens should learn and up to what point they should learn them; and we see even the most highly esteemed of capacities to fall under this, e.g. strategy, economics, rhetoric; now, since politics uses the rest of the sciences, and since, again, it legislates as to what we are to do and what we are to abstain from, the end of this science must include those of the others, so that this end must be the good for man.
>
> (tr. Ross, 1094a18–1094b7)

This tension, according to which the philosophical concept of politics is both subordinate to metaphysics and superior to it, could be followed throughout the tradition in various forms: the relation between law and being, ought and is, theory and praxis, knowledge and action and so on, could be said to derive from this split in philosophy's understanding of itself and its relation to its usually reproachful other. The political demand made of Derrida is a repetition of this long tradition: if Derrida were ever simply to *answer* to that demand, to provide an answer which that demand could hear and accept, then his own thinking could safely be located in the metaphysical tradition he has always claimed to outflank. In this sense, Derrida providing a political answer to his political critics would prove just the opposite of what they would take it to prove, and so we might say that he stands a chance of proposing something radical about the political just to the extent that his texts do *not* answer simply to that demand.[15]

The fact remains, however, that Derrida himself nowhere produced an analysis of politics in this vein in the '60s and '70s. One reason for this may have been itself 'political': a sense of political strategy and solidarity may have dictated prudence about criticising the arguments of the Left. But a more powerful reason lies in just the fundamental ambiguity we have located in the concept of politics itself, which, perhaps more clearly than any other (with the possible exception of 'law'[16]) betrays a radical instability in the metaphysical concept of concept itself – and one plausible way of reading Derrida's work as a whole is that it shows up an irreducible conceptual politics even in the most theoretical or speculative domains of philosophy. In a way that is not at all a reduction in the sense of the 'human science' gestures mentioned earlier, Derrida on this account would liberate a sort of energy in the metaphysical concept of politics, so that *all the conceptual dealings deconstruction has could be taken to be political*.[17] Within this generalised 'politics' that deconstruction just is, conceptual dealings with what metaphysics defines as strictly political concepts would have a limited but important, perhaps exemplary, place.

Politics is the privileged domain of self-importance and self-righteousness for a specific reason: its apparently incontrovertible appeal to reality. The point with politics obviously being to change the world and not just to interpret it, interpreters habitually build the point of changing it into their interpretation as though *that* changed anything at all. At the beginning of Chapter 4 of *Politiques de l'amitié*, Derrida slightly wearily breaks off a discussion of some complicated formulations in Bataille, Blanchot and Nancy to reflect on this difficulty: might not this patient, prudent way of dealing with the political issues raised by difficult texts appear too slow, too self-indulgent? Is there really *time* to take this much time in the urgency of contemporary political issues and violences? Following a paradoxical moment in Nietzsche, and aporetical formulations in Blanchot or Nancy, might the reader not become impatient with 'relation without relation', 'inoperative community', and so on? Might it not be urgent (and just that would be politics) to get on to the 'real' issues, with less 'bibliophiliac discretion'? This is, of course, not an idle speculation on Derrida's part, but just the reaction his work has most typically aroused, ever since the famous *il n'y a pas de hors-texte* in *Of Grammatology*.

> Now, what would a 'history', a science and action that wanted to be resolutely and ingenuously extradiscursive and extratextual *do*? What would a finally *realist* history or political philosophy *do in truth* if they failed to take on board, so as to measure up to them, to account for them, extreme formalisation, new aporias, semantic instability, all the

worrying conversions we have just seen at work in these signals? If it did not try to read all the apparently contradictory possibilities ('relation without relation', 'community without community', etc.) these 'sophistical discourses' remind us of? Let's say it: very little, hardly anything. They would miss what's hardest, most resistant, most irreducible, most other about the 'thing itself'. They would dress up as 'realism' at the very moment they fall short of the thing – and repeat, repeat, repeat without even the awareness or memory of that repetition.[18]

As with the remarks about the human sciences, where the way to avoid *simply* inheriting from metaphysics was actively to assume (and thereby modify) the heritage of metaphysics, here the chance to engage with reality, with 'the thing itself'[19] is given by a rigorous reflection on any possible means of access to that 'thing'.

The traditional view would be that a certain amount of theorising or interpretation is no doubt necessary as a preparation for action: Derrida will maintain the paradox that theorising and interpretation are structurally interminable and can *never* prepare for the interruptive and precipitate moment of decision and action, but that the decisiveness of the decision depends none the less on its structural relation to interminable analysis. Traditional political thinking believes it can determine decisions by writing the theory of their practice: Derrida believes that a decision is only a decision to the extent that it cannot be programmed in this manner – as he often repeats, a decision that was determined by prior theories or reasons would not be a decision, but the simple administration of a programme, so for a decision to be worthy of its name it must supervene in a situation of undecidability, where the decision is not given, but must be taken.[20]

It is this deceptively simple argument which provides the core of Derrida's thinking about politics, and which will lead to the radical thinking of a 'democracy to come'. Let us approach it through the analysis of Nietzsche and a certain transcendental 'perhaps' in *Politiques de l'amitié*. Derrida is reading a fragment from *Beyond Good and Evil* in which Nietzsche talks about a new type of philosophers capable of thinking the 'perhaps', in the context of an attack on so-called 'free spirits' and the 'taste for democracy', a thought Derrida wants to link to a responsibility toward the future, in a passage I must cite at length to show how these motifs intertwine:

Shall we say that this responsibility which inspires (in Nietzsche) a discourse of hostility about the 'taste for democracy' and 'modern ideas' is exercised against democracy in general, against modernity in general? Or else does it respond *on the contrary* to the name of a hyperbole of democracy or to the modernity to come, respond *before* it [*devant elle, avant elle*], a hyperbole of which the 'taste' and 'ideas', in the Europe and America named here by Nietzsche, are merely mediocre caricatures, chattering self-righteousness, perversion or prejudice – abuse of the term *democracy*? Are not these lifelike caricatures, just because they are lifelike, the worst enemy of what they look like, whose name they usurp? The worst repression, the very one that must, right up against the analogy, be opened up and really *unlocked*?

(Let us leave this question suspended; it is breathing the *perhaps*, and the *perhaps* which is coming will always have come before the question. The question seconds, it is always tardy and secondary. The moment it is formed, a *perhaps* will have opened it. It will always forbid it from closing, perhaps, at the very place where it forms. No response, no responsibility will ever abolish the *perhaps*. That a *perhaps* forever open and precede questioning, that it in advance suspend – not so as to neutralise or inhibit them but to make them possible – all the determined and determining orders that depend on *questioning* (research, knowledge, science and philosophy, logic, law, politics and ethics, language even and in general), that's a necessity to which we attempt to do justice in several ways.

For example:

1. By recalling that acquiescence (*Zusage*) which is more originary than the question and which, without saying *yes* to anything positive, can only affirm the possibility of the future by opening itself to determinability, and therefore by welcoming what still remains indeterminate and indeterminable. This is indeed a *perhaps* which cannot yet be determined as dubitative or sceptical,[21] the perhaps of what *remains* to be thought, to be done, to live (to death). Now this *perhaps* not only comes 'before' the question (enquiry, research, knowledge, theory, philosophy); it would also come, making it possible, 'before' the originary acquiescence which in advance engages the question to the other.[22]

Derrida's 'political' thinking, explicitly here preceding the *metaphysical* order of the political as determined by the question, will exploit this radical 'perhaps', the only condition of possibility for an event of any sort (including an event of decision) to arrive, and the thought of the future it entails, to formulate a notion of democracy which is the closest his thought ever gets to a political projection or programme.

This thinking about 'perhaps' has some startling consequences. For it is not

26

enough simply to stress that undecidability is a condition of decision, or radical possibility (and therefore unpredictability), for events and decisions nonetheless occur, and must occur, and when they occur they are quite determinate. Derrida will say that an event that occurs out of the condition of the perhaps *lifts* that condition (but remembers it *as* its condition): 'If no decision (ethical, juridical, political) is possible without interrupting determination by getting into the *perhaps*, on the other hand the same decision must interrupt the very thing that is its condition of possibility, the *perhaps* itself' (p. 86).[23] Radicalising this thought about events in general in the context of *decisions* leads to a reinscription of the concept of decision away from the concept of the subject to which it is tradition-ally bound. For if an event in general has to be thought of in this way, then the traditional way of thinking about decisions can be said to neutralise just what makes the event an event by referring it to the subject:

> The decision makes an event, of course, but it also neutralises that supervening that must surprise both the freedom and the will of any subject, in a word surprise the very subjectivity of the subject, affect it where the subject is exposed, sensitive, receptive, vulnerable and funda-mentally passive, before and beyond any decision, even before any subjectivation, or even any objectivation. Doubtless the subjectivity of a subject, already, never decides about anything; its self-identity and its calculable permanence turn every decision into an accident that leaves the subject indifferent. *A theory of the subject is incapable of accounting for the slightest decision* … nothing ever happens to a subject, nothing worthy of the name 'event'.
>
> (87 [68])

So where the classical theory of the subject (still operating in Schmitt's decisionism, which Derrida discusses at length in *Politiques de l'amitié*) tends to reduce the eventhood of the event of decision by referring it to a subject, Derrida is trying to 'eventise' the decision, and this means it can no longer be quite *my* decision. On this view, decisions are taken *by the other*, my decisions, my most sovereign decisions, cannot be decisions if they are taken by some self-coincident agency, but are decisive only if there is a diremption between 'me' and the decider (in me):

> The passive decision, condition of the event, is always in me, struc-turally, an other decision, a tearing decision as decision of the other. Of the absolute other in me, of the other as the absolute that decides about me in me. In principle absolutely singular, in its most traditional concept, the decision is not merely always exceptional, *it makes an exception of me.*

27

In me. I decide, I make up my mind, sovereignly, would mean: the other than me, the other-me as other and other than me, *makes* or *make* an exception of the self-same. This presupposed norm of any decision, this normal exception does not exonerate from any responsibility. Responsible for myself before the other, I am first of all and also *responsible for the other before the other*.

$$(87-8 [68-9])^{24}$$

Now this thought, which is no doubt the key to Derrida's thinking about politics, is in fact a rigorous consequence of the quasi-concept of *différance*, at least as developed through the notion of the 'trace' in *Of Grammatology* in 1967. There, Derrida famously claims that 'the general structure of the trace links in the same possibility, and without one's being able to separate them except by abstraction, the structure of the relation to the other, the movement of temporalisation and language as writing'.[25] And the trace-structure of the relation to the other is such that the 'presentation of the other as such, i.e. the dissimulation of its "as such" has always already begun and no structure of beings escapes this' (*ibid.*). It is just this dissimulated (ghostly[26]) presentation of the other as other in me which determines the analysis of decision we have just seen almost thirty years later.

A further consequence has to do with violence. This description of events and decisions as radically unpredictable arrivals of the other[27] entails a thought that this arrival is irreducibly violent. Reflection on violence has a long history in Derrida's work, and it could be said that in a certain sense violence is the condition of possibility of history and politics. The analysis of Lévi-Strauss in *Of Grammatology*, for example, distinguishes three levels of violence: an originary 'violent' non-appropriation (first level) is violently organised into effects of propriety (in this instance by the classificatory system of secret proper names – second level), which can then be violently disclosed (third level) to the guilty ethnographer.[28]

But perhaps more importantly for thinking about politics, 'Violence and Metaphysics' establishes, apparently against what can appear too irenic in Lévinas, the primordiality of an 'economy of violence' (again this flows directly from the thought of trace and *différance*). It also suggests something like a categorical imperative in terms of a 'lesser violence in an economy of violence'.[29] Positing a primordial 'violence' in this way upsets *all* traditional political philosophies, which are bound up in a teleological structure prescribing that *arkhe* and/or *telos* be thought of as peaceful. The metaphysical thought of origin and end entails non-violence, and duly prescribes politics either as the unfortunate and degenerative decline from a peaceful origin (Rousseau), or as the redemptive drive towards an achieved peace (Kant). Even political philosophies which appear in one way or another to give greater thought to violence (Hobbes, Hegel, Marx) cannot think violence other than in the teleological perspective of non-violence. Political philosophy as such is wedded to this metaphysical scheme, and this has the paradoxical consequence that political philosophy is always the philosophy of the end of politics, or that the metaphysical concept of politics is the concept of politics *ending*.[30] Derrida's thinking of primordial violence disallows this teleological scheme, or at least complicates it to the extent that what the remarks about violence amount to is an affirmation of the *endlessness* of politics,[31] and thereby of freedom.

This thinking of violence also has consequences for the political analysis of *foundation* or *institution*. Just because of this originary or pre-originary violence, political institutions are always instituted *in violence* in a way which goes beyond the traditional (Kantian or even Hegelian) recognition of the empirical or contingent violence that *in fact* presides at moments of political foundation or institution. If it is possible to say more generally that institutions, or the institution of institutions, is ('transcendentally') violent, this is because of a formal argument to the effect that, because the institution is, by definition, *not yet* in place at the instant of its institution, it cannot *comprehend* its institution. At its inception, the law of the institution is written, as Joyce has it, in the language of the outlaw.[32] Derrida demonstrates this point not only with respect to an institution such as the University,[33] but more generally and more ambitiously in an extraordinary analysis of the American Declaration of Independence.

This short text, presented as little more than a polite introduction to a lecture on Nietzsche which happens to coincide with a visit to Charlottesville during the bicentennial celebrations of Independence in 1976, shows how the moment of the declaration, by which the 'people' who sign it come into existence *as* a people capable of signing, is struck by a necessary undecidability (between the sense that the declaration *describes* a state of affairs and the sense that it *produces* the state of affairs is appears to describe):

> There was no signatory, by right, before the text of the Declaration which remains itself the producer and the guarantor of its own signature. By this fabulous event, by this fable which implies the trace and is in truth possible only through the inadequation to itself of some present moment,[34] a signature gives itself a name. It opens a line of credit *for itself*, *its* own credit, from itself *to* itself. The *self* rises up here in all cases (nominative, dative, accusative) as soon as a signature credits itself, through a single *coup de force*, which is also a writing *coup*, as right to writing. The *coup de force* makes right, founds right, gives right, *gives rise to the law*.[35]

This founding violence, whereby no institution can quite close on itself and integrate all its moments,[36] implies that right will never quite be entirely right, but always opened up by this moment of violence at its foundation. This is not a negative or regrettable situation, however, because if institutions could so close in on themselves in total self-understanding or self-legitimation, then right would simply be transformed into necessity, there could be no question of freedom, and politics as such would simply disappear.[37] The *chance* of politics is given by this founding impossibility at the moment of institution of the institution, which also means that institutions are essentially historical and never entirely stabilised, haunted by the *coup de force* that institutes them. This aporetical moment at the 'origin' (what we might call the 'absolute past', insofar as this moment cannot be gathered into the form of the present, never really happens as such, precedes the institution as its fabulous dream-time) opens up all institutions in general to time as the radically unpredictable arrival of the event we have described. The absolute past communicates in this way with what we might be tempted to call the 'absolute future', which provides the *à-venir* Derrida regularly associates with democracy, and explains Derrida's recourse to the motif of the *promise*.[38]

* * *

It seems just possible to derive from this configuration, which we have seen involves the thought of deconstruction in general, something resembling a politics with which to return to our initial demand. For Derrida indeed attempts, on the basis of just this thinking of other, event and founding violence, to develop a notion of democracy, which runs like the unifying thread throughout *Politiques de l'amitié*, picking up on earlier, more informal developments in *L'autre cap* and *Du droit à la philosophie*. By 'democracy' here, Derrida means not so much a particular political regime as a *tension* derived in the first instance from Plato and Aristotle:

> No democracy without respect for singularity or irreducible alterity, but no democracy without 'community of friends' (*koina ta philon*), without calculation of majorities, without subjects which are identifiable, stabilisable, representable and equal among themselves. These two laws are irreducible to one another. Tragically irreconcilable and wounding for ever. The wound itself opens with the necessity of having to *count* one's friends, count the others, in the economy of one's own, where every other is entirely other [*là où tout autre est tout autre*].
>
> (40 [22])[39]

Derrida shows at length how the inherited concept of democracy is inseparable from values of nationality and rootedness, and a value of fraternity which excludes (or at least prejudges) the place of sexual difference in politics by normalising the political relation according to a model of community grounded on the example of the relation between *brothers*. As in every deconstruction (and the case of 'democracy' would in that case be exemplary) the point is to exploit other resources in the inheritance, and so the maintenance of an 'old word' for a 'new concept' requires *strategic* justification:

> If [in Plato's *Menexenus*], between the name ['democracy'] on the one hand, the concept or the thing on the other, the play of a discrepancy gives rise to rhetorical effects which are also political strategies, what lessons can we draw from this today? Is it still *in the name of democracy* that one will try to criticize such and such a determination of democracy or of aristodemocracy? Or, more radically, closer, precisely, to its fundamental *radicality* (where for example it *roots* in the security of the autochthonic foundation, in the stock and genius of filiation), is it still in the name of democracy, of a democracy to come, that we will try to deconstruct a concept, all the predicates associated in a generally dominant concept of democracy, that in the heritage of which we find without fail the law of birth, natural or 'national' law, the law of homophylia or of autochtony, civic equality (*isonomia*) grounded on the equality of birth (*isogonia*) as condition of the calculus of approbation and therefore of the aristocracy of virtue and wisdom, etc.?
>
> What still remains or resists in the deconstructed (or deconstructible) concept of democracy to orient us without end? To order us not only to start a deconstruction but to keep the old name? And still to deconstruct in the name of a *democracy* to come? That is still to enjoin us still to inherit that which, forgotten, repressed, misrecognised or unthought in the 'old' concept and in its whole history, would still be awake, delivering up signs or symptoms of survival to come through all its old, fired features? Would there still be in the concept of *eudoxia* (reputation, approbation, opinion, judgement), and in the concept of equality (equality of birth (*isogonia*) and equality of rights (*isonomia*)) a double motif which could, interpreted differently, withdraw democracy from autochtonic and homophyliac rootedness? Is there another thought of calculus and number, another way of apprehending the universality of the singular which, without giving politics over to the incalculable, still justifies the old name 'democracy'? Will it still make sense to speak of democracy in a situation in which it would no longer be a question (essentially and constitutively) of country, of nation, even of state and of

citizen, in other words, *if at least one still holds to the received acceptation of this word*, in which it would no longer be a question of politics?

(126–7 [103–4])

On the one hand, then, this is a specific issue around the specific concept of democracy as it is inherited from the tradition. We shall see in a moment how Derrida develops this deconstruction via the motif of the 'to come' we have already noted. But on the other hand, we said that this specific case was *exemplary*. This means, following an ambiguity Derrida himself has often exploited,[40] not only that democracy is one example among others of deconstruction, a sample, but that it is exemplary, the best example, a paragon, for deconstruction in general.[41] Which need not surprise us if we bear in mind our earlier suggestion that one effect of deconstruction was to suggest an irreducible conceptual politics, and that the metaphysical concept of politics carried a privileged ambiguity with it. This is enough to suggest, not just that deconstruction is in one sense a fundamentally political mode of thought, but that it is bound up with this issue of democracy in a more intimate way:

> In reaffirming that the maintenance of this Greek name, democracy, is a matter of context, rhetoric or strategy, even of polemics, in reaffirming that this name will last the time it takes but scarcely longer, in saying that things are getting singularly faster these days, one is not necessarily giving in to the opportunism or the cynicism of the anti-democrat not showing his hand. Quite on the contrary: one is keeping one's right to question, to critique, to deconstruction (rights which are in principle guaranteed by every democracy: no deconstruction without democracy, no democracy without deconstruction). One keeps this right in order to mark strategically what is no longer a matter of strategy: the limit between the conditional (the edges of the context and concept of democracy which enclose the effective practice of democracy and feed it on soil and blood) and the unconditional which, from the start, will have inscribed an auto-deconstructive force in the very motif of democracy, the possibility and the duty for democracy to de-limit itself. Democracy is the *autos* of deconstructive auto-delimitation. A delimitation not only in the name of a regulative idea and an indefinite perfectibility, but each time in the singular urgency of a *here and now*.

(128–9 [105])

Deconstruction then, on the one hand generalises the concept of politics so that it includes all conceptual dealings whatsoever, and on the other makes a precise use of *one* particular inherited politico-metaphysical concept, democracy, to make a pointed and more obviously political intervention in political thought. 'Democracy' is an old name retained because on the one hand it allows a thought of an endless progress towards a better political state, but on the other, cutting into the teleologism of the structure of the Kantian Idea, obliges an interventionist perception of the here and now, always *in the name* of the democracy-to-come which will never finally arrive, but never claiming to have established a satisfactory democracy. In this way, politics, beginning to drift away from its metaphysical determinations, is projected as *endless* (it never will come to an end, cannot really still be thought within the terms of the regulative Idea, is *perpetually* a promise, never fulfilled), and also endlessly singular (so that politics is happening each time *now*). Derrida's many more or less visible interventions in concrete political situations (most recently, for example, around new immigration laws enacted in France in 1996), are to this extent not merely the circumstantial acts of a philosopher elsewhere, and more importantly, developing theories or knowledge, but continuous with each act of deconstruction from the start, always more or less obviously marked by a strategic event of decision in a given context. This does not provide a theoretical model for politics so much as it strives to keep open the event of alterity which alone makes politics possible and inevitable, but which political philosophy of all colours has always tried to close.

3

DECONSTRUCTION AND ETHICS

Deconstruction cannot propose an ethics. If the concept − all the concepts − of ethics come to us, as they do, as they cannot fail to, from the tradition it has become commonplace to call 'Western metaphysics', and if, as Derrida announces from the start, deconstruction aims to deconstruct 'the greatest totality',[1] the interrelated network of concepts bequeathed to us by and as that metaphysics, then 'ethics' cannot fail to be a theme and an object of deconstruction, to be deconstructed, rather than a subject of its admiration or affirmation. Ethics is metaphysical through and through and can therefore never simply be assumed or affirmed in deconstruction. The demand or desire for a 'deconstructive ethics' is in this sense doomed to be disappointed.

And yet, through the naivety of certain reactions to deconstruction which have wished to present it as more or less straightforwardly ethical, as though the burden of deconstruction consisted in delivering us from metaphysical illusion into the clear light of ethical felicity and self-righteousness,[2] we might also detect a certain truth worthy of elaboration. Deconstruction deconstructs ethics, or shows up ethics deconstructing (itself), in deconstruction, but *some* sense of ethics or the ethical, something archi-ethical, perhaps, survives the deconstruction or emerges as its origin or resource. Deconstruction cannot be ethical, cannot propose an ethics, but ethics might nonetheless provide a privileged *clue* for deconstruction, and deconstruction might provide a new way of thinking about some of the problems traditionally posed by ethics.

The form of this argument is familiar from other deconstructive movements. Writing, for − the perhaps most famous − example, is itself a metaphysical concept which nonetheless, through its very metaphysical determination, provides important resources for the deconstruction of metaphysics. Similarly for the concept of the sign or of metaphor. Concepts constitutively 'secondarised' by metaphysics can be shown to be paradoxically primary, constitutive themselves of the very primary concept (and in the end, always, 'presence') from which they cannot fail to appear to be derived. In this sense, 'ethics' too always might provide deconstruction with resources repressed or left unexploited by its metaphysical determination, and these resources might then be shown to be in some way 'more powerful' than that metaphysical determination, in excess of it. In which case deconstruction might after all be describable as ethical, and perhaps as ethics itself. In 'Force of Law', Derrida famously and mysteriously claims that justice (as distinct from right or law) is the undeconstructible condition of deconstruction, and it seems that this must have some ethical resonance if it is to be intelligible.[3]

There is of course at least one salient difference between writing and ethics as potential deconstructive resources, and that is their very different status in metaphysical thought. Writing is at best a secondary concept in a domain (that of language) itself made secondary in traditional thinking, whereas ethics is, from the start, one of the basic divisions of philosophy, one of its major branches. It might then be expected that it will be a more complex and differentiated notion than was 'writing', and provide a concomitantly harder task for deconstruction. And further, whereas 'writing' is used explicitly and consistently in Derrida's work as a means into deconstructive thinking, exhaustively unpacked in both its traditional and its deconstructive guises, 'ethics' is never treated in such a way, and indeed, as we shall see, its *explicit* incidence in Derrida's work is essentially concentrated in his discussions of the work of Emmanuel Lévinas, whose thought is precisely dedicated to displacing the traditional metaphysical sense of ethics in the name of a redefined notion of metaphysics. It is these discussions of Lévinas that will provide us with our guiding thread.

On the other hand, if Derrida has been at all successful in carrying out or promoting the deconstruction of 'the greatest totality', then we would be right to expect that his thinking *in general* will not fail to have effects in the philosophical domain traditionally called ethics, and indeed that it would not be false to spread a discussion of 'deconstruction and ethics' across his work as a whole (the footnotes here will try to give a sense of this possibility). And indeed we shall see that this is the case: the very general concept of the 'originary trace' as developed in *De la grammatologie* in fact *immediately* engages with the 'relation to the other' which we can follow Lévinas in seeing as the basis of the ethical. This will have two distinct consequences: (1) deconstructive thought *in general* has an ethical import just because of this status of the originary trace; and (2) deconstructive thought will have *specific* interventions to make in the traditional metaphysical vocabulary of ethics, around concepts such as responsibility, decision, law and duty.

* * *

The non-ethical opening of ethics can be seen straightforwardly and yet intractably in the fact of reading, for example this, here, now.[4] Any text, 'before' affirming or communicating anything at all, is constituted as an appeal to a reading always still to come.[5] No text can make any particular reading of itself *necessary* (the text of laws is perhaps the clearest example here: laws attempt to exclude any reading other than the one 'intended' by the legislator, to constrain reading to *only this one* reading, but show up in the extraordinary textual efforts this involves the very impossibility of the task), but equally no text can open itself up to *just any* reading (no text is *absolutely indeterminate* with respect to its reading). Texts appeal to reading, *cry out for reading*, and not just for any reading, but leave open an essential latitude or freedom which just is what constitutes reading *as* reading rather than as passive decipherment. There would be no practice, and no institutions of reading, without this opening, and without the *remaining* open of this opening. (Hermeneutics is the dream of closing that opening.) Any reading at all, however respectful of the text being read (however respectful, that is, of the way the text reads itself) takes place in this opening, and this is why texts are not messages, and why the classical concept of 'communication' is unhelpful in discussing them. It follows that reading has a duty to respect not only the text's 'wishes' (the reading of itself most obviously programmed into itself) but also the opening that opens a margin of freedom with respect to any such wishes, and without which those wishes could not even be registered or recognised. Readers recognise those wishes (traditionally thought of as the 'author's intentions') only by opening themselves to the opening which constitutes the very *readability* of the text – however minimal that readability may be in fact – and that readability is, as such, already in excess of those wishes. A text is a text only as at least minimally readable in this sense, and that means it always can be read *differently* with respect to the way it would wish to be read. An *absolutely* respectful relation to a text would forbid one from even touching it. The ethics of reading would, then, consist in the negotiation of the margin opened by readability.[6]

Derrida on occasion formulates this situation in terms of legacies or inheritance. Here, for example, in *Spectres de Marx*:

> An inheritance is never gathered, it is never one with itself. Its presumed unity, if there is one, can only consist in the *injunction* to *reaffirm by choosing. You must* [il faut] means you must filter, select, criticise, you must sort out among several of the possibilities which inhabit the same injunction. And inhabit it in contradictory fashion around a secret. If the legibility of a legacy were given, natural, transparent, univocal, if it did not simultaneously call for and defy interpretation, one would never have to inherit from it. One would be affected by it as by a cause – natural or genetic. One always inherits a secret, which says 'Read me, will you ever be up to it?'

(40 [16])

and a little later:

> Inheritance is never a given, it is always a task. It remains before us, as
> incontestably as the fact that, before even wanting it or refusing it, we
> are inheritors, and inheritors in mourning, like all inheritors. In partic-
> ular for what is called Marxism. *To be* ... means ... *to inherit*. All
> questions about being or what one is to be (or not to be) are questions of
> inheritance. There is no backward-looking fervour involved in recalling
> this fact, no traditionalist flavour. Reaction, reactionary or reactive are
> only interpretations of the structure of inheritance. We *are* inheritors,
> which does not mean that we *have* or that we *receive* this or that, that a
> given inheritance enriches us one day with this or that, but that the *being*
> we are *is* first of all inheritance, like it or not, know it or not.
>
> (94 [54])

The concept of inheritance also appears at a key moment in a text on Nelson
Mandela: having pointed out Mandela's admiration for the European tradition of
parliamentary democracy, Derrida goes on: 'But if he admires this tradition, does
that mean he is its inheritor, simply its inheritor? Yes and no, according to what
one understands here by inheritance. One can recognise an authentic inheritor in
he who conserves and reproduces, but also in he who respects the *logic* of the
legacy to the point of turning it back on occasion against those who claim to be its
holders, to the point of showing up against the usurpers the very thing that in the
inheritance, has never yet been seen: to the point of bringing to light, by the
unheard-of *act* of a reflection, what had never seen the light'.[7]

It follows from this situation not only that reading-as-inheritance is itself an
ethical relation, but that it can be taken to *exemplify* the ethical relation as asymmetrical relation to an unmasterable and unassimilable other. That other is not
absolutely other (if it were, the text would be unrecognisable as a text, would not
even call for reading) but its otherness (the insistence and ultimate indecipher-
ability of the *call* for reading, the fact that reading is not just a tranquil act of
deciphering) is irreducible.[8] In this situation in which one's duty is to read in
respect for what makes reading possible (i.e. for the very thing that makes it
impossible for reading to be mere deciphering, the thing that reading can never
read as such), one's duty, or the duty of that duty, is to be *inventive*. Being inventive means not being merely *dutiful*. A dutiful (for example scholarly) reading
never *begins* to fulfil its duty, insofar as it tends to close down the opening that
makes reading possible and necessary in the first place:[9] and indeed this logic can
be extended to the concept of duty in general – Kant famously says that I must act
not just *in accordance with* duty but *from* duty, for the sake of duty (otherwise I
always might simply be aping what I take to be dutiful conduct);[10] but the further

logic of this is that I must in fact, in the name of duty, act not just *from* duty, but *out of* duty in the sense of inventing something that falls outside what duty might be taken to dictate or prescribe. Simply following one's duty, looking up the appropriate action in a book of laws or rules, as it were, is anything but ethical – at best this is an *administration* of rights and duties, a *bureaucracy* of ethics. In this sense an ethical act worthy of its name is always *inventive*, and inventive not at all in the interests of expressing the 'subjective' freedom of the agent, but in response and responsibility to the other (here the text being read). For I am, after all, reading the other's text, not simply attempting to 'express myself': and this situation is general. I can in fact 'express myself', exercise my freedom, only in this situation of response and responsibility with respect to the always-already-thereness of the other text as part of a 'tradition' to which I am always already indebted.

This 'ethics of reading' informs Derrida's formulations from his early work. In discussions of Freud or Lévi-Strauss, for example, it is clear that there is no escaping from 'complicity' with the tradition (it alone provides us with all our concepts and vocabularies), so the issue becomes one of rigorously and inventively negotiating that necessary complicity (what we have here been calling inheritance or just reading). 'Freud and the Scene of Writing', for example, begins by seeming to condemn Freud on the grounds that all of his concepts are inherited from the metaphysical tradition, and cannot therefore be as radical or as new as is often thought. But Derrida immediately goes on to recognise that *in itself* this situation of inheritance cannot be a ground for complaint or criticism, just because this situation is unavoidable: everyone must of necessity inherit their concepts from the tradition, so the ground of complaint is displaced, and the objection to Freud becomes the fact that he 'never reflected the historical and theoretical necessity' of this situation.[11] Similarly, in the famous early essay on 'Structure, Sign and Play in the Discourse of the Human Sciences', Derrida rapidly establishes around Lévi-Strauss the inevitability of a certain 'complicity' with the tradition: and, given that inevitability, the issue becomes one of how it is negotiated and reflected upon. Like Freud, Lévi-Strauss cannot do other than inherit his concepts from the tradition; what he might have been expected to do (and this, then, is an ethical complaint) is to reflect on that very inevitability. Only thus, the argument goes, would there be a chance of doing something about, and with, the inheritance one cannot choose not to take on.[12]

* * *

This situation of reading, then, provides a certain *matrix* for thinking about the inherited nature of concepts in general, the obligation (not a necessity, so at most what Derrida would call a *chance*) to read and thereby to give oneself the possibility of displacing them. On this construal, a certain apparent *irresponsibility* (what I have been calling reading) opens the possibility of responsibility as response to the other as necessarily not absolutely other. But if this situation is general, and places one's conceptual dealings in general in a *milieu* that might reasonably appeal to a displaced (responsibly read) sense of ethics to describe it,[13] that sense of ethics *doubles up* when the specific conceptuality being read and inherited is that of ethics itself. For Derrida's work does not just reflect, in a way we might want to call ethical, on the relation to the traditionality of thought *in general*, but also, on occasion, within that *milieu*, reflects on the traditionality of ethical concepts in particular, and indeed has done so increasingly in recent years. This more explicitly ethical reflection can rapidly be characterised as taking place in a space between a 'phenomenological' critique of the traditional division of philosophy (including the place that division gives to the ethical), and a Lévinasian attempt to retrieve a sense of the ethical as 'first philosophy'. Derrida wants both to register the force of Husserl's or (more radically) Heidegger's suspicion of the place of ethics in the traditional figuring of philosophy,[14] and Lévinas's powerful claim that ethics be re-considered as *first* philosophy, prior to what he calls ontology. The reference to Lévinas seems almost as essential to Derrida as the reference to Heidegger, and one way of tracking a path through Derrida's work is to follow the three great essays devoted to Lévinas.[15] We have already seen some of the doubts raised in 'Violence and Metaphysics' about Lévinas's basic conceptuality, and used 'En ce moment même ... ' to establish a certain originary ethicity in the textuality itself: let us now turn to 'Le mot d'accueil' for an elaboration of some more 'positive' ethical moments in Derrida.

The central argument of this text goes as follows: according to Lévinas, ethics begins in the welcome or reception of the other, who 'appears' non-phenomenally in the *face*.[16] This primary receptivity defines the ethical relation as the face-to-face, a non-symmetrical dual relation. Lévinas argues very forcibly that only this relation, as essentially ethical, provides the possibility of *sense* in a situation which is otherwise one of *disorientation*.[17] This face-to-face relation with the other is marked as asymmetrical by the other's transcendence, which in this context means that the other has a radical prior claim on me, or even allows 'me' to exist as essentially responsibility to and for the other. I do not exist first, and then encounter the other: rather the (always singular) other calls me into being as always already responsible for him.[18] In 'Le mot d'accueil', Derrida insists on how this dual (if asymmetrical) relation is from the start affected by the *third party*. This possibility of the third party (another other, the other's other) haunting my face-to-face with the other gives the possibility of *justice*, at least in the sense of *right*, i.e. some codifiable formulation of what, in the face-to-face itself, would have to remain singular to that relation, uncommunicable and above all unformulatable *as* ethics. If the face-to-face is immediately the place of response and responsibility, the third party is the possibility of raising questions about that response and responsibility (p. 63). Reading beyond the obvious intention of Lévinas's text, Derrida wants to say that this originary presence of the third party haunting the face-to-face with the other may appear to compromise or contaminate the purity of the properly ethical relation, but that that possible contamination, that compromise of purity, is *necessary* if the ethical relation is to avoid the possibility of an absolute violence of that purity itself.[19] For if the singular encounter with the other in the face-to-face were not always already compromised by this haunting third party (and, therefore, by communicability, intelligibility, but also institutionalisation and politicisation), then the supposedly pure ethical relation always might be that of the worst violence:

> The third party does not wait, his illeity calls from the moment of the epiphany of the face in the face-to-face. For the absence of the third party would threaten with violence the purity of the ethical in the absolute immediacy of the face-to-face with the unique. No doubt Lévinas does not say it in this form. But what is he doing when, beyond or through the duel of the face-to-face between two 'unique beings', he appeals to justice, affirms and reaffirms that justice 'is necessary' [*il faut*]? Is he not, then, taking into account this hypothesis of a violence of pure and immediate ethics in the face-to-face of the face? Of a violence potentially unleashed in the experience of the neighbour and of absolute uniqueness? Of the impossibility of discerning good from evil, love from hatred, giving from taking, desire for life and death drive, hospitable welcome from selfish or narcissistic enclosure?
>
> The third party would thus protect against the vertigo of ethical violence itself. Ethics could be doubly exposed to this same violence: exposed to suffer it, but also to exercise it. Alternatively or simultaneously. It is true that the protective or mediating third party, in its juridico-political becoming, in turn violates, at least virtually, the purity of the ethical desire for the unique. Whence the terrifying fatality of a double constraint.
>
> (66)

This analysis, which in typical deconstructive style pushes the text read beyond its own explicit claims, but in so doing respects the logic of the text's own economy and answers to the 'ethics of reading' scenario we have sketched out above, generates a situation which can be found in all deconstructive situations: one of an essential *contaminability* which aims to account *both* for the possibility of any purity whatsoever, *and* for the *a priori* impossibility of the (even ideal) achievement of any such purity. The logic here, which is just what is elsewhere formulated as the *quasi-transcendental*, states in general a complicity (even an identity) between conditions of possibility and conditions of impossibility, such that the *necessary possibility* of the failure, compromise or contamination of the supposedly (or desiredly) pure case is sufficient to justify the thought that that purity is *already* compromised in its very formulation. The very thing which is supposed to protect the purity in question is the thing that compromises it.[20] In this case, the ethical relation of the face-to-face constitutes itself *as* ethical only by protecting itself from itself in the figure of the third party: but that same figure will always prevent the ethical being quite the pure relation it was supposed to be, and to that extent casts doubt on its priority *as* ethical.

The paradoxical or aporetical consequences of this situation are considerable, but it is in them that we can find the core of deconstructive thought about ethics. For example, it follows from the situation just described (through and beyond Lévinas, in a version of Lévinas that already appeals to the third party beyond for its legitimacy) that justice finds its condition of possibility in what Derrida calls *perjury*. The ethical nature of the primary ethical relation in the singular face-to-face with the always unique other depends on that ethics' being protected from itself by the appeal to, and of, the third party: but appealing to that third party means that I am *eo ipso* being unfaithful to the other, failing in my implicit promise of an unconditional fidelity and respect. Ethics has a chance of being ethical only in this becoming-justice which is already also the becoming-right of justice, the becoming-formal of the absolutely non-formal relation of the face-to-face, the becoming-institutionalised of the pre-institutional 'absolute anteriority' of the relation to the other, and thus in the betrayal of my primary engagement to the other *as this* singular other. Ethics begins with this archi-betrayal or archi-perjury which functions as its condition of possibility and (therefore) of impossibility:

> Lévinas never designates this double bind in this way. I shall however take the risk myself of inscribing its necessity in the consequence of his axioms, axioms established or recalled by Lévinas himself: if the face-to-face with the unique engages the infinite ethics of my responsibility for the other in a sort of oath [*serment*] before the letter, a promise of respect or unconditional fidelity, then the ineluctability of the third party, and with him of justice, signs a first act of perjury ...
>
> Thereafter, in the deployment of justice, one can no longer discern fidelity to one's promise from the perjury of false witness, but primarily one can no longer discern betrayal from betrayal, always more than one betrayal. One ought then, with all the necessary analytical prudence, to respect the quality, the modality, the situation of the failings with respect to this 'original word of honour' before all oaths [*serments*]. But these

differences would never erase the trace of this inaugural perjury. Like the third party who does not wait, the agency [*l'instance*] that opens both ethics and justice is, in them, in a situation of [*en instance de*] quasi-transcendental or originary, even pre-originary, perjury.

(68)

Ethics, then, is ethical only to the extent that it is originarily compromised or contaminated by the non-ethical. According to a logic laid out more than thirty years earlier in 'Violence and Metaphysics', the chance of avoiding the worst violence is given by a compromise involving an acceptance of, and calculation of, the lesser violence.[21] As with all other apparently purely positive concepts analysed deconstructively, ethics in this Lévinasian sense can be made coherent only by allowing that it protect itself from itself by a necessarily risky innoculatory contamination of itself by its apparent other(s). In this case, Derrida will say that ethics is essentially *pervertible*, and that this pervertibility is the positive condition (to be affirmed, then) of all the 'positive' values (the Good, the Just, and so on) ethics enjoins us to seek.

This affirmation of pervertibility as a positive condition of what appeared to be opposed to it (so that, for example, a positive condition of promising is that I always might not keep my promise, for without such a necessary possibility, if the object of my promise necessarily followed from my promising it, my promise would not be a promise at all, but a necessary causal sequence[22]) does not of course commit one to welcoming *actual* perversions of ethical values. Saying that a positive condition of ethics is an inaugural – structural – perjury does not mean that I am henceforth ethically bound to *approve* actual acts of perjury. This production of a condition of possibility is the aspect of the analysis that prompts its qualification as transcendental. But its specifically *quasi*-transcendental character means that, as always in deconstructive thought, it is impossible rigorously to separate the transcendental from the factical or the empirical,[23] and this entails that, uncomfortably, I cannot use the transcendental aspect of the analysis to provide *a priori* knowledge of which empirical cases, which events arriving, in fact constitute acts of perversion or perversity. The positive necessary possibility of perjury affects, in the modality of necessary possibility, all empirical acts of promising or swearing, for example, but leaves open the singular judgement each time as to the actual perversity of this or that act. The quasi-transcendental analysis opens up, as a condition of ethics, the possibility of *the worst* perjury or perversion of ethics. The necessary possibility of the worst is a positive condition of the (unconditionally demanded) better. The necessary possibility of what Kant called radical evil is a positive condition of the good. The non-ethical opening of ethics, as 'Violence and Metaphysics' called it, consists in just this: that the *chance* of ethics (i.e. its necessary possibility as non-necessary[24]) lies in its hospitality to the possibility that the event to come is the worst, that the primary 'yes' it says to the other, the stranger,[25] the *arrivant*,[26] *always might* be a welcome to something or someone who will simply blow away my home, my welcome, the threshold at which I extend the greeting and the offer of food and drink in the primary ethical gesture according to Lévinas. Ethics means, then, on this view, that I know *a priori* that ethics is constitutively pervertible, but that I *never know* in advance when it is perverted in fact. As we saw earlier, any *knowledge* in this respect would immediately evacuate the specificity of the ethical in favour of an administrative or bureaucratic application of cognitive rules.

This situation appears to promote what might be called a *decisionistic* view of ethics. Without the sort of supposedly binding prior *test* of what is ethical provided by the so-called Kantian formalism, and without the sort of securities offered by the sort of ethical thinking that grounds ethics unproblematically in a particular *ethos* or even *ethnos*,[27] it looks unavoidable that ethics come to be a matter of singular decisions taken on the occasion of singular events. And, as is also the case with Carl Schmitt's decisionism in the realm of political theory, this always might seem to run the risk of promoting a particular understanding of the sovereignty of the deciding subject.[28] It is not hard to see that Derrida's doubts about Lévinas's granting primacy to the other in the ethical relation, with its concomitant (and attractive, seductive) demoting of the subject from its classical voluntaristic position, always might seem to risk returning to a sort of subjectivism without any doctrine of subjectivity to back it up. It is, then, of the utmost importance that Derrida explicitly and quite consistently argues that the logic of decision called for by the position we have summarised here is more powerful than the resources of the classical doctrine of the subject. For what would a decision that simply deployed my own subjective, egological possibilities be, if not a refusal of the very event of alterity that is here being radicalised as the (non-ethical) condition of the ethical? If 'decision' simply meant the expression of my subjective will, then it would be no decision at all, but again, in a different register, the mere application of given possibilities to a situation which consists precisely in a certain challenge to what is merely possible.[29] Derrida argues that the concept of responsibility, which is one way into what is here being described, exceeds the resources of the concept of the subject to such an extent that the subject functions as a *de-responsibilising* concept, a concept which closes off the infinite nature of responsibility which it is Lévinas's strength to bring out so forcibly. And if Derrida's 'defence' of Husserl in 'Violence and Metaphysics' seemed to run the risk of reinstating the primacy of the subject against Lévinas's more audacious insight, 'Le mot d'accueil' makes clearer what the economy of the earlier text might have obscured a little: if we are to talk intelligibly of decisions and responsibilities, then we must recognise that they take place *through the other*, and that their taking place 'in me' tells us something about *the other (already) in me*, such that, following another 'axiom' of deconstructive thought, 'I' am only insofar as I already harbour (welcome) the other in me, if only, as we pointed out at the beginning of this sketch, insofar as to be me I must accept as mine the alterity of the 'tradition' (minimally in the form of the language I speak but never chose to speak,[30] and under the name I am given but have never given myself).[31] Here too, Derrida is explicitly extending (and thereby also, respectfully, contesting) Lévinas:

> If one pursues them with the necessary audacity and rigour, these conse-
> quences ought to lead us to an other thinking of the responsible
> decision. Lévinas would no doubt not say it like this, but can one not
> claim in that case [Derrida has just been quoting Lévinas to the effect
> that: 'It is not I – it is the Other who can say *yes*'] that without exoner-
> ating me in any way, decision and responsibility are always *of the other*?
> That they always come back down to the other, from the other, be it the
> other in me? For would it really be a decision, an initiative that remained
> purely and simply 'mine', in conformity with the necessity which yet
> seems to require, in the most powerful tradition of ethics and philos-
> ophy, that the decision always be 'my' decision, the decision of one who
> can freely say 'I', 'me', *ipse, egomet ipse*? Would what comes back down to
> me in this way still be a decision? Does one have the right to give this
> name 'decision' to a purely autonomous movement, be it one of
> welcome and hospitality, which would proceed only from me, myself,
> and would merely deploy the possibilities of a subjectivity that was
> mine? Would we not be justified in seeing in that the unfolding of an
> egological immanence, the autonomical and automatic deployment of
> the predicates or possibilities proper to a subject, without that tearing
> that ought to advene in any so-called free decision?
>
> (52–3)

This radicalisation by Derrida of Lévinas's thought consists in a way of no more than a rigorous unwrapping of the concept of alterity which it is Lévinas's im-measurable merit to have brought out as the constitutive moment of the ethical. That 'radicalisation' can always look (and to Lévinasians has often looked) like just the opposite, a reduction of the radicality of Lévinas's own thinking, insofar as it seems to protest against Lévinas's absolutising of the other, and to that extent make the other *less other* than is the case in Lévinas. But in this paradoxical domain we should be wary of such a linear logic: Derrida's construal of alterity as *always less than absolute* in fact constitutes a thought of the other as *more other than the absolute other*. This apparent 'less is more' logic flows from Derrida's earliest insights into the notion of difference, and the quasi-concept of *différance* which

I have suggested elsewhere can helpfully be thought of as a name for the non-absolutisability of difference.[32] *Différance* is what saves a thought of difference from the Hegelian arguments about absolute difference collapsing into indifference and absolute identity, or rather affirms the difference *in* indifference and absolute identity as not amenable to the dialectical resolution Hegel thinks inevitably follows from the truth of difference supposedly residing in opposition and contradiction. The apparently maximal thought of difference as contradiction in fact always leads to a reaffirmation of identity beyond difference, whereas the apparently minimal thought of difference *this side of* opposition and contradiction releases a more radical and intractable concept of difference which is not to be teleologically or dialectically gathered up in a greater identity.[33]

In the present context, the consequence of this thinking of difference or alterity as non-absolute is what saves Derrida from Lévinas's attempt to situate the ethical as such as 'first philosophy', against ontology, and also from the ultimate piety of the appeal to God as the almost inevitable figure of absolute alterity, and thereby as the truth of the singular face of the other which grounds ethics, gives sense, and supposedly saves us from disorientation. But it also, and this too is a general feature of deconstructive thought, makes it difficult to maintain with any confidence the inherited metaphysical distinctions between, for example, ontology, ethics and politics. Derrida's radicalisations of Lévinas in the first part of 'Le mot d'accueil' tend to complicate the distinction between ontology and ethics,[34] and the second part goes on to suggest that Lévinas will be unable, in spite of himself, to maintain the sorts of distinctions between ethics and politics which are, however, crucial to his philosophy, at least from the opening paragraph of *Totality and Infinity*.[35]

Derrida's point derives from what we have just seen about the figure of the third party: for if the third party makes possible the ethical relation as such by instigating an originary and necessary contamination of its purity, then the defining feature of the ethical (the dual figure of the face-to-face, however asymmetrical) tends to be lost in the perspective of a multiplicity of relations introduced by the opening to the third party in general. In which case we might want to say that we are as much in the domain of politics as of ethics.

This disturbing pluralisation and even scattering of the figure of the other (to which Lévinas appealed to secure a principle of sense in a situation of distressful disorientation) gives rise, in other recent essays by Derrida, to the striking formula *tout autre est tout autre*.[36] This formula, translated by David Wills as 'Every other (one) is every (bit) other', introduces simultaneously a certain irreducible *singularity* and a certain *plurality*. One of the challenges of Derrida's thought has always been to grasp together singularity and plurality or multiplicity, and this challenge can be followed in recent work both through the questioning of Kierkegaard's distinction between the ethical and the religious in 'Donner la mort', and through the attempt to rethink the concept of democracy in *Politiques de l'amitié*. The principle whereby the very (irreplaceable) singularity of the other (the principle of its difference) is thinkable only in the context of that singularity's potential equalisation with every other singularity (the principle of its indifference) will pose difficult challenges to our thinking for some (incalculable) time to come. In the context of 'deconstruction and ethics', it is this principle that ensures the possibility both of the ever-singular 'ethical' relation and of its perpetual transgression and dispersion in 'political' multiplicity.

4

DERRIDA'S MALLARMÉ

Although 'La double séance' has often appeared to be a daunting and rather mysterious text, its structure and principal arguments seem relatively clear.[1] Analytically speaking, Derrida wants to interrogate the relation between litera- ture and truth, and to show how literature escapes (or can escape) the hold of the ontological question ('What is ... ') in a way which can nonetheless provide something like a 'formalisation' of the question of truth. To do this, Derrida is concerned (1) to explicate a traditional, Platonic, schema of *mimesis*; (2) to estab- lish the *theoretical* possibility of this schema's being disrupted by a feature or process he calls the re-mark; (3) to posit Mallarmé as an *exemplary* instantiation of that theoretical possibility; (4) to show (a) that this cannot be accounted for by a thematic reading, and (b) that it entails a practice of reading which takes more seriously than a thematic one ever could the play of (i) syntax, and (ii) sub-lexical items in the text. Each of these points is presented in recognisably argued form, and could in principle be the object of critical debate and refutation.

If 'La double séance' has been a daunting text, however, this is not without good reason. Among the many doublings and duplicities the text's title[2] indicates is a basic doubling of the analytical structure I have just outlined, by a structure we might be tempted (ill-advisedly) to call more 'properly' deconstructive. According to this second, overlaid structure, Derrida wants to show that the disruptions of the Platonic model it is heuristically simpler to refer to Mallarmé must in fact already be at work in that Platonic model, so that it is, already and intrinsically, double and duplicitous. According to this structure of argument, the failure or disruption of the Platonic schema is part of that schema from the start, and so Mallarmé's status as exemplary disruptor is rendered more complicated. According to a duplicity which inhabits the very concept of example, Mallarmé will on the one hand be presented as exemplary in the sense that he would be the *best* example, or at least a shining example, to that extent more than *just* an example, but a sort of paragon; and on the other as really no more than a *sample*, exemplifying the disruption of *mimesis* just as any text (including Plato's) might be taken to exemplify it, an example more or less randomly picked from a whole range of possibilities.

I want to argue not only that the interest of 'La double séance' lies primarily in the way in which Mallarmé is thus presented as duplicitously *exemplary*, but also that the logic of exemplarity at work in Derrida's text follows, in its structure, that of the 're-mark' Derrida finds exemplarily at work *in* Mallarmé's text (that re-mark being the essential feature of the theoretical possibility of disrupting the Platonic schema of *mimesis* posited in (2) above). This structure places Mallarmé in a curious position which I shall try to explicate, and dictates a certain convergence, both between Mallarmé's more theoretical remarks about language and Derrida's own, and between Mallarmé's textual *practice* and Derrida's own.[3] This will mean that Derrida's text cannot in principle be read exhaustively as theoretical or argumentative (although that is how I shall almost exclusively be reading it, for reasons which go beyond issues of personal competence), and that in some sense it too is, still in this double sense, *exemplary* of the theoretical positions for which it argues.

To make these points, let me first quote Derrida's formalisation of the Platonic view of *mimesis*:

1. *Mimēsis* produces the thing's double. If the double is faithful and perfectly like, no qualitative difference separates it from the model. Three consequences of this: (a) The double – the imitator – is nothing, is worth nothing in itself. (b) Since the imitator's value comes only from its model, the imitator is good when the model is good, and bad when the model is bad. In itself it is neutral and transparent. (c) If *mimēsis* is nothing and is worth nothing in itself, then it is nothing in value and being – it is in itself negative. Therefore it is an evil: to imitate is bad in itself and not just when what is imitated is bad. 2. Whether like or unlike, the imitator is something, since *mimēsis* and likenesses do exist. Therefore this nonbeing does 'exist' in some way (*The Sophist*). Hence: (a) in adding to the model, the imitator comes as a supplement and ceases to be a nothing or a nonvalue. (b) In adding to the 'existing' model, the imitator is not the same thing, and even if the resemblance were absolute, the resemblance is never absolute (*Cratylus*). And hence never absolutely true. (c) As a supplement that can take the model's place but never be its equal, the imitator is in essence inferior even at the moment it replaces the model and is thus 'promoted'. This schema (two propositions and six possible consequences) forms a kind of logical machine; it programs the prototypes of all the propositions inscribed in Plato's discourse as well as those of the whole tradition. According to a

complex but implacable law, this machine deals out all the clichés of criticism to come.

(D, 212–13 n. 8 [186–7 n. 14])

Let us accept for now that this is an accurate description and that it does indeed provide the means for accounting for all subsequent doctrines of mimesis.[4] We shall see in due course that part of Derrida's point is that this doctrine *cannot* in fact account for mimetic practices in general, so it is predictable that all subsequent doctrines of mimesis (and indeed Plato's own) will in some sense always be escaping its terms, and Derrida's schematic footnote will to that extent come to have a slightly parodic ring, as he shows how Plato's discourse is *also* necessarily escaping the hold of this 'logical machine'. For now, however, this doctrine (insofar as it can be made coherent) is essentially determined by the fact of its referring itself to the *truth*, and, according to our point (2),

> this reference is discreetly but absolutely displaced in the workings of a certain syntax, whenever any writing both marks and goes back over its mark with an undecidable stroke. This double mark escapes the pertinence or authority of truth: it does not overturn it but rather inscribes it within its play as one of its functions or parts. This displacement does not take place, has not taken place, as an *event*. It does not occupy a simple place. It does not take place *in* writing. This dis-locution (is what) writes/is written. This redoubling of the mark, which is at once a formal break and a formal generalisation, *is exemplified by the text of Mallarmé, and singularly by the 'sheet' you have before your eyes* (but obviously every word of this last proposition must by the same token be displaced or placed under suspicion.)

(D, 220 [193–4])

We need to understand a number of things in this passage. Let's try first to explicate the theoretical possibility of this double mark, and its undecidability, before attending to the status of Mallarmé as an exemplary instance of the practice of it, and, finally, to the problem of knowing what to make of the final parenthetical *mise en garde*.

Mallarmé's text 'Mimique' describes the scene of a sort of radical imitation which in fact imitates nothing, no thing. The 'mime' described acts out, represents, a drama which has no fixable prior referent, no anterior 'reality' of which it is the representation. Mallarmé, as read by Derrida, sets up a scene in which *there is* miming, but in which no thing is mimed. Derrida's description, with subordinate demonstrations spread over several pages, is as follows:

There is no imitation. The Mime imitates nothing. And to begin with, he doesn't imitate. There is nothing prior to the writing of his gestures. Nothing is prescribed for him. No present will have preceded or supervised the tracing of his writing. His movements form a figure that no speech anticipates or accompanies ... The Mime is not subjected to the authority of any book ... In the beginning of this mime was neither the deed nor the word. It is prescribed ... to the Mime that he not let anything be prescribed to him but his own writing ... The Mime ought only to write himself on the white page he is ... Mallarmé ... writes upon a white page on the basis of a text he is reading in which it is written that one must write upon a white page.

(D, 221–5 [194–8])

And faced with the possible objection that the text Mallarmé is reporting on in 'Mimique', the *livret* for the performance of the mime, however complex that text may in turn be in its own structure[5] – faced with the possible objection that this text would nonetheless be the final referent of Mallarmé's (thereby still mimetic) writing, Derrida complicates the analysis in a way which will help us to understand the sense we can give to the 'double mark' we quoted earlier: 'Telle écriture qui ne renvoie qu'à elle-même nous reporte *à la fois*, indéfiniment et systématiquement, à une autre écriture. A la fois: c'est ce dont il faut rendre compte' (229). [A writing referring only to itself *simultaneously* refers us, indefinitely and systematically, to another writing. Simultaneously: that is what we have to account for' (D, 229 [202]).] This seems to be the difficult point to grasp: Derrida is not getting excited in a *general* way about the discovery of what was at the time of 'La double séance' being taken up enthusiastically, by for example Barthes and Kristeva, under the name of 'intertextuality': the point is not (as might seem to be the case in some of Barthes's work, for example) to celebrate self-conscious intertextuality *in general*, but to stress the *singularity* (this will lead us to the *exemplarity*) of *each* referral. Whence a difficult and perhaps rather awkward *enchaînement*:

A writing that refers only to itself and a writing that refers indefinitely to some other writing might appear noncontradictory: the reflecting screen never captures anything but writing, indefinitely, stopping nowhere, and each reference still confines us within the element of reflection. Of course. But the difficulty arises in the relation between the medium of writing and the determination of each textual unit. It is necessary that while referring each time to another text, to another

determinate system, each organism only refer to *itself* as a determinate
structure; a structure that is open and closed *at the same time*.

(D, 229–30 [202])

This 'en même temps' and 'à la fois' of the open and the closed (this simultaneity
or undecidability being just what Derrida will attempt to formulate with the
word 'hymen' a little later, bespeaking both the maintenance of a distinction and
its transgression) constitutes the double mark, or the re-mark we are trying to
understand: just as a vague sense of intertextuality will not make Derrida's point,
so it is not enough to invoke a vague sense of *self-referentiality* whereby writing
refers to itself as writing by referring in general to writing in an indeterminate
way: the point is that *this* singular writing here both refers to itself as this singular
writing here *and in so doing* refers itself to other writing too.[6]

This demonstration is part of a more general Derridean claim about identity in
general: the self-referential 'ceci' in the sentence from *Les mots anglais* ('Lecteur,
vous avez sous les yeux ceci, un écrit ... ' [Reader, you have before you this, a
writing ...]) confirms the identity of the 'écrit', or at least of the word 'ceci'
itself, only by *getting outside itself* to point to itself from the position of the other,
the reader explicitly addressed by the sentence apparently referring only to itself.
The mark ('ceci') is re-marked as itself ("ceci") by a ghostly doubling whereby the
mark marks itself as marking, refers to itself referring to itself, only by the fact of
separating itself enough from itself to open the gap across which reference can
function: but the 'end' of that reference, the referent to which that reference is
supposed to refer, is nothing other than the fact of reference or referring itself.[7]
This 'miming' of reference (without which no reference at all could take place,
for want of sufficient self-identity in the mark doing the referring) is the principle
according to which mimesis's referral to truth will never quite be successful.[8]

What the 'official'[9] Platonic doctrine of *mimesis* cannot contain, then, is this
simultaneity of reference (be it thought of as reference to 'reality' or simply to
other texts) and self-reference. 'Giving itself to be read for itself and doing
without any external pretext, *Mimique* is also haunted by the ghost or grafted onto
the arborescence of another text' (D, 230 [202]). More importantly, Mallarmé's
text is not only structured in this way (it only takes a moment's reflection to
realise that any text must *a priori* be so structured), but it writes that fact into
itself: 'Mimique' is not only a growth grafted on to the complex branching structure of the history of Pierrot, but a grafted growth which 'remarks' the fact of
that grafting:

Bibliographical investigation, the search for sources, the archeology of
the Pierrots would be both endless and useless, at least for our concerns

here, for the process of referral and graft is *remarked in* Mallarmé's text, which has, then, no more an inside than it is properly by Mallarmé.

(D, 233 [205])[10]

So, Mallarmé's text refers to a performance which is apparently to be a pure production with no prior text determining its acts, but does so by referring itself to another text (Paul Margueritte's *livret* with its complex internal structure and endless referrals to the tradition of the *commedia dell'arte*), and yet folds back onto itself insofar as it refers to its own gestures of referral. Derrida's contention is that this structure cannot be described either by the official Platonic doctrine of *mimesis* as adequation, or by the associated view that this would therefore be the pure production of truth itself as an inaugural unveiling (truth as *aletheia*). The point is that the Mime *mimes*, but mimes nothing, no-thing: this is what Derrida calls a 'reference without referent',[11] whereby the apparent structure of *mimesis* is maintained, and indeed generalised, so that what we have is an imitation without a model, a ghost which is there from the start, the ghost of no once living (and now dead) thing. This *generalised mimesis*, obtained by the re-marking in the text of the referral of the text to another text (by the apparently reflexive re-marking, then, of the failure of the text to achieve closure and self-identity) is here presented as powerful enough to suspend the subordination of literature to truth, insofar at least as that truth is secured by an ontology or a dialectics.[12]

But it follows directly from this suspension of the ontological referent ('being') that it will be impossible to maintain the structure used so far to establish a contrast between a Platonic doctrine and a Mallarméan contestation of that doctrine: generalised *mimesis* will be general only if this type of structure is itself complicated or disrupted too. Derrida's prose presents this consequence as a sort of theoretical narrative within a paragraph we may ourselves take as provisionally *exemplary* of the deconstructive manner:

> Mallarmé thus preserves the differential structure of mimicry or *mimēsis*, but without its Platonic or metaphysical interpretation, which implies that somewhere the being of something that *is*, is being imitated. Mallarmé even maintains (and maintains himself in) the structure of the *phantasma* as it is defined by Plato: the simulacrum as the copy of a copy. With the exceptions that there is no longer any model, and hence, no copy, and that this structure (which encompasses Plato's text, including his attempt to escape it) is no longer being referred back to any ontology or even to any dialectic. Any attempt to reverse mimetologism or escape it in one fell swoop by leaping out of it *with both feet* would only amount to an inevitable and immediate fall back into its system: in suppressing the double or making it dialectical, one is back in the perception of the

thing itself, the production of its presence, its truth, as idea, form, or matter. In comparison with Platonic or Hegelian idealism, the displacement we are here for the sake of convenience calling 'Mallarméan' is more subtle and patient, more discreet and efficient. It is a simulacrum of Platonism or Hegelianism, which is separated from what it simulates only by a barely perceptible veil, about which one can just as well say that it already runs – unnoticed – between Platonism and itself, between Hegelianism and itself. Between Mallarmé's text and itself. It is thus not simply false to say that Mallarmé is a Platonist or a Hegelian. But it is above all not true.

(D, 235 [206–7])

In accordance with what Derrida means by deconstruction more generally, apparent escape from the closure of metaphysics leads inevitably to a fall back into it: the apparently greater difference falls back into no difference, in-difference, sameness.[13] A more radical difference, then, is made by making an apparently smaller difference, an apparently minor displacement, or even what may look like a re-doubling confirmation. Mallarmé *looks just like* an Idealism or a Hegelianism, but just because of that insistence on mimetic doubling, that insistence on looking just like itself, Mallarmé makes a bigger (because 'more subtle and patient') difference. Mimesis is exceeded by a mimesis of mimesis, a second-order mimesis, a miming of mimesis, that takes as its reference the act of reference of first-order mimesis (which has a referent as *its* reference). But bringing out the 'truth' of mimesis in this way displaces the truth: at what it can only be a provisional convenience to call this second level, mimesis is shown to have no truth other than the referring movement itself whereby it always might *not* be truthful. And this must be just as true of first-order mimesis too, so that in Plato too there is a doubling up of mimesis, so that the most official examples of it always might be just mimickry or false imitations.

At which point there is a possibility and a danger. The *possibility* (of which Mallarmé would, then, be *exemplary*) is that *there be* some sort of 'escape' from philosophy (metaphysics), here showing up as the generalisation of mimesis and therefore of 'literature'. This possibility is the more alluring in that it looks as though its necessary *generalisation* means simply that *there is no philosophy*, so that Plato too would turn out to be just another instance of what is now a general literature. The *danger* is that just this alluring possibility pitches the analysis back into the very problem Derrida has just been praising Mallarmé for avoiding (by keeping the mime in mimesis) and leads simply to a sameness in which all differences are lost. To avoid this consequence, or rather to face up to this danger, Derrida appeals to a notion of *strategy*, which will lead to a reintroduction of something like history into the account, which appeared earlier to be bracketing history out in the name of a transcendental structure of the re-mark. The danger would consist in declaring *straightforwardly* that all texts necessarily escape metaphysics, which could then simply be forgotten in the name of something like a general literature or textuality in which we could henceforth triumphantly or blissfully install ourselves, with Mallarmé our hero. Such a declaration would have at least the heuristic advantage of dramatizing a 'performative contradiction': the thetic form of a metaphysical proposition would have been borrowed just long enough to declare the subsequent (and antecedent) invalidity of any such thetic metaphysical statement. The only valid metaphysical statement would be the eminently metaphysical statement that all metaphysical statements are invalid. Deconstruction is the ongoing and necessarily interminable demonstration (or enactment) of the over-hastiness of this consequence, the perpetual holding back short of this apparent *telos* of its arguments. Whence the need for a long footnote about this notion of strategy, appended to the paragraph we have just quoted:

> Just as the motif of neutrality, in its negative form, paves the way for the most classical and suspect attempts at reappropriation, it would be impudent just to cancel out the pairs of metaphysical oppositions, simply to *mark off* from them any text (assuming this to be possible). The strategic analysis must be constantly readjusted. For example, the deconstruction of the pairs of metaphysical oppositions could end up defusing and neutralising Mallarmé's text and would thus serve the interests invested in its prevailing traditional interpretation, which up to now has been massively idealist. It is in and against this context that one can and should emphasise the 'materialism of the idea'. We have borrowed this idea from Jean Hyppolite (' ... within this materialism of the idea he imagines the diverse possibilities for reading the text ... ' 'Le coup de dés de Stéphane Mallarmé et le message', in *Les Etudes Philosophiques*, 1958, no.4). This is an example of that *strategic dissymmetry* that must ceaselessly couterbalance the neutralising moments of any deconstruction. This dissymmetry has to be minutely calculated, taking into account all the analysable differences within the topography of the field in which it operates. It will in any case be noted that the 'logic of the hymen' we are deciphering here is not a logic of negative neutrality, nor even of neutrality at all. Let us also stress that this 'materialism of the idea' does not designate the content of some projected 'philosophical' doctrine proposed by Mallarmé (we are indeed in the process of determining in what way there *is* no 'philosophy' in his text, or rather that this text is calculated in such a way as no longer to be situated *in* philosophy), but precisely the form of what is at stake in the operation of

writing and 'Reading – That practice –,' in the inscription of the 'diverse possibilities for reading the text.'

(235 n. 18 [207 n. 24])

This notion of strategy or calculation is of course itself not simple.[14] But it leads to a thought that each textual occasion is *singular*, and of course just this was the point Derrida was making about the generalising *reference* he was also describing in Mallarmé's text. This singularity of textual occasions opens the field of 'strategic calculation' as to the best example on a *given* occasion: we may then want to say that it is no accident that Derrida is choosing to read Mallarmé in 1969, in the context not only of the 'massively idealist' reception of Mallarmé, but also of a *Tel Quel* 'textual materialism' he is also discreetly and patiently displacing.

The same configurations can be seen at work in the second part of the text, in the critique of Jean-Pierre Richard. The argument here is that Richard's two exemplary 'themes', *blanc* and *pli*, cannot in fact satisfactorily be thought of as themes, on the one hand because, as Richard himself recognises, they are, like all 'themes', defined diacritically rather than substantively, but on the other, more importantly, because these are 'themes' only to the extent that they *also* say something about the possibility of all other 'themes', or the possibility of anything like 'themes' in general. Let us rehearse briefly this argument, which relies on the structure of what it has become commonplace to call 'quasi-transcendentality' in Derrida's thought.

The point here is that, whatever thematic series or perspective Richard sees fit to insert *blanc* into (the *Tableau* text suggests 'neige, froid, mort, marbre, etc.; cygne, aile, éventail, etc.; virginité, pureté, hymen, etc.; page, toile, voile, gaze, lait, semence, voie lactée, étoile, etc.' [snow, cold, death, marble, etc.; swan, wing, fan, etc.; virginity, purity, hymen, etc.; page, canvas, veil, gauze, milk, semen, milky way, star, etc.] (p. 372)) all the terms in that series or perspective are separated from each other by blanks or gaps. A thematic series can only be recognised as a series if its members are articulated among themselves, and the minimal condition of such an articulation is that they be at least relatively separable, to be recognised as the terms that they are: this separability entails that there be a gap or space, however construed, between them. It will follow that any thematic term which can be thought to refer to just that space or gap will have a privilege over other such terms, and just this is the case with *blanc*. *Blanc* is of course a common 'theme' in Mallarmé, and can convincingly be placed in a series or perspective with other *blanc*-related terms, but it also, in an apparently transcendental manner, refers to the gapping or spacing that is a condition of possibility of that series in which it is also only one member or term. *Blanc* is to be found on the same level as all the other textual signifiers identifiable as themes in Mallarmé, but, still occurring in the text, provides the 'supplementary re-mark' of the spacing or gapping which is a condition for all textual signifiers to take their place in the text at all.

Now this double or duplicitous position of *blanc* is the same as that of Mallarmé himself as exemplary of a certain excess of Platonic *mimesis*: Mallarmé is on the one hand merely a sample of that excess, one of a series insofar as any text at all might be taken more or less clearly to show that excess, insofar as it just is a necessary condition of textuality. But Mallarmé is a good, perhaps the best, example, because his text brings out that condition in an unusually salient way, making it difficult to avoid. Similarly, it can in principle be shown on the basis of any theme at all how themes work and that in fact *there is no theme* (no atomic thematic unity identifiable as such outside the network of other 'thematic' 'unities'),[15] but *blanc* is a better example than others from this point of view, because it quite literally refers, beyond the figural richness Mallarmé's text invests it with, to the spacing that is the condition and undoing of themes in general. As always in Derrida, the quasi-transcendental gives us conditions both of possibility (there can be no theme without a spacing or gapping of themes) and of impossibility (just that spacing disallows atomic thematic identity to any theme whatsoever). But it also generates an undecidability on each occasion of *blanc* (but by extension too of all the words that might be its figural substitutes), insofar as each such occasion refers the reader both to the 'theme' in question *and* to its condition of (im)possibility. Further, this undecidability is not just a modish way of referring to an additional semantic resource in the text, because *blanc* as condition of any meaning at all is itself *meaningless*, not a meaning at all, but the spacing that Derrida here consistently refers to as a *syntactic* excess over any semantics.[16] As such, it cannot become the Great Transcendental Blank it might be tempting to see as the final – nihilistic – signified of Mallarmé's work, because all it does is to refer *back down* into the actually occurring signifiers in the text. After all, *blanc* is still just one term among many, Mallarmé still only an example among others.

Just this double or duplicitous structure of the *blanc*, the rising and falling movement or *rhythm*[17] of the quasi-transcendental make it possible to argue that it is already, from the start, affected by a *pli*. *Blanc* is constantly folded back into the text whose (im)possibility it also indicates while more or less exuberantly confirming that text's 'figural' movement, moving us down the 'thematic' axis of *blanc* and *pli* to *éventail* and soon to *page*, *plume* and so on.

> The blank is folded, is (marked by) a fold. It never exposes itself to straight stitching. For the fold is no more of a theme (a signified) than the blank, and if one takes into account the linkages and rifts they propa-gate in the text, then *nothing* can simply have the value of a theme any more.

And there is more. The supplementary 'blank' does not intervene only in the polysemous series of 'white things,' but also *between* the semes of *any* series and *between all* the semantic series in general. It therefore prevents any semantic seriality from being constituted, from being simply opened or closed. Not that it acts as an obstacle: it is again the blank that actually liberates the effect that a series exists; in marking itself out, it *makes us take* agglomerates for substances. If thematicism cannot account for this, it is because it overestimates the *word* while restricing the *lateral*.

(D, 285 [253–4])

It remains to show how this leads necessarily to the reading of sub-lexical features of the text. The logic here is as follows: once it is recognised in this way that themes have no identity outside the textual – syntactic – system in which they are at work, then 'themes' are no longer essentially to do with meaning at all. In the *Tableau* text, Derrida says quite straightforwardly that critical and rhetorical reading methods have always relied on the determinability of meaning (however much they may celebrate semantic wealth, complexity or polyvalence): but once the operation of the re-mark obliges the reader to attend to the failing structure of thematics in general, then it will follow that the traditional structure of the sign (textual signifiers name signifieds which we organise thematically) can no longer be relied upon. A first consequence is that syncategorematic terms (which resist nominalisation) can come to the fore in a way thematic criticism would find difficult to read.[18] But this functioning in Mallarmé is further complicated by exploitation of possible play between different syntactic values of the 'same' word, or words sounding the same (the *Tableau* looks briefly at *elle/aile* [she/wing], *lit/lis/lys* [bed/read/lily], and, like 'La double séance' itself, *or* [gold/thus]), and this leads inexorably to a break-up of the unity of words which thematic criticism must presuppose, so that, for example, 'or', appears not only as a word which might be a noun or a conjunction, but *within* other words such as 'dehors, fantasmagoriques, trésor' [outside, fantasmagorical, treasure], etc., and in complicated plays with *son or, sonore* [his gold, sonorous], and even the *English* word 'or'. And this leads further still to an insistence on the letter 'o' or 'i', so that Mallarmé's texts become in some sense ('ceci, un écrit') *about* the disposition on the page of letters which in and of themselves have no meaning whatsoever, still less a *thematic* value.[19]

Again, Mallarmé is *exemplary* in this respect. No text can function to generate effects of meaning, however literal, without disposing pre-semantic marks on the page. In principle, any text, including the texts of Plato himself, can show this, however much the meaning-effects they generate may seem dedicated to repressing it (but that's metaphysics, and most of literature). But despite the best efforts of idealistic thematic critics, Mallarmé, whose texts cannot of course *prevent* themselves from being read thematically, dialectically and metaphysically, provides ample material to make the accomplishment of such readings difficult to maintain.

How, finally, are we to understand the relationship between Derrida's writing and Mallarmé's? Given the progressive suspension by Derrida of all the usual critical *points de repère*, it is difficult to believe that the categories of commentary, interpretation or analysis[20] will suffice to describe that relationship. It seems more plausible to suggest that Derrida's text has a relationship to Mallarmé's which is somewhat of the order of the relationship he describes as holding between Mallarmé's text and Margeritte's *livret*, or more generally of the order of what Mallarmé's text calls 'mimique'. It would not be difficult to find evidence in Derrida's text of a more or less marked mimicry of Mallarmé. This does not of course mean that Derrida is somehow simply repeating Mallarmé or doing no more than quoting Mallarmé against, say, Plato. But it follows from everything we have seen that, while being concerned to stress an exemplary singularity of Mallarmé, Derrida is also committed, among other things just through the careful reading of Mallarmé, to the disappearance of anything as easily identifiable as 'Mallarmé' or 'Derrida'. If one of the paradoxes of Mallarmé is that he signs and affirms the 'disparition élocutoire' of the poet, then we might think we can read 'Mallarmé' wherever such a disappearance leaves its trace. This is why Derrida suggests that we cannot think of Mallarmé straightforwardly as an 'event' befalling Platonism. And by extending and generalising that structure, Derrida would on this account be usurpatorily signing all the texts he reads just as he withdraws from them and puts them before us in their incontrovertible and shocking literality. Or, which we will have tried, still, here to do, to him.

Part II

ALLOGRAPHICS

5

R.I.P.

For the clarity we are aiming at is indeed *complete* clarity. But this simply means that the philosophical problems should *completely* disappear.

The real discovery is the one that makes me capable of stopping doing philosophy when I want to. – The one that gives philosophy peace ...

(Wittgenstein, *Philosophical Investigations*, §133)

Let me begin with some violently dogmatic quasi-axioms.[1]

Philosophy knows all about the future, or at least about *its* future. It knows, and has always known, that it has no future. Philosophy knows that the future is death. Philosophy is always going to die. Always has been going to die. Always will have been going to die. From the beginning, its future will have been its end: and from this end, its future will have been always to begin its ending again. The end of philosophy is the end of philosophy.

The concern philosophy has always shown with what we might naively call *literal* death (my death, Socrates's death, the death involved in being-towards-death individuating *Dasein* in its *Jemeinigkeit*) is (also) a displaced figure of what we might equally naively call philosophy's *figural* (or at least non-literal) death, which death is analytically inscribed in the philosophical concept of philosophy. But this primary possibility of figural displacement, between death and 'death', the death of the philosopher and the death of philosophy, leaves the rich philosophical lexicon of death curiously indeterminate as to its sense and reference. 'Death is a displaced name for a linguistic predicament', wrote Paul de Man.[2]

Philosophers philosophise because the future is death, they philosophise to overcome death, so as not to be afraid of death. The *locus classicus* here is Socrates in the *Phaedo*:

Ordinary people [other people, i.e. people other than philosophers: του αλλου] seem not to realize that those who really apply themselves in the right way to philosophy are directly and of their own accord preparing themselves for dying and for death. If this is true, and they have actually been looking forward to death all their lives, it would of course be absurd to be troubled when the thing comes for which they have so long been preparing and looking forward.

Simmias laughed and said, Upon my word Socrates, you have made me laugh, though I was not at all in the mood for it. I am sure that if they heard what you said, most people [τους πολλους] would think – and our fellow countrymen would heartily agree – that it was a very good hit at the philosophers to say that they are half dead [θανατωσι, moribund, as good as dead] already, and that they, the normal people, are quite aware that death would serve the philosophers right.

And they would be quite correct, Simmias – except in thinking that they are 'quite aware'. They are not at all aware in what sense true philosophers are half dead [θανατωσι again] or in what sense they deserve death, or what sort of death they deserve.[3]

That 'true' philosophers are half dead will perhaps not come as a surprise to most of us: but it's worth stressing that this 'half death' – and this is no doubt in part why it must escape the awareness of 'normal people' – also affects all moral qualities as their condition of logical consistency. Socrates proceeds to argue that only the philosopher thus defined by the relation to death can possess the virtues of courage, self-control and temperance (and by extension all the others) in a form which is not 'illogical': in the non-philosopher, for example, courage is always dictated by fear (of something worse than that in the face of which courage is shown, and that 'worse' taken to an absolute is death) – but that courage be thus dictated by fear is illogical.[4] Only philosophers, in the half-death that defines them *as* philosophers, can exhibit a philosophically acceptable (i.e. logical, non-contradictory) virtue, and they can do so only because of the horizon of death that makes philosophy philosophical in the first place. The half death of the philosopher is the half life of philosophy. Taking something philosophically, then, *always* involves this more or less hidden relationship with death.[5] Or, by a slightly violent *contraction*, whatever I take philosophically is death. Death is the only subject of philosophy, by which it knows the future and can allow philosophers to be moral. The philosophers' stone is an inscribed headstone.

The 'logic' invoked here by Socrates, and the logic of that invocation of 'logic', with the concept of 'half death' that supports it, are both absolutely familiar and extremely disconcerting, as *Unheimlich* as the double of what is most homely and reassuring. What looks at first like a dialectical pattern whereby life and death can exchange their attributes to the point that Socrates will depart for a fuller life in death than in life (which was, after all, half-death, and so only half life), where 'those who have purified themselves sufficiently by philosophy live thereafter altogether without bodies' (114c) – this apparently dialectical pattern (which could no doubt be described as dialectical only on the basis of death conceived in this way, and of which the Hegelian life of Spirit that endures and maintains itself in death would be the continuous and programmed development[6]) can always pitch catastrophically, like the souls of the damned into Tartarus (113d), into a non-dialectizable aporetics which leaves philosophy (or at least the philosopher) in a zone which is less 'between' life and death,[7] than strictly uncognizable in terms of the concepts 'life' and 'death', (and here we would have to stress the fact that Socrates's *viva voce* doctrine of life, death and philosophy – in which those concepts 'life' and 'death' and 'philosophy' receive a determination definitive of the Western tradition – is relayed, according to the fiction of the dialogue, still *viva voce* by Phaedo to Echecrates, but beyond that in writing by Plato (absent of course on the fateful day), according to the relay-structure analysed in 'Plato's Pharmacy' and the 'Envois' section of *The Post Card*). In this aporetical reading (and I use the term 'aporetical' in homage to Derrida's recent *Aporias*, which is all about death), the soul is *both* essentially separate from the body, pure of the body's contingent taint, *and* essentially corruptible or contaminable by the body: the philosopher is half dead because he strives to keep the soul pure of such contamination, but *only* half dead in that the soul cannot be pure of the body until death, after philosophy, which is thus also always the fading compromise of its own contamination and taintedness.[8] The philosopher may 'practise death', as Socrates says a little later (81e), may rehearse death in life, but cannot ever quite *practise* it until the death that philosophy never quite achieves but which releases the philosopher for a pure practice of philosophy as a wisdom which would henceforth be endless and pointless.

Death, then, cuts both ways. Death interrupts, cuts the thread or tears the cloth of living existence, puts an end always too soon, brings up short. Nothing more inevitable, nothing more unpredictable. Death is both absolute necessity and absolute contingency. But death, cutting the thread or ripping the yarn of my life, tearing it off, brings peace or at least repose. Philosophy is organised around or towards death, but also, thereby, around or towards peace. When Kant, for example, opens his text about Perpetual Peace with a joke about the Dutch innkeeper whose inn of that name carried a sign depicting a graveyard, he introduces an image that repeatedly returns to haunt not only that text, but his whole philosophy.[9]

This situation generates several paradoxical consequences which mark out the history of philosophy and maybe just are the history of philosophy. I philosophise *for* death and from death, but because I philosophise death as peace or repose, I philosophise that death *as* life. Transcendental life is death conceived in this way. As transcendentally alive, I am, essentially, dead. Jacques Derrida's demonstrations in 'Cogito and the History of Madness', 'Freud and the Scene of Writing', *Speech and Phenomena*, and 'Signature Event Context' show this, I am tempted to say, *conclusively*, with lethal – mortal – accuracy, and one evaluation of this 'early' work would say that its importance lies precisely in this simultaneous confirmation and displacement of the philosophical thinking of death or of philosophy as a thinking of death. Deconstruction would, on this view, be less a thinking of language or meaning, as it is often still taken to be, than a thinking of death.

But the point, for Derrida, would be to get out of what he might call the turnstile or merry-go-round of these consequences,[10] and this leads towards other consequences (or perhaps something other than consequences), whereby death can be thought radically *as* death, and not as dialectically exchangeable with life in the Socratic-transcendental-dialectical set-up: and according to a familiar paradox of deconstructive thought, death is thought *more* radically than in the tradition by being thought of in a sense *less* radically, neither rending nor repose, neither RIP nor R.I.P. Derrida is the death of death. It is on the condition of this 'less is more' radicalism that the perhaps optimistically plural title of this conference, *futures*, can be given some ... future.

One feature of this curious situation is that the founding philosophical *pathos* of the future-as-death is somewhat modified. It is difficult to sustain at least certain versions of existential earnestness or even excitement about death in the face of the demonstration that death is entailed in every use of a proper name or of the pronoun 'I'. No doubt Derrida's complaint in 'Circumfession' that in 'Derridabase' I deprived him of any future[11] is a way of saying that I presented him as a philosopher (and therefore enacted a wish for his death), forgetting that his thinking of death must displace the whole of philosophy with it (and therefore keep him alive to the extent that, as I also – be fair – tried to argue, enacting a wish for his long life – *il nous enterrera tous, d'ailleurs* – that deconstruction is the least philosophical discourse imaginable).

But this deconstructive displacement may seem to replace a thinking of the future as death with a thinking of the future as birth, that runs the risk of generating an at least equal pathos.[12] Derrida may easily seem to buy into some such pathos at least in famous comments about the future being *monstrous*, especially perhaps at the end of the *exergue* to the *Grammatology*.[13] For my purposes here, however, the version of this pathos to be found at the end of the 'Structure, Sign and Play' essay is more interesting. Here, you will remember, Derrida has invoked 'two interpretations of interpretation' in one of the more celebrated half-read (rather than half-dead, though the two probably go together) paragraphs of his work. No question of choice here, he says, *first* because the category of choice appears thin in this context; *second* because we must first try to think the common ground and the *différance* of that irreducible difference; *and because* (less a third reason, this, than a supplement to the second),

> And because this is a type of question – let's call it historical still – whose *conception, formation, gestation, labour*, we can today only glimpse. And I say these words with my eyes turned, certainly, towards the operations of childbirth; but turned too towards those who, in a society from which I do not exclude myself, are still turning them away [so I'm turning my eyes towards people who are turning their eyes away from something: so none of us is looking at it] before the still unnameable which is looming [*qui s'annonce*, still: it's not clear to me in the optics or catoptrics of this scene whether the people I've turned my eyes towards have turned theirs away from the still unnameable or from whatever it is that *announces* the unnameable] and which can only do so, as is necessary every time a birth is at work, in the species of the non-species, the formless, mute, infant and terrifying form of monstrosity.
>
> (ED, 428 [293])

The version from the *Grammatology* made no reference to childbirth, and the emphasis given to it here, in a text written at about the same time, has always seemed rather mysterious to me. Even if there were contingent, perhaps biographical, reasons for this reference to childbirth (though even they would not explain the presence of this reference in the one text and its absence in the other) and even if those same contingent reasons might motivate the link of childbirth with the terror of the monstrous, it might still seem curious to choose such figures to say something about the radical futurity of the future. However terrifying the prospect of childbirth in general and the reality of the birth of one's own children in particular, childbirth might seem to be part and parcel of the most naturalistic and reassuring temporality imaginable, rather than a sign of the formlessness of the radical future.

The slight oddness of this reference can be brought out by juxtaposing Derrida's childbirth passage with a remark in Kant's *Prolegomena to any Future Metaphysics that Will be Able to Come Forward as Science*. In the course of his famous and intensely problematical attempt to distinguish *Grenze* from *Schranke*,[14] bounds from limits as the standard translation has it, Kant stresses a difference between mathematics and natural science, which know limits but not bounds (in that, for example, what cannot be an object of the senses cannot fall within their grasp, and they are therefore *limited* with respect to such objects, but they do not lead necessarily to the thought of such objects), and metaphysics, which cannot but lead us to a thought of bounds by inevitably transgressing the limits of what can be given in intuition:

> But metaphysics leads us towards bounds in the dialectical attempts of pure reason (not undertaken arbitrarily or wantonly, but stimulated thereto by the nature of reason itself). And the transcendental ideas, as they do not admit of evasion and yet are never capable of realisation, serve to point out to us actually not only the bounds of the use of pure reason, but also the way to determine them. Such is the end and the use of this natural predisposition of our reason, which has brought forth metaphysics as its favourite child, whose generation [*Erzeugung*], like every other in the world, is not to be ascribed to blind chance but to an original germ [*nicht dem ungefähren Zufalle, sondern einem ursprünglichen Keime zuzuschreiben ist*], wisely organised for great ends [*zu großen Zwecken*]. For metaphysics, in its fundamental features, perhaps more than any other science, is placed in us by nature itself and cannot be considered the production of an arbitrary choice [*das Produkt einer beliebigen Wahl*], or a casual enlargement [*zufällige Erweiterung*, contingent widening] in the progress of experience from which it is quite disparate.[15]

For Derrida in the 'Structure, Sign and Play' essay, childbirth is the very figure of what looks as though we could call a radical contingency of the future; for Kant, a figure of the very opposite of that – a wise teleological organisation of nature. What are we to make of this apparent divergence in the use of the same figure?

Let us note first of all that Kant's use of this figure of non-contingency does not itself seem to be at all arbitrary or contingent. Childbirth comes along quite naturally here, because it is an essentially teleological figure of teleology itself[16] as the 'truth' of metaphysics itself, insofar as metaphysics just is the inevitably teleological movement of thought definitive of finite rational beings to the extent that they *are* rational. The dialectic of pure reason, necessarily generated by the fact that the pure principles of possible experience are not themselves given *in* experience, and therefore seem to lead beyond it, resolves itself in the third *Critique* into the merely regulative use of the reflexive judgement, as laid out more especially (or so it seems to me) in the antinomy of teleological judgement. The end of Kant's thought, its *telos*, is teleology itself.[17] The image of childbirth here captures this sense in which metaphysics, teleologically produced in us through reason by the agency Kant calls 'nature', is *itself* essentially teleological: Kant chooses to figure metaphysics just the sort of natural object (i.e. an organism) that in the third *Critique* will call necessarily for teleological judgement (see §65). It might, then, come as no surprise that Derrida should diverge from Kant in his mobilisation of this figure, for the infinitesimal and seismic shift that deconstruction marks in the thinking of death I have just alluded to carries with it a similarly infinitesimal and seismic shift in the relation thinking might bear to teleology, the originary complicity of philosophy with its end, *telos* or death, being just the type of archaeo-teleological determination of which one would be quite justified in thinking that Derrida is most suspicious.

It is, however, entirely in the baffling logic of what I just called the 'less is more' radicalism of the deconstructive thinking of death that this apparent shift or displacement with respect to the metaphysical, teleological determination of the future, must already be more or less surreptitiously at work *in* that metaphysical determination. I shall be trying to suggest very briefly that the traces of this ateleological work can be read in what Kant calls judgement. I can attempt to formulate briefly the sort of thing I shall be trying to find Kant saying: for example, that the end of teleology is the end of teleology, or even that the end of the end is the end of the end. I hope the following fragment of a reading of Kant will make these formulations seem less gratuitously provocative, and hint at least at a *rapprochement* with what Jacques Derrida's recent work takes the (I think considerable) risk of calling a messianicity without messianism.[18]

* * *

Let me begin by recalling some elementary features of Kant's thinking about judgement. Judgement first appears early in the transcendental analytic in the first *Critique* in the context of Kant's insistence that human knowledge is *discursive*. The understanding is a discursive and not intuitive faculty in that it gives rise to knowledge by concepts which it does not *construct*, as is the case with mathematics. *All* the understanding can do with these concepts is judge with them:

> Now the only use which the understanding can make of these concepts is to judge by means of them. Since no representation, save when it is an intuition, is in immediate relation to an object, no concept is ever related to an object immediately, but to some other representation of it, be that other representation an intuition, or itself a concept. Judgement is thus the mediate knowledge of an object, that is, the representation of a representation of it. In every judgement there is a concept which holds of many representations, and among them of a given representation that is immediately related to an object ... Now we can reduce all acts of the understanding to judgements, and the *understanding* may therefore be represented as a *faculty of judgement* [*ein Vemögen zu urteilen*]. For, as stated above, the understanding is a faculty of thought. Thought is knowledge by means of concepts ... (etc.)
>
> (A68–9/B93–4)

Thought is knowledge by concepts; for us these concepts are of a discursive use, and we therefore use them to judge. But what is proper to the act of judging, is the fact of identifying for a concept a *case* of this concept. Judgement always has to do with the case, which gives rise, a little later in the first *Critique*, to a more detailed description of its operation, at the very beginning of the chapter entitled 'Transcendental Judgement in General', where the word 'judgement' now translates *Urteilskraft*, the word used in the title of the third *Critique*. The understanding being the faculty of rules, judgement is the power of subsuming under those rules, i.e. of recognising cases for them. General logic cannot contain rules for judgement, because (according to a formula that Wittgenstein was also to make famous) we would need a rule to teach the application of rules to cases, and therefore also a rule to teach the application of that rule to its cases, and so on *ad infinitum*.[19] Judgement can only be an innate capacity, a talent or natural gift which cannot be taught (which is why, much later, Kant will say no less famously that philosophy cannot be learned, and why it is possible to become erudite without ever supplying the lack of judgement – this is what justifies Kant's objections to historians of philosophy, especially in the *Prolegomena*, and gives some substance to the sense that erudition is intrinsically *stupid*, stupidity (*Dummheit*) being the term Kant uses to characterise lack of judgement) – the *Mutterwitz* that no amount of knowledge can ever make up for.

Transcendental judgement, however, appears to have the considerable advantage of being able to give itself its object without exposing itself to the risk that the *Mutterwitz* will let it down. As transcendental logic is concerned only with the relation of knowledge to a possible object of experience in general (which is why it is transcendental), it can, as Kant says (A135/B174–5) 'specify *a priori* the instance to which the rule is to be applied'.

But the comforting aspects of this claim (from which it seems to follow that transcendental logic is one area where stupidity is not a problem, or even that transcendental philosophy would be the natural vocation for those most lacking in judgement, which might of course just be those who are half-dead) have, at least by the time of the third *Critique*, been somewhat troubled by a sense that judgement, even of this determinant type, always, and constitutively, bears a difficult relationship to the singular and the contingent which both constitutes and unsettles the transcendental itself. According to a set-up which pervades Kant's thought, the end (*telos*) of transcendental philosophy is the end (*finis*) of transcendental philosophy: or would be that end, were it not for the structure of a generalised teleology without *telos* I shall attempt to point to.[20]

According to the definitive introduction to the third *Critique*, judgement has no place in *doctrine*, in the accomplished system of a metaphysics, but only in *critique*. From the point of view of doctrine, there are only two sorts of concepts (of nature on the one hand, of freedom on the other): in the system of a completed philosophy, judgement, which is *between* these two domains, can be attached to the one or the other, as needed. The introduction to the third *Critique*, having first repeated and justified this division of philosophy into *two*, then draws back to treat of 'the domain of philosophy in general, *Vom Gebiete der Philosophie über-haupt*'. This is where we find a famous passage which attempts to trace the frontiers of this domain, containing the objects of a possible application of concepts:

Insofar as we refer concepts to objects without considering whether or not cognition [*Erkenntnis*] of these objects is possible, they have their field [*ihr Feld*: Pluhar translates as 'realm']; and this field is determined merely by the relation that the object of these concepts has to our cognitive power [*Erkenntnisvermögen*] in general. [So the field would be the place in the 'general domain' where there is a still indeterminate relation between concept and object. Kant does not say if the general domain of philosophy extends still further, but one might imagine that what Kant elsewhere calls 'general logic' might occupy those parts of the domain not covered by the field.] The part of this field in which cognition is possible for us is a territory [*Boden*] (*territorium*) for these concepts and the cognitive power we need for such cognition. That part of the terri-tory over which these concepts legislate is the domain [*Gebiet*: the same word Kant used for the encompassing domain of philosophy in general, and this reappearance of the outside in the middle in the context of legislation seems to me to be anything but fortuitous] (*ditio*) of these concepts and the cognitive powers pertaining to them. Hence empirical concepts do have their territory in nature, as the sum total of all objects of sense, but they have no *domain* in it (but only residence [*Aufenthalt*], *domicilium* [this domicile would then appear to be that part of the terri-tory not occupied by the domain]; for though they are produced according to law, they do not legislate; rather, the rules that are based on them are empirical and hence contingent.

Let's take this distribution as literally as possible. Kant is implicitly inviting us to draw a plan, which we might do as in Figure 1 on page 70. However, we must immediately complicate this, because Kant opens the next paragraph by saying that 'Our cognitive power as a whole has two domains, that of the concepts of nature and that of the concept of freedom, because it legislates *a priori* by means of both kinds of concept.' But the terrain or territory of these two domains is the same (the terrain of objects of a possible experience), and we must expect that they will be able, and even that they must, share certain objects, which would give Figure 2 on page 70:

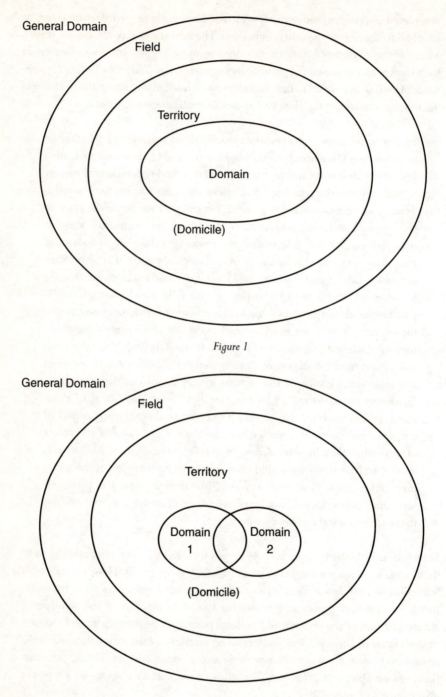

Figure 1

Figure 2

We shall see this topography, which is still quite simple here, get more and more complicated as Kant advances in his description. The fact that these two legislations bear on domains in the same territory (domains which coincide at least in part, and perhaps totally) does not give rise to interferences at the level of legislation, but to a reciprocal limitation (Kant uses the verb *einschranken*) at the level of effects. But these two domains remain two in that their objects are of a different nature, or at least are considered from different perspectives. The domain of nature presents its concepts to intuition, as phenomena, whereas the concept of freedom presents them as things in themselves, without this presentation taking place in intuition. Where there is theoretical knowledge, there is no thing in itself, and where there are things in themselves, there is no theoretical knowledge. Of such a knowledge (which, if it were to present itself as such would be the transcendental illusion) one must of course have an Idea, which then takes its place in the field, but without giving rise to a territory, nor, *a fortiori*, to a domain:

> Hence there is a field that is unbounded, but that is also inaccessible to our entire cognitive power: the field of the supersensible. [So we were wrong to enclose the field as we did in our diagram, but that leaves the relation between the field and the 'general domain' unclear.] In this field we cannot find for ourselves a territory on which to set up a domain of theoretical cognition, whether for the concepts of the understanding or for those of reason. It is a field that we must indeed occupy [*müßen*: necessity here rather than obligation] with Ideas that will assist us in both the theoretical and the practical use of reason; but the only reality we can provide for these ideas, by reference to the laws [arising] from the concept of freedom, is practical reality, which consequently does not in the least expand our theoretical cognition to the supersensible.

Which already complicates the description Kant has given, for where we thought we were dealing with a concentric arrangement of field, territory and domain, we now see that things are more complicated. Previously, it seemed that theoretical and practical knowledge had each their domain within the territory: now the domain of the practical is, if not identified, at least placed in a strange relation with the (unlimited) field which *surrounds* the territory. To understand what is happening here, we should clearly have to introduce a dynamic element into the representation, allowing practical legislation to happen *from* the field but aiming at the domain within the territory, apparently occupied by theoretical legislation. This is why the celebrated 'abyss', the *unübersehbare Kluft*, the cleft over which one cannot see, is not simply a division or accentuated separation between two sides of the same sort, and this is also why the attempt to throw a bridge across it (which would be judgement) is not so easily conceivable as is sometimes thought, unless we think of a one-way bridge:[21]

> Hence an immense gulf is fixed between the domain of the concept of nature, the sensible, and the domain of the concept of freedom, the supersensible, so that no transition from the sensible to the supersensible (and hence by means of the theoretical use of reason) is possible, just as if they were two different worlds, the first of which cannot have any influence on the second; and the second *ought to* [*soll*, Kant's emphasis] have an influence on the first, i.e. the concept of freedom ought to [*soll* again] actualise in the world of sense the end [*Zweck*] enjoined by its laws. Hence it must [*müßen*] be possible to think of nature as being such that the lawfulness in its form will harmonise with at least the possibility of [achieving] the ends that we are to achieve in nature according to laws of freedom. So there must after all be a ground [*Grund*] *uniting* the supersensible that underlies nature and the supersensible that the concept of freedom contains practically, even though the concept of this ground does not reach cognition of it either theoretically or practically and hence does not have a domain of its own, though it does make possible the transition from our way of thinking in terms of principles of the one to our way or thinking in terms of the principles of the other.

If, then, there is a possibility of transition from one domain to the other, this transition takes place only in one direction (it is impossible to pass from the theoretical to the practical, on pain of transcendental illusion), and it happens, not so much by throwing a bridge over the abyss, but by passing under, *in a tunnel*, for the *Kluft* may be un-see-over-able but it has a bottom nonetheless, is cut into the common (sub)-soil of the field, a *supra*-sensible *sub*-soil divided between theoretical and practical knowledge. This passage, or its possibility, is not itself of the order of theoretical knowledge. That it be possible to pass from the practical to the theoretical (that legislation according to freedom be compatible with legislation according to nature), that the moral law might have effects which can be registered in the natural-mechanical world, is part of the (being-)law of this law.[22] It is duty's duty to realise itself in the world of nature. The moral law *must be able* (or, if 'must' commits us to *müßen*, let's say it *ought to be able*) to realise or actualise itself in the sensory world, following a pre- or archi-moral duty which provides for the pre- or archi-prescriptiveness of prescriptions:[23] duty owes itself the duty of becoming effective. But this primitive *sollen* (which must in fact – in right – precede the distinction between freedom and nature, because it is the principle of their separation as well as of their communication), according to which one *ought to* have effects in the sensory world, provokes another duty in return, which this time owes it to itself to be a *müßen*, according to which the legality of natural legality is such that it must, in its form, lend itself to this reali-sation of moral ends. Only this consequence gives any substance to the archi-duty of duty: for if nature did not *respond* to it, duty could owe itself to itself *ad infinitum* without this duty's being a jot more realisable. The duty of duty, then, *must be* realisable *as it ought to be*, failing which it would not be a duty, and there would be no duty. There ought to be this must, because there must be this ought. This originary connivance between necessity and obligation, nature and freedom, *müßen* and *sollen*, mechanism and ends – it's the law – will make of judgement (which has not yet been named in the Introduction), an essentially teleological judgement.

The sensory world is thus *the end* of duty, or, for duty owes itself to itself from the end, *the end of the end*. What Kant has not yet named as 'judgement' will be in some sense the faculty of this doubled end, or of the movement which carries judgement towards its end and ensures that the moral law will find in nature the condition of its possible realisation. Nature must needs be such that it respond to the moral law. Which means that, contrary to what one might think on reading the typic of the second *Critique*, the form of the law, the *Gesetzmässigkeit* that the moral law is supposed to borrow from the laws of nature (the categorical impera-tive prescribes that I put the maxim of my action through the test of the form of a law of nature), it is the form of law of the moral law which gives its form to natural legality. Nature has a legal form *so as to* be able to respond to the moral law; natural necessity is thus dictated by the moral law, which gives a (suprasen-sible) foundation to its necessity, but at the same time (digging the tunnel) undermines this foundation. For if natural necessity owes itself to duty, it is no longer quite necessary, nor quite natural. That the (legal) form of nature must accord with the possibility of ends is its end. The end of nature is that the law will find its end in it. Which means that even the archi-determining transcendental judgement of the first *Critique* is already teleological, for it must presuppose that nature is such that it will present it with cases adapted to the law that under-standing is in a position to prescribe to nature.

It is just this that allows for the possibility of the transcendental position itself. The understanding is legislative for nature in a strong sense: the understanding pre-scribes itself a nature such that the laws it will pronounce will have at least the *possibility* of finding satisfaction in it. Nature is thus *made for* the judgement that will take its case into account, and this *made for* already gives nature its end as apt to receive moral-practical realisations. Even subsumptive theoretical judge-ment, then, is determined in return by its apparent other, which returns through the tunnel to pop up in the middle – foreign legislator.

This is what Kant will say much later, in §76 of the *Critique of Teleological Judgement*. Reason demands unity, the unification of the manifold. But the understanding, in so far as it is linked to sensibility and is thus subject to a transcendental logic (for the transcendental is less what goes away from than *what returns* to the singular),[24] can only proceed from the universal to the particular, in which it cannot *not* find the contingent. This contingent must be brought under the law, which is done by postulating a finality of the contingent as such:

> Now, as the particular as such contains something contingent with respect to the general, and yet reason demands unity (i.e. legality) in the combination of even the particular laws of nature (which legality of the contingent is called finality), whereas the deduction of particular laws from the general, as regards what is contingent in them, *a priori* through determination of the concept of the object, is impossible, the concept of the finality of nature in its products becomes for the human faculty of judgement with respect to nature a necessary concept ... [25]

Which has as an apparently paradoxical consequence that, to be legal, nature must be fundamentally contingent. If it is to receive the law, nature *must not* be completely necessary. Natural necessity, seen from its end (the law) is that it be contingent. The necessity of necessity is contingency (which calls for teleology). This chance of contingency (the only chance of the law) is not *knowable* as such, but the object of a non-knowledge which calls for what is called judgement. For one to be able to judge *according to the end*, there must be contingency, for only contingency calls for the end as the only chance of its legality. Necessity has no end, it is blind: for the end, this blindness must blind itself again in the contingent.

Nature, then, has a purpose: to be purposive, which it is only in contingency. That there be this purpose-iveness comes under neither theoretical knowledge (for if it were to be demonstrated, contingency would be reduced to natural necessity: this is why Kant keeps on repeating that the principle of judgement – i.e. that you must judge *as if* it were made to be judged – is only subjective, or at least is not objective, while functioning *just as if* it were objective, because without this there would be no 'subject'), nor under practical 'knowledge' (no duty here), but underlies the possibility of these two domains as the presupposition indispensable to their separation. At the end, we know strictly nothing of the end.

This position of judgement, as essentially teleological, is precisely what undermines any clear sense of any *telos* at all for judgement by opening it to an indefinite future in which it seems unlikely that philosophy will ever find peace or repose in the disappearance or doctrinal resolution of its problems. This endless teleology (or thinking of teleology as essentially without *telos*) explains the attraction of thinking judgement in general along the lines of the so-called 'aesthetic' judgement and its purposiveness without purpose or finality without end, or lawfulness without law, as Kant says in §22. This naturally does not mean that all judgement thought in this way is somehow culpably aesthetic, just because this generalised opening of judgement renders quite uncertain the borders of the aesthetic as such. A similar argument can be generated, with no specific reference to the aesthetic at all, from analysis of that most Kantian of motifs, the 'guiding-thread', the *Leitfaden*, which turns out always to be invoked just where guidance is *not* to be had, and any arrival at an end is radically uncertain, or from the question of *orientation* in thought, which turns out to be necessary only where it is impossible to secure.

Which seems to confirm *both* the Derridean *and* the Kantian readings of the figure of childbirth from which I began. Childbirth is unthinkable without *some* appeal to *something like* a teleology: but what provides the opening for the monstrous is that this teleology has no definable *telos*. This monstrosity[26] inscribed in the notion of childbirth is, however, precisely what prevents philosophy from finding itself in its *telos*, which would be its *finis*, its death. Teleology read in this way is just what holds philosophy short of its end and thus gives it the possibility of a future in spite of itself. It is no accident that the 'children' generated by philosophers (*qua* philosophers) should be the books they write.[27] The (half-) death of the philosopher would then never be completed, but would be the (half-) life of philosophy, which half-life lives as a repeated call to reading thrown towards a future in which that reading will never be finished.[28] Derrida's futures are to that extent, like those of every other philosopher, both absolutely predictable and absolutely uncertain: but those futures will, let me hope here and now, already be marked, in reading, by a gratitude for opening just that futurity to reading, always elsewhere, in Plato and Kant for example, in the past.

6

X

'Duralex', said Lex.

X marks the spot.[1] Like the cross-hairs in the telescopic sight, the intersection of the lines marking the point to aim at.

X crosses through, does the *sous rature*, leaving legible what it simultaneously cancels, for example the words 'is' and 'thing' in a famous sentence of Derrida's.

X is the chiasmus, where lines meet at a point and continue, never to meet again, the *quadrifurcum* that will have organised so much of Derrida's writing, the *chi* that drives the reading of Adami's fish-picture, the fish dragged from its element only to fall back in, that will have given me my favourite pedagogical support for the explanation of the quasi-transcendental.

X is forbidden, and therefore desirable, censored, and therefore uncensorable.

X shows which dotted line I have to sign.

I imagine X as a three-dimensional representation: of a pyramid seen from above, rising to its definite point, or of a rectangular shaft disappearing into the infinite depths, the central point a mere perspectival vanishing never arrived at, however long the fall.

Applied Derrida. Derrida applied.

Apply Derrida. Derrida, apply.

The application of Derrida.

Apply Derrida sparingly, liberally, gently, regularly (to the affected parts).

A brief application of Derrida soon brought about considerable improvements.

Judicious application of Derrida should prevent the problem from occurring again.

A short, sharp application of Derrida may occasionally be called for.

What are the immediate, short-term, medium-term, long-term applications of Derrida?

Derrida: for external application only.

Derrida. Apply within. Serious applicants only. Application forms may be obtained by writing to the secretary at the following address. Applicants will be expected to show detailed knowledge of the work of Jacques Derrida.

Confidential reference for Jacques Derrida. The candidate has worked with great application from the outset.

Derrida appliances. (The appliance of science.)

Ap-*pli*-cation. Folding in and folding back. Basic origami: take a square of paper and fold across each diagonal – there's the X.

I imagine Derrida in the title of this conference as an applicant, an application (possibly in the computing sense, with an appropriate icon of course), an applicator, an appliance. Something trying to get in, something to click and run, something (soothing) to put on, and the means of putting it on.

* * *

What does 'Applied Derrida' mean that just 'Derrida' doesn't? What made Julian Wolfreys and his co-organisers decide to call their conference '*Applied* Derrida' and not just 'Jacques Derrida'? And what does it mean to hold a conference *today* (and even more specifically, today *in Luton*, in this place the rough location of which I marked with an X on a large-scale map of England for a French friend who asked where I was going) with such a title (and such a programme – and what a programme! The like of which I for one have never seen)?

Conference titles in general play a specific and original role in intellectual – or at least academic – life (if you can call it life), and it's worth applying oneself to the readings they invite or discourage. They also have a specific pragmatic structure it's worth noting: unlike titles of books, or articles, or even conference papers (which do indeed bear a complex relation to the future from the side both of writing and reading, but which function in general as the proper name of an existing object), titles of conferences are *essentially* proleptic, radically anticipatory of a content yet to come, which content they are designed to *call for* (as in the 'call for papers' regularly issued with announcements of conferences), to call up, but also to control and influence, in a way that is, intuitively at least, not the case for titles of books, articles or papers. Conference titles of course do name the conference they entitle (even if the conference were never to take place, it would still be named by its name), but they also, before naming anything, call for that thing to be. What I've just imprudently called a 'content' is of course not just that of the papers presented at the conference (in many cases quite exhaustively summarised in the programme, to the extent that if it were just a question of content one might be forgiven for simply reading the programme and staying at home), but the *event* of the conference, with all that that entails. Authors do of course issue titles of books or articles (and especially, perhaps, of conference papers) in advance, without always really having much idea of what will be in the finished text – and they sometimes choose deliberately enigmatic or indeterminate titles to allow for subsequent invention or variation (sometimes they even choose titles which try in some way to name this very situation of indeterminacy holding between a text and its title, or a title and its text): but whatever the degree of openness of the future opened up in this way, this functioning of titles is distinct from that of the title of a conference, where the organisers do not know, and cannot know what will happen in a more radical sense than holds for individual authors. Conference organisers issue titles as a way of guiding contributors towards something that functions as a *hope*. Of course the organisers *know* that most conference participants will, whatever the title of the conference, simply present some of their work in progress (and they *fear* that some will only manage to produce something from the dreaded 'bottom drawer'), but they *hope* that the title of the conference will nonetheless oblige speakers to think *towards* something they had perhaps not thought of before, slant their work, as they say, towards the theme or idea that the title presents, so that, in the best (and rarest) cases something new happens during the conference, so that the pull or push of the title brings out something that might otherwise not have been thought at all by anyone (including of course the organisers themselves). The title of the conference *calls*, then, for something new to be brought to thought, and that call is therefore, however gently and non-coercively, prescriptive. Hearing that call involves accepting an obligation at least to *read* the title that calls, and that reading (which must go beyond the pure call itself, insofar as hearing a call is not yet a reading at all) always might – but this is also the chance of something happening – always might interpret the text of the title in a way that goes against the hope of the organisers when they decided, more or less solemnly and hopefully, on the words to send out in search of someone or something.

Across the different ways of applying oneself to the title of this conference with a view to understanding what we might be doing here, or called on to do here, let me provisionally isolate two. First possible application: 'Applied Derrida' functions, alongside or beyond its role as the proper name of an event which has not yet taken place, like a prescriptive sentence. Beyond the sort of archi-prescription inherent, as we have just seen, in any conference title insofar as it is a call, 'Applied Derrida' on this reading carries a further, more or less hidden, more or less secret prescription. 'Applied Derrida' hopes to name proleptically an object or event which will, finally, after all the conferences and books and articles devoted to Derrida, and high time too, have *applied* Derrida, got on and done something with him. Whether impatiently ('there's been too much self-indulgent theorising, it's time to get on to real applications'), or more tolerantly ('we've needed a long time to get Derrida straight, but now we have, it's time to do something with him'), there is, on this reading, a hint of urgency in the call of the title. 'Applied Derrida' says to its putative contributors: for goodness' sake don't just stand there talking about Derrida: *do* something. And this reading would typically go along with a sense that Derrida too has been applying himself more of late, most of all perhaps in the splendidly untimely book on Marx.

But this first reading, or type of reading (for we can imagine its being inflected across many more versions than I have presented here), would have to be tested against another, second, possibility. Here there is no further prescriptive element beyond that inherent in the call of the conference title itself. 'Applied Derrida', on this second reading, doesn't just name the event-to-be of the conference, doesn't just call for that event to be, but alongside that naming and calling, also *describes* something. 'Applied Derrida' would here be saying not so much something about what we should do with Derrida, but something about what Derrida already is or does. Here the claim is not that we should (finally) get on and apply it, but that *there is* already an applied Derrida, or at least *some* applied Derrida. On this construal, the business of the conference would be less to produce something that does not yet exist (except insofar as that is the business of all conferences, to become the event they are going to have been), but to reflect on an already existing object. 'Applied Derrida' is out there somewhere, and we should be identifying it, thinking about it, analysing it. This possibility too opens up to many different inflections, but let's say provisionally that there is a strong and a weak way of reading this descriptive alternative to the prescriptive first reading. The *weak* reading says that, alongside or among (at least one) other Derrida(s), there is an applied one, and that this is the one the conference will be concerned with, to the exclusion of others. The *strong* reading, which forces the syntax of the title a little, but only a little, suggests that Derrida just *is* applied, in which case the qualifier takes on a sort of honorific status, like a title becoming part of a proper name, so that 'Applied Derrida' would be read by analogy with, say, 'Fantastic Mr Fox' or 'Lovely Luton'. In this sense, the qualification is not restrictive, but totalising, and implies an excellence (an X-cellence) of some sort: the salient feature of Mr Fox is that he is fantastic, of Luton that it is lovely, and of Derrida that he is applied. 'Applied Derrida' does not, on this strong version of the descriptive reading, really say any more than just 'Jacques Derrida', and indeed can take over the function of the proper name, but it reminds anyone who might have forgotten, or overlooked the fact, that *Derrida is applied*. For the purposes of this chapter, then, I'm taking the conference title to be a violent but interesting attempt to re-baptise Derrida, who will henceforth be called, not 'Jacques', but 'Applied'.

I imagine that this last reading will seem the most improbable (maybe even eccentric or excessive) *as a reading* of the title, but it will no doubt seem less improbable that this is the reading I shall be defending in this chapter, and I draw strength from the fact that others (Suhail Malik, John Phillips) have been defending a similar line here too. So, reading at least a little against the grain of the call I also hear in that title, I shall be suggesting that any invitation to *produce* an applied Derrida must somewhere lead to confusion, because of the implication in such an invitation that Derrida is *not yet* applied, or has not yet been applied: this implication makes sense only in the context of a number of assumptions about Derrida's thinking, and about thinking more generally, which I think are not only untenable, but which I think are untenable precisely for reasons that Derrida has most clearly brought out. The form of this argument is familiar, and runs as follows: the demand for application presupposes a distinction between something like theory and something like practice or praxis, between something like metaphysics and something like physics, between something like philosophy and something like the real world. But as the distinction between metaphysics and non-metaphysics just is metaphysics, the demand for application typically ends up being the least applicable demand of all (this is why it can be permanently self-righteous), the pretext for smuggling in what Derrida calls transcendental contraband of all sorts. The demand for application – which is as such prior to any particular political identification, as common on the Right as on the Left, as tech-nocratic as it is revolutionary – in fact reinforces the structure which means that nothing ever gets applied and that we spend our time theorising about the more or less tragic or culpable failure to apply. I shall try to show very briefly that this set-up is the structure of (quasi-)transcendentality itself, and that it is precisely this that Derrida helps us to understand and displace. The result is that the 'Applied Derrida' that this chapter is also concerned to defend and even illustrate must be already crossed through with the X of its *own* application, here, now, today in Luton.

Introducing the 'Idea of a transcendental logic' in the first *Critique*, Kant first distinguishes clearly and memorably sensibility and the understanding as the two sources of our knowledge: 'Thoughts without content are empty, intuitions without concepts are blind' (A51/B75). Thoughts spring from the understanding, intuitions from the sensibility. But if knowledge can only arise from the union of these two sources, says Kant, all the more important for a critique to avoid confusing them. The sensibility has therefore a separate science of its rules in the Aesthetic, the understanding in Logic.

Logic in turn divides into two: general logic 'contains the absolutely necessary rules of thought without which there can be no employment whatsoever of the understanding' (A52/B76); special logic contains the rules of thinking proper to this or that science, what Kant calls the *organon* of those sciences. General logic itself divides into two: it can, says Kant, be pure, or it can be *applied* (*angewandte*). Kant's gesture in deploying this distinction will, in the first instance, be straightforwardly and predictably metaphysical. Pure general logic is a *canon* (as opposed to an organon) of the understanding and reason, 'but only in respect of what is formal in their employment, be the content what it may, empirical or transcendental' (A53/B77); applied general logic, not to be confused with special logic, 'is directed to the rules of the employment of understanding under the subjective empirical conditions dealt with by psychology' (*ibid.*). Kant continues:

> Applied logic has therefore empirical principles, although it is still indeed in so far general that it refers to the employment of the understanding without regard to difference in the objects. Consequently it is neither a canon of the understanding in general nor an organon of special sciences, but merely a cathartic of the common understanding [*ein Kathartikon des gemeinen Verstandes*].
>
> (*ibid.*)

Applied logic, says Kant, does not then mean something to do with logical *exercises*, but 'a representation of the understanding and of the rules of its necessary employment *in concreto*, that is, under the contingent subjective conditions which may hinder or help its use, and which are all given only empirically' (A54/B78–9). In other words, and this is in many ways just the gesture of philosophy itself, applied logic falls away, through the very fact of application, into the contingent and the empirical, and thus the non-philosophical. Applied logic in this sense is, however general, almost not quite logic: it stands to pure general logic, says Kant, as the doctrine of the virtues stands to pure ethics – the latter containing 'the necessary moral laws of a free will in general', the former those laws 'under the limitations of the feelings, inclinations and passions to which men are more or less subject. Such a doctrine can never furnish a true and demonstrated science, because, like applied logic, it depends on empirical and psychological principles' (A55/B79).

   As we might expect, then, the pure lines up with the true and the necessary, and the applied with the empirical and the contingent. Kant will be very keen not to have applied logic intrude into the *Critique*. But there's already a hint of a tension in these brief pages, at least where, as we have seen, Kant says that applied logic is (I'm quoting again a phrase I just quoted) 'a representation of the understanding and of the rules of its *necessary* employment [*notwendigen Gebrauch*] in concreto, that is, under the *contingent* [*zufälligen*] subjective conditions … '. The understanding is *necessarily* employed in *contingent* conditions. What are we to make of this necessary contingency, and what has it to do with the question of application?

   Kant doesn't say, but pushes on into Transcendental Logic itself. Transcendental Logic is not General Logic either pure or applied, insofar as General

Logic – even applied – is concerned only with logical *form* independently of its objects, whereas Transcendental Logic is concerned with thought insofar as it relates to an *object*. Again, however, this relation to an object must not be empirical, but pure (the Transcendental Aesthetic having demonstrated the possibility of pure intuitions (of space and time)). Transcendental logic is therefore the science of the rules of thought insofar as it relates non-empirically to an object. What is the nature of this 'relating'? Curiously enough, it appears to be an *application*:

> And here I make a remark which the reader must bear in mind, as it extends its influence over all that follows. Not every kind of knowledge *a priori* should be called transcendental, but only that by which we know that – and how – certain representations (intuitions or concepts) can be applied [Kemp Smith has 'employed', but the German term is *angewandt*, the same qualifier Kant uses for 'applied logic' in the passages I have quoted, but tends, perhaps confusingly, often to use 'application' for *Gebrauch*, which one would normally prefer to translate by 'use' or 'employment'] or are possible purely *a priori*. [And now an extraordinarily obscure definition:] The term 'transcendental', that is to say, signifies such knowledge as concerns the *a priori* possibility of knowledge, or its *a priori* employment [*Gebrauch*].
>
> (A56/B80)

As opposed to the merely a priori, which is just the sort of knowledge it is possible to have without recourse to experience, then, the transcendental is knowledge *about* knowledge (of objects), insofar as that knowledge of objects is *a priori*. Space may be an *a priori* intuition, but it is not (yet) transcendental: what is transcendental is the knowledge *that* space is not itself an empirical intuition but that it nonetheless relates *a priori* to objects of experience. The distinction between the transcendental and the empirical, then, is not a distinction to do with the relation of knowledge to object, but of a different level of knowledge to that knowledge-of-objects; and that different level of knowledge is just what Kant calls *critique*.

Transcendental logic, then, as opposed to general logic, requires a relation of thought to an object, and that relation is in some sense at least an *application*. To that extent, transcendental logic will not be straightforwardly *opposed* to applied logic: applied logic, you remember, considers the necessarily contingent circumstances of the exercise of thought; transcendental logic considers the exercise of thought insofar as it relates *a priori* to objects. Applied logic is to do with contingent conditions on the side of the subject; transcendental logic to do with restrictions on the side of the object, and, as we shall see, the commitment of transcendental logic to empirical application is also a sort of commitment to the necessity of contingency. For now, let's just note that transcendental logic retains a problematic of application just through its restriction to a relation of thought to an object.

This problematic of application is confirmed a little later in this chapter, in the section on 'The Division of Transcendental Logic into Transcendental Analytic and Dialectic'. Kant summarises his procedure: first isolate the understanding from sensibility so as to find 'that part of thought which has its origin solely in the understanding'. But then, so as to avoid the consequence of empty thoughts, re-connect that pure thought with objects *to which it can be applied*:

> In a transcendental logic we isolate the understanding – as above, in the Transcendental Aesthetic, the sensibility – separating out from our knowledge that part of thought which has its origin solely in the under-standing. The employment of this pure knowledge depends upon the condition that objects to which it can be *applied* [*angewandt* again] be given to us in intuition. In the absence of intuition all our knowledge is without objects, and therefore remains empty.
>
> (A62/B87)

Knowledge is empty unless it can be applied to objects, and transcendental logic is the canon of that possible application. Failing this application, the purity of pure knowledge leads to the sort of illusion it will be the task of the Transcendental Dialectic to analyse: without application, transcendental logic stops being a canon and is treated as an *organon* for the production of a sort of knowledge it can never in fact validate. Transcendental logic is therefore not just a logic of the *possibility* of experience, but a logic of the *applicability* of concepts to objects: this means that the transcendental is not *opposed* to the empirical, but bound up with it through this problem of application. Transcendental logic is, in its analytical part, a logic of application to the empirical, and, in its dialectical part, a logic of *misapplication* of concepts to objects which are not, and could never be, given in intuition. True knowledge occurs only on the line or surface of contact of sensibility and the understanding, the point of their application and sticking together, and the critique is carried out only with a view to that application. Knowledge is the skin formed where sensibility and understanding meet.

This point of application, where the transcendental and the empirical, the pure and the applied, the necessary and the contingent meet, is what I call 'X'. X is mysterious and possibly forbidden: the two lines intersect to define a pure, vanishing point. This point is the point of transcendentality itself, in its endless collapse into the empirical. Let's see how X is drawn out in Kant.

Kant's first X comes in a passage from the first edition of the *Critique*, where he is clarifying the distinction between analytic and synthetic judgements. You will remember that, on Kant's construal at least, analytic judgements are those in which the predicate simply unpacks what is already 'contained' in the concept of the subject, and therefore does not in any way extend my knowledge, whereas in synthetic judgements the predicate 'stands outside' the subject, but is connected with it and through that connection extends my knowledge. So, in the examples given by Kant, the judgement 'All bodies are extended' is an analytic judgement, because extension is necessarily thought in the concept of a body, whereas the judgement 'All bodies are heavy' is a synthetic judgement, insofar as the concept of a body in general does not already contain the predicate of weight. And here is the first X:

Thus it is evident: 1. that through analytic judgements our knowledge is not in any way extended, and that the concept which I have is merely set forth and made intelligible to me; 2. that in synthetic judgements I must have besides the concept of the subject something else (X), upon which the understanding may rely, if it is to know that a predicate, not contained in this concept, nevertheless belongs to it.

In the case of empirical judgements, judgements of experience, there is no difficulty whatsoever in meeting this demand. This X is the complete experience of the object which I think through the concept A – a concept which forms only one part of this experience. For although I do not include in the concept of a body in general the predicate 'weight', the concept none the less indicates the complete experience through one of its parts; and to this part, as belonging to it, I can therefore add other parts of the same experience. By prior analysis I can apprehend the concept of body through the characters of extension, impenetrability, figure, etc., all of which are thought in this concept. To extend my knowledge, I then look back to the experience from which I have derived this concept of body, and find that weight is always connected with the above characters. Experience is thus the X which lies outside the concept A, and on which rests the possibility of the synthesis of the predicate 'weight' (B) with the concept (A).

(A8)

As the passage substituted for this one in the second edition of the *Critique* makes clearer, A and B here are connected *contingently* as parts of a whole which Kant calls experience. In the case of synthetic judgements of this sort (i.e. *a posteriori*, empirical judgements), X just is X-perience which always provides the missing term on which the understanding relies for the extension of knowledge. Kant, famously making of *a priori* synthetic judgements the problem of transcendental philosophy, really wants to know about the X without the -perience: when I attempt, for example, to attach the predicate of cause to the subject 'event', as in the claim that every event has its cause, I cannot rely on experience to give the basis for the connection:

> What is here the unknown $= X$ [the first edition has just 'the X'] which gives support to the understanding when it believes that it can discover outside the concept A a predicate B foreign to this concept, which it yet at the same time considers to be connected with it? It cannot be experience ...
>
> (A9/B13)

What is the X when it is not ex-perience? Kant is quite sure that there must be some X to support the understanding, and that failing it, there would be no knowledge, but only what he elsewhere calls a mere aggregate or rhapsody of sensations. X marks a necessary convergence towards a unity, and the point of this unity can be approached from the side of the subject or from the side of the object. From the side of the subject, X is what Kant calls transcendental apperception, the necessarily presupposed unity of consciousness which cannot be an object of experience, but without which experience would not be unified as my experience (as one experience) giving rise to knowledge. From the side of the object, X just is the object *as* object (as opposed to the phenomenal appearance we can intuit), the famous transcendental object $= X$ (Kant says there is only one X, the same transcendental object throughout all our knowledge (A109)) of which we can by definition know nothing.

It is important to be as clear as possible here, because a certain general understanding of Kant talks quickly about things in themselves and noumena without giving enough attention to the X. This common view[2] of Kant, which is no doubt encouraged by a common view of the Hegelian reading of Kant, thinks that the transcendental object $= X$ is some *thing* that lies behind or beyond any experience we might have, in an intelligible realm to which our access is barred only by the peculiar constitution of our faculties. On this view, which can find some support in Kant's text, our understanding encounters a limit conceived of simply as a barrier, beyond which another world lies, but to which we cannot reach. Hegel takes this structure to be what generates the 'ought' in Kant: the reading of Kant in the *Greater Logic* sees the limit set to knowledge (the limit drawn by the strictures of possible experience) as *ipso facto* projecting a supposedly superior but in fact unrealisable world beyond that limit, towards which we ought to strive but which we are condemned, by the limit itself, never to reach. Whence the supposed perversity of Kant's philosophy, especially in its moral dimension.[3] But Kant's many formulations of the X, and of the limit it marks *and crosses*, are perhaps more complex than this view allows for, and indeed there is already a partial response to this Hegelian critique in the first edition of the *Critique of Pure Reason* itself.

First, it is important to recognise that the transcendental object = X is *not* immediately or simply the same as the thing-in-itself (the assumed substrate of appearances) or the *noumenon* (a supposed intelligible object beyond the realm of experience), although it explains how the latter comes to be (and, according to Kant, must be) thought. Kant is not always consistent on these points, but here's a clear enough statement from the first edition of the *Critique*:

> All our representations are, it is true, referred by the understanding to some object; and since appearances are nothing but representations, the understanding refers them to a *something*, as the object of sensible intuition. But this something, thus conceived, is only the transcendental object; and by that is meant a something = X, of which we know, and with the present constitution of our understanding can know, nothing whatsoever, but which, as a correlate of the unity of apperception, can serve only for the unity of the manifold in sensible intuition. By means of this unity the understanding combines the manifold into the concept of an object. *This transcendental object cannot be separated from the sensible data*, for nothing is then left through which it might be thought. Consequently it is not in itself an object of knowledge, but only the representation of appearances under the concept of an object in general ...
>
> (A250–1, my emphasis)

And, a little further on:

> The object to which I relate appearance in general is the transcendental object, that is the completely indeterminate thought of *something* in general. It cannot be entitled the *noumenon*;[4] for I know nothing of what it is in itself, and have no concept of it save as merely the object of a sensible intuition in general, and so as being one and the same for all appearances.
>
> (A253)

The X, then, is not some *thing*, but the indeterminate thought of *something*. But if, as Kant has just said, it 'cannot be separated from the sensible data', this is because, according to a folding-back movement, an ap-pli-cation which just is that of the transcendental as such, the transcendental is transcendental only *for* the empirical, for there to be something empirical. What Kant calls transcendental illusion is the tendency to take the transcendental transcendentally or, as he says in a celebrated but obscure distinction, to make transcendent use of the transcendental. The transcendental cannot not give rise to illusion, and to the suggestion of another realm of objects lying beyond those we can know, but in the strictest Kantian sense the transcendental is 'properly' transcendental (rather than transcendent) only in the folding back onto the empirical, only in the *application* it can find in the field of experience. The transcendental is not beyond the limit of experience, but what applies or adheres to experience as limited. To be transcendental, the transcendental must just be the experience of experience as limited. The X allows the application of transcendental to empirical which is the singular (and unpredictable) point or spot of possible knowledge. (If we had the time, we'd have to pursue the mysterious and vanishing point of contact, the cross of the X, into the schematism, supposed to link concept and object.)

This is perhaps why, in the *Opus Postumum*, Kant returns so often to the X, and where the interpretation of it as pure *relation* or even pure *application* becomes dominant. Here there is indeed a tendency to identify X, thing in itself and noumenon, but only insofar as the X interpretation now subsumes the other two. For example:

> In the knowledge of an object there are two sorts of representations, 1) of the object in itself, 2) in the phenomenon. The former is the one through which the subject posits itself originarily in intuition (*cognitio primaria*), the second, the one in which it makes itself mediately into an object according to the form in which it is affected (*cognitio secundaria*). This latter is the intuition of oneself in the phenomenon, the intuition through which the sensory object is given to the subject; it is the representation and composition of the manifold in accordance with the condition of space and time. But the object in itself = X is not a particular object, but rather the mere principle of synthetic *a priori* knowledge, which contains in itself the formal side of the unity of this manifold of intuition (not a particular object).
>
> (XXII, 20)

Or again,

> Every representation as a *phenomenon* is thought as being distinct from what the object is *in itself* (the sensible over against the intelligible); but this latter = x is not a particular object existing outside my representation, but merely the idea of the abstraction of the sensible, an abstraction recognised as necessary. It is not a *cognoscibile*, as intelligible [this would be the earlier position of the noumenon], but an x, because it is outside the form of the phenomenon, but yet it is a *cogitabile* (and precisely as

necessarily thinkable) which cannot be given, but must yet be thought, because it can present itself in certain other relations which are not sensory ...

The distinction between the supposed object *in itself* as opposed to the object in the phenomenon (*phaenomenon adversus noumenon*) does not signify a real thing standing over against the sensory object, but rather, as $= x$, merely the principle that there is nothing empirical which contains the basis for the determination of the possibility of experience.

(XXII, 23–4)

And a little further on:

Objects of the senses, the manifold of which in intuition is determinable only through the relation of this manifold in space and time, find themselves *a priori* under principles of the representation of their objects as phenomena; there also corresponds necessarily with them in the idea another sort of representation: consider them as *things in themselves*, whereby however the thing in itself $= X$ does not signify another object, but merely another point of view, a negative one, from which precisely the same object is considered. – This latter is the principle of the ideality of sense objects considered as phenomena.

(XXII, 42)

And finally, just a little further on, a reference to 'transcendental philosophy, where the thing in itself $= X$ is merely a pure concept of relation'.

X, then, is not a thing, but a relation to an object simply taken *qua* object, i.e. in abstraction from its particular sensory aspect as phenomenon. It seems, then, as though Heidegger, who quite rightly insists in §5 of *Kant and the Problem of Metaphysics* on the fact that the thing in itself is not a *different entity* from the phenomenon, may be being imprudent in claiming that the phenomenon is the entity seen from the perspective of finite (human) knowledge, whereas the thing in itself is the same entity seen from the perspective of infinite knowledge.[5] Whatever the extensive use Kant may indeed make throughout his thought of the idea of rational beings differently constituted from ourselves, and not subject to the same restrictions on their knowledge, it seems clear from these passages in the first *Critique* and the *Opus Postumum* (from which Heidegger also quotes part of one of the passages I've just given) that the thing in itself, as X, is inseparable from the finitude affecting phenomenal knowledge, and constitutes the possibility of that knowledge by giving the principle of the unity of the manifold without which there would not even be phenomena. Kant's point is that phenomena can only be thought of *as* phenomena through the X. Only by this minimal in-

88

finitising X-cess of finitude over itself can finitude be thought (or even experienced as such), and it is just this excess of finitude which immediately folds back and applies to finitude – and only this constitutes finitude as finite – just this that Kant calls the transcendental.

How does this sketch of a reading of Kant's X help us with applied Derrida? It doesn't seem to be in any straightforward sense an application of Derrida to Kant, though it would not be difficult to show that the principle of this reading is Derridean through and through, and that it might all be taken as an oblique commentary on the claim from *Speech and Phenomena* that 'Infinite différance is finite'. But what it does suggest is that what it has become fashionable to call the 'quasi-transcendental' thinking that Derrida puts forward, whereby apparently transcendentalising terms are constantly pulled back down into the finite facticity and contingency of the texts they are also used to read, is already at work in Kant. Not only is the quasi-transcendental already in Kant, but, in a certain sense, the quasi-transcendental just is what the transcendental is. This seems to mean two things, though they no doubt come down to the same: *on the one hand*, on the side of the signifier, as it were, the *term* or signifier 'transcendental' in Kant functions quasi-transcendentally. Like many other terms identified in specific contexts in Derridean readings, the term in question – which in this case just happens to be the term 'transcendental' – tries to achieve a transcendental status (the transcendental signifier become a signified through its very transcendentality), but 'only' manages to function quasi-transcendentally. 'Transcendental' is not quite transcendental. But, *on the other hand*, (what would have to be the side of the signified) the term 'transcendental' as deployed in the specific economy of Kant's text is already advancing a *thinking of* the quasi-transcendental. The claim here would be that the only coherent reading of Kant's many confusing attempts to explain the transcendental is that the transcendental itself (and no longer just the *term* 'transcendental') is already (only) quasi-transcendental. The transcendental is only *really* transcendental (and not transcendent) to the extent that it is (only) quasi-transcendental, which now seems to name the crossing of the X at the point of application of transcendental and empirical. In this sense, we are talking not just about the functioning of a *term* in Kant, but about a thinking (or at least a readable economy) of a sort of implosive in-de-term-ination of all terms, including the term 'transcendental'. Formulations such as these naturally ruin the distinction between signifier and signified that allowed us to produce them, but ruin too all the distinctions Kant seems bent on establishing (including the distinction between the transcendental and the empirical, but also the distinctions between the understanding and reason, between the determinative and the reflective, the constitutive and the regulative, and so on), but they ruin them on the authority, as it were, of a 'logic' that is demonstrably at work in Kant's texts, a logic which, if we had the time and patience, I would try to show is essentially an endless ana-logic which means in principle, and among other things, that Kant can never progress from critique to doctrine, which in turn means that critique is not really critique (insofar as critique only makes sense in Kant insofar as it does lead to doctrine). X, which Kant constantly links to the possibility of the transcendental question itself (i.e. how are *a priori* synthetic judgements possible?), turns out to cross the transcendental through just by aiming it at its vanishing point, so that the X of the transcendental object is invisibly overlaid by the X of its crossing through, its becoming quasi-transcendental. This crossing through of X by X is invisible, cannot be seen, but must be *read*. At which point even distinctions such as that between the finite and the infinite cannot be sustained, but cross over (into) each other in an inextricable chiasmus.

This situation is typically complex, and hints at the reasons why Derrida's work is such a threat to the historicism and culturalism still so prevalent in intellectual discussion, and which still largely informs the piece by Richard Rorty about which I shall be making a few (applied) remarks in conclusion. I said that the reading of the conference title I was going to defend was one where 'Applied Derrida' meant that Derrida just is applied. All of Derrida's texts are already applications, so there is no separate 'Derrida' in the form of theory who might *then* be applied to something else. Insofar as 'Deconstruction' tends to become a method or a school, we might say that it has forgotten this, and has begun at least to make Derrida into a theory which it wants to put into practice. The structure of the quasi-transcendental is such that we cannot be content simply to claim that Derrida (sometimes) applies his own theory, or unites theory and practice, or performs theoretical practice, but that all such oppositions are drawn into the indeterminating X which is also their *sous rature*. This is why we should resist any temptation to follow Rorty's understanding of the quasi-transcendental. In a piece about the book *Jacques Derrida*, called 'Is Derrida a *Quasi*-Transcendental Philosopher?',[6] Rorty at first seems to understand my foregrounding in that book of the notion of the quasi-transcendental as suggesting a sort of middle ground between transcendental and empirical approaches: 'Quasi transcendentality is what you go in for if you … respect philosophy enough to realize that it is inescapable, but not enough to take the idea of conditions of possibility as seriously as Kant did' (180), but a little later, having quoted and glossed a bit, he says 'I do not know how to use the notion of "quasi transcendentality", except as a name for the advantage Bennington claims for Derrida over all the other philosophers whom I have just listed' (185; referring to, among others, Heidegger, Dewey, Habermas, Foucault, Davidson, Wittgenstein), only then to use that falsely modest 'I do not know' as the ground for a more aggressive counter-claim whereby not only should Derrida be seen as cooperating rather than competing with the other philosophers named (this justified by the perspective of 'the intellectual historians of the end of the twenty-first century', as though the truth lay with them – I imagine Rorty would like to think of himself as part of the same cooperative), but that

> There is no need to worry about how to locate a middle ground called 'quasi transcendentality,' intermediate between taking the transcendental/empirical distinction with full Kantian seriousness and simply forgetting it. More specifically, there is no need to be more precise about the nature and procedure of deconstruction than to say, 'You know – the sort of thing Derrida does'.
>
> (186)

But as I hope to have shown, 'taking the transcendental/empirical distinction with full Kantian seriousness' already involves recognising that there is no simple distinction to be made between the transcendental and the empirical, that there can therefore be no simple 'middle ground', and that the transcendental *itself* cannot but be affected by the complication the 'quasi-' points up, *especially* if it is taken with full Kantian seriousness, in other words if we take the trouble to *read* Kant's text. The result is that the sorts of classifications Rorty proposes cannot hold, and that, for example, 'quasi-transcendental' does not name a philosophical position or strategy one might choose to adopt, and certainly not a middle ground, but a sort of necessity (the necessity of the meeting of necessity and contingency we have begun to follow in Kant) which, on a deconstructive construal (but maybe Rorty already understands this when I say 'You know – the sort of thing that Derrida does') affects all philosophical thinking of sufficient complexity. This would mean that even a self-proclaimed pragmatist like Rorty cannot help being a quasi-transcendental philosopher himself, even if he claims not really to know what that is, so long, that is – but this is not always the case – as his arguments reach a certain level.

   This still leaves us, and 'Applied Derrida', with a serious problem. If it is true that Derrida *is* applied in any case, not at all after the fashion of a technical aid one would bring to bear from outside on some problem, but in that 'Derrida' only *happens* textually in a dispersal of 'applications' across texts read, and even in texts he has not explicitly read or in readings like this one which he has not signed but for which he might in some sense be held responsible, then the location of anything like Derrida's *signature*, the identification of anything like 'Derrida himself', becomes harder than ever. The last way to go about understanding this situation is Rorty's, for whom,

> The effect of 'Circumfession' is to rub one's nose in the fact that all the quasi-transcendental, rigorous philosophizing which Bennington describes

is being done by a poor existing individual [Rorty has earlier referred to Kierkegaard's having used these terms of Hegel, and elsewhere he uses the term 'nerd' in this sense – one thing Rorty is keen to argue is that philosophers are just nerds like any others, and this seems to go along with the need, as he puts it on two occasions, for philosophers to 'get a life', whatever that is supposed to mean], somebody who thinks about certain things in certain ways because of certain weird, private contingencies.

(197: Rorty has in general great faith in the distinction between private and public, though he clearly likes it when the private *goes public*, which is how he reads *Circumfession*, while not quite admitting to liking what he describes as the 'nerd-with-a-gimmick' practice of intellectual biography.)

A different approach would be to note the following paradox: the more applied Derrida is, the more he applies himself to his reading, the more he disperses into the texts of the tradition, then the more *and* the less he signs what he writes. Plato or Kant turn out to be signed by Derrida: but by the same token Derrida has only signed 'Plato' or 'Kant'. This generalised counterfeiting of signatures (by all concerned – the counterfeiting doesn't *start* with Derrida, nor even with, say, Rousseau, but is already written into what Plato writes about writing, and almost explicitly by Kant into what he says about reading, among others, Plato)[7] – this generalised counterfeiting ruins Rorty's apparently modest liberal-historicist position. Turning writing into ghost-writing like this, so that Kant has in a certain sense already written Derrida, but already in a sense been written by Plato, and yet still needs Derrida to sign what he has written – this is the double-edged gesture 'Applied Derrida' has brought off. X marks the spot – today, in Luton – where metaphysics still applies itself to itself as never quite itself, dotted line waiting for a definite signature that can never quite be relied upon to sign anything, where responsibilities must nonetheless be taken, where the 'poor existing individual' is written in and out, inside and out, getting and losing more than one life, and where applications cannot but continue, excessively, to fold themselves round.

7

CIRCANALYSIS
(THE THING ITSELF)

What will he have given to psychoanalysis? (What does psychoanalysis owe him?)[1]
What will he have taken from psychoanalysis (What does he owe psychoanalysis?)
What will he have made over to psychoanalysis (Are they quits?)
What will he have made of psychoanalysis (In what state will he have left it?)

Freud is never named in 'Circumfession'. This text, which seems – more than any other text of his, perhaps – to *turn around* psychoanalytic themes,[2] as though offering itself to a psychoanalytic reading, does so without any direct reference to Freud.[3] Derrida speaks, for example, of himself as 'author of more or less legitimate writings about Plato, Augustine, Descartes, Rousseau, Kant, Hegel, Husserl, Heidegger, Benjamin, Austin' (JD, 110 [115]), but omits Freud from his list, which is striking in the context of the list, given that Derrida is saying that he is the only philosopher who will have dared to describe his own penis. This marked absence of Freud works as though he was saying: 'Here, analyse me, I'm happy to lend myself to it, I even demand it, I'm giving you something to work on, you see – unlike the patient Freud talks about at the beginning of the text on negation, I don't even say "It is not my mother" so you can immediately mutter "So it was his mother", I say myself, without waiting, "It's my mother, I speak only of her, you ought to know what that means"; and look, to make life easier for you, I'm not even going to speak of analysis or Freud in this text, I'm not even going to begin to call into question the concepts you will not fail to invoke in your analysis. I expose myself in all inno-cence to your ear.' Analysis becomes so easy as a result that we might suspect that it will be impossible.

The scene thus played by 'Circumfession' is like the exasperation of a situation so well described by Serge Leclaire almost thirty years ago: how to analyse, once

93

the patient already more or less shares the analytic knowledge of the analyst? That is, once analysis theorises itself sufficiently for such a sharing to be in principle possible and therefore inevitable? 'How are we to conceive', writes Leclaire, 'a theory of psychoanalysis which does not cancel, by the fact of its articulation, the very possibility of its exercise?'[4] And Leclaire goes on to show how a simple absence of theorising would leave analytic practice in 'a sort of two-person fantasmatisation', but that on the other hand a 'closed formalisation' would exclude 'the very possibility' of analysis seeking for extreme singularity'.[5] It is impossible not to see in the very brutality of these remarks the possibility of an articulation with Derridean themes,[6] and one might even be tempted to re-read Leclaire's text as a significant moment in what will have been the troubled history of the relations between psychoanalysis and Jacques Derrida, bringing out especially the moment at which Derrida is invoked in a note which claims a certain 'proximity of trajectory', but where Leclaire admits that he would find it 'for the moment, impossible really to take stock of this encounter'.[7] I do not know if stock of this encounter, if it really is an encounter, if it really took place (supposing we even know what that means), has ever been taken, for example here, during this ongoing conference, and I do not here intend to go into the stories one might tell – which have indeed been told – about 'Derrida and psychoanalysis'; but it is important for me to note that by all accounts, and for non-contingent reasons, there will have been complex relations between Derrida and psychoanalysis, a problematic proximity, and that – such at least will be my hypothesis today – it is these relations which matter more than any other to the more general question of this colloquium: that is, too bluntly: since Lacan, there will have been, and there will be still, Derrida.[8] In order to approach this question, I do not intend to pick up even part of what analysts of all camps – and especially the Lacanian camp, if there is *one* such camp, but I imagine it is poorly represented here today – have said about Derrida's work, but, more modestly, no doubt too modestly, by insisting on what is perhaps already obvious, to lay down some elements for the analysis of what Derrida says about psychoanalysis, and more especially about Freud himself.

* * *

What, first of all, of Derrida's *declarations* about psychoanalysis? I ask the question knowing (I am not so naive as to think I am teaching you analysts anything) that we must always be wary of declarations, be they declarations of war or (especially) of love (in fact a declaration is perhaps always a declaration of war or of love, and doubtless both at once), that Derrida himself is wary of them (declaration is not at all his preferred manner) and that this wariness ought to involve close attention to what we might call the pragmatic structure of declaration as speech act, to the grammar (in the Wittgensteinian sense) of the verb 'declare'.

From this pragmatics or grammar, let us provisionally retain this simple fact that in declaring something one is doing something more than, and other than, *stating* [constater] something. Where current French usage means one can *constater* something, in the sense of noticing it, without stating it (whence the somewhat metaphysical idea – that the theory of speech acts is, precisely, trying to contest – that the verbal *constat* would be the degree zero of the speech act, scarcely a sentence, scarcely an act), or at least where one might think that the essential resides less in what one says than in what one sees or understands, independently of what one says, the very term 'declaration' involves an *essential* reference to the act of speaking, or at least to the fact of perpetrating a speech act. To declare something is of course to say it, but to say it clear and loud, 'announce, proclaim, or publish especially by a formal statement or official pronouncement' (Webster). A declaration is therefore in principle double, it always involves, over and above an act of speech or language strictly speaking, a supplementary act which could be termed an act of subscription: I do indeed say something, but I also say that I say it, I add to what I say an implicit: 'there, that's indeed what I intend to have understood, make no mistake about it, I say it solemnly, I say it in truth, I subscribe fully to it, I persist and sign'.

Now among Derrida's declarations with respect to psychoanalysis (and I'll venture the hypothesis that Derrida has made more declarations with respect to psychoanalysis than with respect to other movements of thought), I'll pick out one to start with, which has never to my knowledge been publicly archived or recorded, but the authenticity of which could be confirmed, if needs be, by our host René Major, for the declaration in question was made after a lecture Major gave at the Sorbonne in 1988.[9] In the following discussion, Derrida was moved to say, in response to a question or suggestion of Major's – and whoever heard it will be able to say whether 'declaration' is the name for what he said – he was, then, moved to make the following declaration: 'I have never subscribed to any proposition of psychoanalysis.'

This declaration, this solemn, signed and subscribed affirmation about a certain non-subscription, was no doubt diversely received by the audience present that day. There was, let's say, a slight commotion in the hall, a little nervous laughter, a small collective intake of breath, as though what had just been said was of the order of an event, i.e. something irremediable. But for us here, it has the indubitable advantage of posing quite sharply the problem of Derrida's 'relation', if there is one, if there is *one*, to psychoanalysis.

If this declaration was able to surprise or even shock more than one listener, this is no doubt because one might have thought, and for good reason, that Derrida's thought was, if not an offshoot of Freud's, at least deeply related to psychoanalysis. Does he not say, for example, in *Of Grammatology*, that the best chances of achieving a breakthrough with respect to metaphysics are to be found,

95

alongside linguistics, in psychoanalysis (GR, 35 [21])? Does he not devote to Freud, alongside Heidegger and Lévinas, some very important pages in the seminal text 'La Différance'? Does he not invoke Freud at a crucial moment in his reading of Husserl (and therefore of all the others) in *Speech and Phenomena*, decisively questioning phenomenological temporality (VP, 71 [63]; cf. GR, 98 [67])? Does he not appeal all over the place to Freudian conceptuality, the very conceptuality he had just, that day in 1988, refused or denied so abruptly? My hypothesis today will be that the relationship Derrida entertains with psychoanalysis is an *original* one, i.e. that on the one hand this relationship is his alone (no-one else has that relationship with psychoanalysis), and on the other hand that this relationship is not the same as the relationship he entertains with other authors or currents of thought he reads, so that he would not make this declaration about Heidegger or Lévinas or Nietzsche.[10] And also, no doubt, that the relationship of Derrida with Freud is *original* in the sense that it is there at the origin, from the start, that there is, and would have been, no Derrida without Freud.

Let us try to schematise a little brutally the relations Derrida entertains in general with the texts he reads, remembering that everything he thinks is done *essentially* and *irreducibly* in reading the text of the other, or rather the texts of the others. Let us posit provisionally that the readings carried out by Derrida (his readings of non-literary texts, at least, if I can make use of such a problematic classification) can be broadly classified into two groups. On the one hand, reading texts which propose overtly 'metaphysical' theses (Plato, Rousseau, Kant or Hegel: a series I shall call, a bit for provocation's sake, the series of fathers) – in these cases, the reading works subversively to discover something else, movements or moments which are difficult to think of as metaphysical, and which even exceed or precede the declared metaphysical themes of the texts in question. *On the other hand*, reading texts which announce or declare themselves more or less directly to be non- or anti-metaphysical (Austin, Benveniste, Foucault, Lacan, even Bataille or Benjamin or Lévinas: I shall call this, still by way of provocation, the series of brothers, enemies of course),[11] Derrida shows how, in spite of their more or less noisy declarations, these texts really do rely on metaphysical foundations, or at least show up an unthought solidarity with the metaphysical tradition. In both cases (let's pretend to believe that there are only these two cases, and say nothing, for example, of the still more mysterious series of *sons*), the reading posits that the text read is at least double (and in fact multiple), divided between what *Of Grammatology* calls the *propos*, the 'statement' and 'another gesture', or else between what is *declared* and what is *said*: but in the first group an apparent metaphysical closure is opened up by other textual resources onto something more mysterious and originary, whereas in the second group the situation is the opposite – brave declarations of independence with respect to metaphysics are undermined by the unobtrusive signs of belonging discovered by Derrida.

How might we situate the reading of Freud in this perspective?

The opening of 'Freud and the Scene of Writing' appears to be unequivocal, and to place Freud firmly in the second group I have postulated: Freudian concepts, he says, 'all belong, without exception, to the history of metaphysics, i.e. to the system of logocentric repression ... ' (ED, 294 [197]). But how could we – with the irreducible psychoanalytic culture which is ours, and to which we shall return – not pick up from these pages, in the very decisiveness of this declaration, as in the one we began by citing, a tension which is, let's say, defensive, the trace already of a resistance, or of resistances in the plural, which will be thematised as such only thirty years later (RES), a tone that is a little brittle and tense in the declaration: '*In spite of appearances*, the deconstruction of logocentrism is not a psychoanalysis of philosophy' (ED, 293 [196]; my emphasis). The gesture is the same in *Of Grammatology*, in which the key 'Question of Method' chapter will tell us that '*in spite of certain appearances*, our picking out of the word *supplement* is anything but psychoanalytic' (GR, 228 [159]). One *could* then be mistaken, and take deconstruction to be a psychoanalysis of philosophy, there are appearances which might run the risk of giving this false impression, it's important not to be taken in by them: beware, says Derrida, I can see what you're going to think, deconstruction looks very much like psychoanalysis, it could even seem to be a species or scion of it, well no, above all do not be taken in, deconstruction *is not* psychoanalysis, and is so much not psychoanalysis that it is deconstruction, and deconstruction alone, which shows that the Freudian concepts belong 'all of them, without exception' to the history of metaphysics. Get that: *without exception*.

And yet, this declaration which is apparently so clear and decisive in 'Freud and the Scene of Writing' is immediately complicated by a concession. Before reading it, I should like to spend a few minutes on the famous 'Question of Method' chapter in *Of Grammatology* which I have just been quoting, and which will help us to clarify the claim that we are interested in here, and in which psychoanalysis figures as pretty much the only example, but it is an insistent, repeated example which does not stop returning, not only one example but the best example, the exemplary example, the paradigm, of what deconstruction *is not*. And if deconstruction is not, is *especially not* psychoanalysis, we can imagine that they must be very close. This is the whole difference between a 'rien moins que ... ' and a 'rien *de* moins que ... '.[12] The 'Question of Method' begins (this is the 'appearances' sentence I have just quoted) with a restricted description of what a psychoanalytical picking up of the word *supplement* would be, as distinct from a deconstructive one: ' ... is anything but psychoanalytic, if one means by that an interpretation transporting us out of writing towards a psycho-biographical signified or even a general psychological structure one could in principle separate from the signifier' (GR, 228 [159]). So that is a first reason. But there is a second reason, a more complex one, why the reading that Derrida is going to attempt will not be, or will above all not be, in spite of certain appearances, psychoanalytic in nature: this second reason (which will extend rather mysteriously into a third reason in a moment) is the following, and I must quote it at length:

> If the path we have followed in the reading of 'supplement' is not simply psychoanalytical [there's already been a small displacement, then: before, it was anything but psychoanalytical; now it is 'not simply' psychoanalytical], this is no doubt because the usual psychoanalysis of literature begins by bracketing out the literary signifier as such [so this is the first reason we have just seen]. No doubt too [second reason, then] because psychoanalytic theory itself is for us a set of texts belonging to our history and our culture. To this extent, if it marks our reading and our interpretation [these marks being, then, on the face of it, the appearances already invoked which could give rise to misunderstanding], it does not do so as a principle or a truth that could be withdrawn from the textual system we inhabit in order to illuminate it in all neutrality. In a certain way, we are *in* the history of psychoanalysis as we are *in* Rousseau's text. Just as Rousseau drew on a certain language which was already there – and which happens to be, to a certain extent, ours, thus providing us with a certain minimal readability of French literature – so we circulate today in a certain network of meanings marked by psychoanalytic theory, even though we do not master that theory, and even if we are sure of never being able to master it completely.
>
> (GR, 230 [160–1])

This second reason (already a complex one, because at first blush it does not seem obvious that we ('we'?) have the same type of relation to psychoanalytical conceptuality as Rousseau could have to the French language or that we might have to Rousseau's texts, that the already-there in question in these three cases is no doubt very different in each case) – this second reason extends, then, into a third one, which is presented as conclusive in the rhetoric of this passage. Recall: the *first* reason why our reading will not be psychoanalytical, is that psychoanalysis (at least in its habitual form) brackets the literary signifier as such; *second* reason, that we have just seen: we cannot go in for a reading that would be psychoanalytical in principle, because psychoanalysis forms to such an extent part of our general textuality that it cannot separate sufficiently from it to gain an overview or mastery of that textuality (which amounts to saying to some extent that our reading cannot be psychoanalytical to the very extent that it cannot *not* be psychoanalytical – which is evidently the reason for the transition from the 'anything but' to the 'not simply'); *third* reason, finally, new paragraph: 'But it is for another reason that we are not dealing with a psychoanalysis, even a stuttering one, of Jean-Jacques Rousseau.' Following what is quite a common procedure with Derrida, and which would need analysing for itself, he first gives arguments which are sufficient without being immediately conclusive, and then acts as though he did not need those arguments, because there is a still stronger argument, a killing argument.[13] What is this third reason which ought finally to establish what the other two have not quite managed to conclude (for I imagine that one might reply to the first reason that there are, perhaps, that there certainly are psychoanalytical readings which do not jump so rapidly over the 'literary signifier' (and we know that it will have taken 'The Purveyor of Truth' and a few other texts to answer this possibility); and reply to the second that the fact that psychoanalysis forms part of our general textuality would rather encourage the idea that the reading could not fail to be psychoanalytical, just as Rousseau could not *not* write in French)? Well, this third reason, as I have said, takes up and prolongs the second: a psychoanalytical reading would have to decide, in the case of Rousseau, between what truly belongs to him, what is properly his (this would be the 'extreme singularity' Leclaire was mentioning just now, what Derrida will subsequently call the signature) rather than everything that belongs to the 'already-there of language and culture', everything that Rousseau's writing 'inhabits' rather than 'produces', and

> Even supposing that psychoanalysis might in principle be able to complete this division and interpretation, even supposing that it accounted for the whole history of western metaphysics which entertains with Rousseau's writing relations of habitation, it would still have to elucidate the law of its own belonging to metaphysics and to western culture. Let us not proceed in this direction.
>
> (GR, 230–1 [161])

This third reason, then, rejoins the passage from 'Freud and the Scene of Writing' that we were in the middle of reading, and which, for its part, does indeed proceed in the direction here abandoned by *Of Grammatology*. We had left this passage between an apparently irrevocable condemnation of Freud and all-his-concepts-without-exception, and a concession which will moderate the force of that condemnation. In fact, that concession, even though not explicit, is already programmed into the argumentation from *Of Grammatology* we have just been reading, for in that case the three moments of the explication with what we might call 'the psychoanalytical appearance' are, rather brutally summarised, as follows: (1) deconstruction is not psychoanalysis because it does not leap over the signifier as such; (2) it is *still less* psychoanalysis because it already inhabits psychoanalysis, is marked in advance by it, as though by a language one does not choose and cannot place in an external position; (3) it is *still less still* psychoanalysis, because psychoanalysis has not elucidated, and no doubt will not be able to elucidate, the law of its own belonging to metaphysics. The concession that awaits us in 'Freud and the Scene of Writing', then, is programmed by the interweaving of these two last points, which say in sum that (a) we inhabit psychoanalysis and cannot therefore avoid it (nor assume it); (b) psychoanalysis inhabits metaphysics and cannot therefore avoid it (nor assume it). It would appear to follow, and this would be just the point of originality we are trying to pin down, that psychoanalysis is, for 'us', (like) our metaphysics, and therefore just as inevitable. All I am trying to articulate today probably comes down to a sentence one could formulate thus: 'We inhabit (psychoanalysis just like psychoanalysis inhabits) metaphysics.' Which means that it is by understanding our relationship with metaphysics that we will be able to understand the relationship of psychoanalysis to metaphysics – and thereby our own too. And so, to understand everything deconstruction advances with respect to the already-there of metaphysics in general we must (this would be a singularity of Derrida's) understand why deconstruction is precisely not, above all not, psychoanalysis. For this understanding to be possible, it would be necessary for psychoanalysis *not* to be completely saturated by metaphysics. So the concession that follows the apparent accusation or condemnation is not, as it were, accidental, for it is constitutive of the thought of deconstruction as such, which will give back to the relations between deconstruction and psychoanalysis all their originality and ambiguity: 'No doubt [this is the beginning of the concession, then] Freud's discourse – its syntax or, if you prefer, its work – is not to be confused with these necessarily metaphysical and traditional concepts.' So the rather loud declaration that all-Freudian-concepts-without-exception belong to the history of metaphysics already sounds less like an accusation and more like an acknowledgement of inevitability: all concepts *in general* belong to the history of metaphysics, and so one cannot particularly complain of Freud that *his* concepts belong to that history. He could not do otherwise, any more than any other could. And this is what will be repeated thirty years later in *Resistances*:

> Under the old name, the paleonym 'analysis', Freud has certainly not introduced or invented a brand new concept, supposing that such a thing ever exists. Who, save for God, has ever *created*, genuinely created, a concept? [Derrida is evidently aiming at Deleuze here: Derrida, Deleuze and Freud would give us more than one circumvolution to follow here.] Freud was obliged, in the first place in order to make himself understood, to inherit from the tradition.
>
> (RES, 33 [19])

The text of 'Freud and the Scene of Writing' now continues:

> No doubt it is not exhausted in this belonging. [Let us hold on to this
> motif of exhaustion, which will return in a moment.] The precautions
> and the 'nominalism' with which Freud handles what he calls conceptual
> conventions and hypotheses already bear witness to this. And a thinking
> of difference is less interested in concepts than in discourse. [End of the
> concession which, as we shall not cease to see confirmed, concedes a
> great deal.] But the historical and theoretical sense of these precautions
> was never reflected upon by Freud.
>
> (ED, 294 [198])

If, then, deconstruction is not, is above all not psychoanalysis (and if, therefore,
psychoanalysis is not deconstruction, cannot explain or comprehend deconstruction), this is not, as we might have thought on reading the first declaration,
because all Freudian concepts without exception belong to the history of metaphysics (because that is true of all concepts in general), but because this very
necessity, and the strategies it thereby dictates to any new conceptual elaboration,
were not *reflected* by Freud. Like any thinker, including Derrida, Freud must draw
his concepts from the metaphysical tradition; and like any thinker who thinks
something new, who invents something, he must invent on the back of these
inherited concepts. And Freud does so. But what he does not do is to reflect this
double necessity: he fails, then, in this double reflection, and fails in it doubly, on
the historical as much as on the theoretical level. (Historical and systematic, as *Of
Grammatology* will say, only to call that distinction immediately into question.) And
so this is, it would appear, essentially what distinguishes deconstruction from
psychoanalysis: not really thinking through both the necessary belonging of its
concepts to the history of metaphysics and its necessary strategic displacement of
those concepts, psychoanalysis *understands less* than deconstruction:

> For example, logocentric repression is not intelligible on the basis of the
> Freudian concept of repression; on the contrary, it allows us to under-
> stand how an individual and original repression is made possible in the
> horizon of a culture and a historical belonging.
>
> (ED, 294 [197])

Psychoanalysis understands less than deconstruction: let's understand by that that
psychoanalysis will not understand – will never be able to understand – deconstruction, whereas deconstruction already understands psychoanalysis; but also –
and this would be a consequence of that – psychoanalysis does not understand
itself either, does not understand what it is doing in necessarily inheriting its

concepts and then in inventively being clever with this heavy legacy. And, not understanding itself according to this law (which just is the law that Derrida will later call quasi-transcendentality, or more precisely transcendental contraband) psychoanalysis as such will be unable to escape from what I would call (but in a sense quite different from the sociological sense given to this word by Robert Castel some twenty-five years ago)[14] *psychoanalysm*, which would be the more or less inevitable consequence of the systematising and theorising tendency mentioned by Leclaire.

What will Freud have thought, being clever with metaphysics in this way, without knowing what he was doing or without at least reflecting what he was doing? His true discovery (the one that would make psychoanalysis 'not a simple psychology, nor a simple psychoanalysis' (337 [228])) would be not so much the unconscious and repression, but *Nachträglichkeit*, which gives rise to the following development in the main text of 'Freud and the Scene of Writing':

> That the present in general be not originary but reconstituted, that it not
> be the absolute, fully living and constitutive form of experience, that
> there be no purity of the living present, such is the theme, formidable
> for the history of metaphysics, that Freud calls upon us to think via a
> conceptuality unequal to the thing itself. This thinking is no doubt the
> only one that does not exhaust itself in metaphysics or science.[15]

This passage calls for two remarks, one bearing on the theme, which we have already noted, of exhaustion, and the other on the theme, or the words, of the thing itself.

First: as we have already seen, in the general characterisation of the relations between psychoanalysis and deconstruction, in the concession-sentence: psychoanalysis is not exhausted by the belonging to all its concepts without exception to the history of metaphysics. Here, still in the mode of a *no doubt* (but a 'no doubt' that would apparently be more one of concession than of probability, because unlike the other one, this 'no doubt' is not picked up by a 'but … '), we have a further specification of this non-exhaustion. There would be, no doubt, *only one* thinking which does not exhaust itself in metaphysics: this thinking, which is only one but complex (Derrida shows this through three formulae in 'That … ', and it is hard to tell here if they are supposed to be equivalent to each other or not: 'That the present in general be not originary but reconstituted, that it not be the absolute, fully living and constitutive form of experience, that there be no purity of the living present … '), this unique thinking will have been a thought which Freud might not have *had* or *thought* himself, but at least a thought that he will have called *us* (?) 'to think via a conceptuality unequal to the thing itself'. So non-exhaustion is translated by a *call* which relates to the thing itself.[16]

Second: This last sentence is still ambiguous. First possibility: is it that Freud would have called us, via a conceptuality unequal to the thing itself, to think fully that same thing itself; or, second possibility, is it that Freud would have called us to think this same thing itself via a conceptuality which would be *always* unequal to it? In other words, is Freud's call or appeal supposed to consist in the fact that he thought what he thought only through this conceptuality unequal to the thing itself (the appeal then being situated precisely in the gap between the thing itself and the thought called to think it)? Or, in more complex fashion, does he call us to think this same thing itself through a conceptuality which will always, constitutively but perhaps differently, be unequal to it? In the first case, there would be something like a relay-baton being handed on from Freud to us: on this view, he has not quite succeeded in thinking what he calls us – and is called himself – to think, but we can do it for him, in his place, following him or inheriting from him; in the second case, the inequality or the inadequation between the thought and the thing itself would be irreducible, and Freud's call will remain an appeal that we can certainly hear, maybe even renew, but never convert into a thought that would finally be clear and adequate to the thing itself that it must however try to reach. It is difficult, in the context of 'Freud and the Scene of Writing', and the scene this text is making around Freud, not to lean towards the first reading, according to which we could take up Freud's appeal and think for him what he was not really able to think for himself, because of the unreflected belonging of all his concepts without exception to the history of metaphysics. This would, basically, be a classical arrangement of inheritance or filiation in philosophy, a family scene in sum, of the same sort as those later ruthlessly dismantled by Derrida himself around Searle and Austin, for example, but also – and this will be the sense of *The Post Card* – around Plato and Socrates. And it will suffice to remember the penultimate sentence of *Speech and Phenomena*, i.e. that 'the thing itself always escapes' to suspect that this first possibility, *in spite of certain appearances*, is not the right one. And, as we shall indeed verify in a moment, everything becomes still less clear as to this tempting reading of 'Freud and the Scene of Writing' when we open 'To Speculate – on Freud' at the page where Derrida is still talking about the same thing, the selfsame thing, i.e. the thing itself, and where he says, more precisely, 'Everything hangs on the difficulty of properly *naming* the thing itself. In truth this difficulty is an impossibility' (CP, 407 [382]). What is this thing itself that Freud calls on us to think, without managing to think it himself? What is its *impossible name*?

We are here, of course, in *Beyond the Pleasure Principle* (but we almost always are when dealing with Derrida and Freud, in this text that Derrida later claims, in a tone it is difficult not to hear as rather sadly reproachful, regretful, that it is never mentioned by Foucault (RES, 130 [104]; cf. too 144–5 [116–17]), this text where psychoanalysis resembles less than ever a simple psychoanalysis, and here too we would find a certain Deleuze, among others). Derrida is commenting on a famous passage from the end of Chapter 6, in which Freud invokes the imaged or figurative nature of scientific language. There are many obscurities in our speculation, says Freud, but we should not let that disturb us, for they are due solely to the obligation we are under of using the scientific, therefore figurative, language of depth psychology. Now Freud is here a whisker away from replying to Derrida's objection that he failed to *reflect* the necessity of using concepts inherited from metaphysics, for he indeed recognises in this situation a necessity which Derrida again mentions in the text from *Résistances* to which we have referred, where he says that 'Freud really had to inherit from the tradition, in the first place in order to be understood'. For Freud here says explicitly that he had to borrow this figurative (and therefore obscuring) language in order to *describe* the processes in question, and in fact even to *perceive* them.

I cannot here reconstitute in detail Derrida's reading of this passage in Freud. Let me schematise a little violently, and take from it simply this: according to Derrida, (1) Freud seems at first to distinguish a first moment, that of simple perception, of scientific observation, and a second moment, in which this observation has to be translated into words, when the metaphorical and speculative drift, first of the language of observation, then of theoretical or scientific language, would begin; (2) but, in saying that one must resort to this figurative language, to all these *trans-* or *über-* movements even to *perceive* the things in question, Freud recognises that this necessary drift starts right at the origin. (3) This recognition still remains ambiguous, for Freud tends to think of it as 'an external and provisional fatality' (CP, 410 [384–5]) which it will one day be possible to overcome through biological progress. Which, says Derrida, brings Freud's sense of the structural necessity of the *trans-* or *über-* back to what he calls a 'very classical logic', according to which this necessity would be merely provisional, and in which the suspense and the borrowing would in the last analysis be guaranteed by a proper origin or end.

Let us pause a moment on this last point, for one might suspect that Derrida moves rather quickly over the articulation of Freud's text here. Freud says that we need not worry unduly about the fact that our speculation contains so many enigmatic and obscure processes, for this is due simply to the fact that we are obliged [*wir genötigt sind*, we are under the necessity] to use the scientific terms proper to psychology (or more precisely, he says, to depth psychology). This is where Freud says that without this, we would not be able to describe the processes in question, nor even perceive them. If we could replace these psychological terms by physiological or chemical terms, we would indeed not have *escaped* the fatality of figurative language, but we would have the relative advantage in that case of using a figurative language which has long been familiar, and which is perhaps simpler; which, says Freud, would mean that the 'deficiencies' [*die Mängel*] of his position would, probably, disappear. So there is here a sort of interrupted or frustrated teleology: we would make progress in the clarity of our thinking if we were in a position to replace the figurative language of (depth) psychology with the still figurative (but less figurative, or less disturbingly figurative) language of physiology or chemistry, but this progress would in principle be limited by the fact that this language would remain figurative nonetheless. Freud does not speak directly of *borrowing* here, as Derrida perhaps implies.

New paragraph. On the other hand [*Hingegen*] says Freud, our speculation, caught up in this way in an economy of figuration between a more of figuration given by the language of psychology and a less of figuration given by the language of psychology or chemistry, has seen its uncertainty considerably increased by the need [*Nötigung*] to borrow from biological science. So there is here a difference, if not an opposition, between psychological-physiological-chemical languages on the one hand, all figurative to a greater or lesser extent, and biological *science* on the other. Freud does not here speak directly of biological *language* (which must also be figurative, as a scientific language, a point that is now accepted), but of biological *science*. Now these borrowings (one imagines that these are essentially to do with what Freud has said about *protozoa* and more generally about unicellular organisms) have considerably increased the obscurity of our speculations (a certain discursive obscurity of which, coming from the figurative nature of scientific language, should not worry us unduly, even if we should no doubt aim to minimise the obscuring effects of this by moving towards a less psychological and more physiological or chemical language). What means that this increase of uncertainty is considerable [*zu einem hohen Grade ... gesteigert wurde*: not really 'by degrees', as Derrida translates or allows to be translated, but literally 'intensified to a high degree'], is evidently not that there would be a continuity between the discursive uncertainties and these borrowings from biology, but because these borrowings from biology are of a different order and a different status. What gives biology this new status is, as Derrida says, that according to Freud the possibilities of biology are open to infinity, that biology is a realm of unlimited possibilities [*ein Reich der unbregrenzten Möglichkeiten*] and that, therefore,

> We may expect it to give us the most surprising information, and we cannot guess what answers it will return in a few dozen years to the questions we have put to it. They may be of a kind which will blow away the whole of our artificial structure of hypotheses.[17]

Can one claim, with Derrida, that in saying this Freud is bending what he has just recognised with respect to a certain originary metaphoricity of scientific language to a 'very classical logic' according to which 'the suspense is provisional, the borrowing presupposes the proper fund, the drafts and money must be guaranteed in the final analysis'? Could one not legitimately think that, on the contrary, by blowing away our structure of hypotheses, biology would oblige us, not, as Derrida suggests, to bow to a truth finally proper and scientific, but to relaunch the process immediately by constructing new structures which would still be hypothetical, enigmatic and obscure? In which case, Freud would have advanced, if not something entirely different from what Derrida has him say, then at least a thinking that is a little less classical than 'To Speculate – on Freud' suggests, a thinking that would go a little further towards the 'thing itself' constituted by the escape of the thing itself, according to the structure of the call that we brought out in 'Freud and the Scene of Writing'.

So we could legitimately think that Freud, whose every concept without exception belonged to the history of metaphysics, had indeed thought or reflected, a little, if not the thing itself, at least the impossibility of acceding to the thing itself, of naming it properly, and thus of perceiving it clearly. As much as to say that here the thing itself – and contrary to Husserl, this would be explicit in Freud – is that there is no thing itself, because of an originary complication named by Freud in the note that closes this chapter of *Jenseits*, and which Derrida says little about; a note in which Freud, careful to clarify his terminology, says that his speculations 'seek to solve the riddle of life by supposing that these two instincts ['life instinct' and 'death instinct', placed in inverted commas by Freud himself, as if the better to show to what extent he takes seriously what he has just been saying about terminology in general in his text] were struggling with each other from the very first' (*ibid.*). It would be just this inequality or originary non-originarity that would constitute Freud's call, of which we could now say that the fact of its being unequal to the thing itself constitutes, precisely, its originality.

* * *

Let us be clear. The point here is not to reproduce a schema that has been quite common in reading Derrida, and which consists in saying that the authors whom he appears to reproach with a certain metaphysical blindness in fact escape from it, that they had already thought what Derrida appears to argue against them. Thus, the oldest and best-known example, Paul de Man on Rousseau,[18] but also, more recently, and among many other examples, especially perhaps in English, Slavoj Zizek on Hegel or Lacan.[19] This type of reading always does well out of Derrida, and no doubt always will (this is the matrix of all the announcements of the imminent death of deconstruction that we have heard over the last thirty years, i.e. since its birth[20]), and it has the merit of bringing out, negatively, a certain negative truth of deconstruction, namely the already-there that we have already invoked, for these cases proceed by taking everything Derrida's readings bring out of the texts read, then credit it to the account of the author in question (who wrote the texts, after all!), and then express surprise that Derrida appears to be opposing that very thing to the text in which, obviously and even explicitly, he learned it. So Derrida will supposedly have helped us find Derrida all over Plato, Rousseau, Hegel and the others, without Zizek and the rest ever drawing the consequences of the fact that these authors would clearly never have subscribed to (countersigned) these things they may have said, but certainly never intended or declared.

This is all the less the point of what I am here proposing that nothing at all is gained by pushing Freud further towards indeterminacy in the belief that he is thus made more 'Derridean'. For just as Freud was unable not to borrow all his concepts without exception from the history of metaphysics, so he can only do justice to the stealing away of the thing itself by making *that* his thing itself, in the very unevenness of his conceptuality. As Derrida says in another text of the same period, and in a slightly different context,

> This necessity is irreducible, it is not a historical contingency; we should have to meditate all its implications. But if nobody is, then, responsible for giving in to it, however little, that does not mean that all the ways of giving in to it are equally pertinent. The quality and fecundity of a discourse are perhaps to be measured by the critical rigour with which this relation to the history of metaphysics and to inherited concepts is thought through.
>
> (ED, 414 [282])

To say, then, that a text (in this case, Freud's) had escaped metaphysics would be meaningless: but it follows, too, that one cannot posit a one-dimensional economy in which there would be simply a linear more or less of belonging to metaphysics. This is why Plato, for example, is both very near and very far from metaphysics, and why one can the better escape the thing itself by delimiting it very tightly. And this is also why Lacan, 'so much more philosophical' (RES, 65 [47]) than Freud, and therefore well placed to avoid the latter's philosophical naiveties, runs the risk of enclosing psychoanalysis all the more securely in the metaphysical closure that Freud managed to open, if only slightly. So the point is not to praise Freud for going further in a given direction than Derrida says, but to pick up from the tiny and unusual tensions we have noted, the trace of a singular, original, nervous relation between psychoanalysis and deconstruction.

If we had time, I would try to show that this original tension is maintained in the most recent texts. Is it by chance, for example, that in the text presented to the 'Lacan avec les philosophes' conference, Derrida, regretting that the time-scale of conferences does not allow one to deal with 'the things themselves', adds immediately, in brackets, in a surely ironic but no doubt, nonetheless, insistent way '(ah, the things themselves!)' (RES, 58 [40]).[21] And such a reading would tend to suggest that the thing itself in question is perhaps *resistance*, which would then be what I have been talking about here for about an hour, and which would knot together very precisely the 'anything but' and the 'not simply', accusation and concession, the declaration of non-subscription and the already. This resistance, which Derrida admits he loves (the word and 'perhaps the thing', the thing itself, he also talks in 'Circumfession' about his dreams of resistance), would become something like a principle of undecidability or interminability, both what undoes the very principle of analysis and affirms it in its very interminability, a so to speak internal resistance of psychoanalysis to psychoanalysis, the relaunched singularity that relaunches the theory as a call always, structurally, unequal to the thing itself. The interminable and repeated resistance of Derrida to psychoanalysis would thus be the fertile principle of their relations.

* * *

Two remarks in conclusion.

1 If, in 'Etre juste avec Freud'[22], Derrida was able to pick up in Foucault an oscillating movement with respect to Freud, making Freud pass constantly from the side of the discourse analysed to that of the analysing discourse without this movement being thought by Freud, and if, politely but clearly, Derrida reproaches Foucault with this as a lack of fairness or rightness [*justice ou justesse*], can we conclude that Derrida, for his part, will have been fair to Freud and therefore to psychoanalysis? Clearly not, if we understand by 'being fair' the fact of emitting, from some tribunal, of reason or history, a last judgement, of deciding once and for all. Clearly not, if we understand by 'being fair' the gesture of giving Freud his due, of awarding him points for having had a few pre-philosophical thoughts from which philosophy could then profit. But if we can think a rightness and a fairness which would consist in responding to the call of the other, a call always unequal to the thing itself (but there is a call only in this unequalness), so as to maintain a listening to that call without immediately cancelling it by agreement or refusal, and without sending back in inverted form, but in making the call ring out in its unequalness, and thus in interminably resisting the very thing the call cannot fail to call for, resisting the call of the call, maintaining, then, the reciprocal debt that will never be paid off, refusing to add the last signature to the subscription – if we can think a rightness or a justice of this sort, then we might at least envisage the thought whereby Derrida's circanalysis, his way of turning around psychoanalysis without ever getting round it or claiming to have completed the tour, would be the only way to be fair with Freud, to give

oneself the time (which will, alas, always be lacking) for the thing itself in its stealing away. And this circanalysis would then be exemplary of a more general thought of justice which would have to be attributed not to Freud, nor simply to Derrida, but to their relation.

2   I have often wondered what would change if, by an extraordinary discovery, it turned out that everything Derrida puts forward about the metaphysical tradition were a fiction. Let us imagine that he had invented a novel about philosophy, with characters called Plato, Kant, Hegel, etc. And within this fiction about a fiction, one could then wonder what would happen if such and such a character were removed from the story. At risk of falling into an absurd hypothesis, I would suggest that if the character 'Rousseau' were no longer to figure in the novel, there would of course be changes, and quite considerable ones, but that nothing fundamental would be changed: narratological analysis would discover the same story in spite of the change made to the discourse. But – such at least would be my hypothesis – if the character Freud were no longer to be included, Derrida's novel would be entirely transformed, to the extent that the very structure of the narration would be turned upside down. I would not say that Freud is the only such character (Heidegger would be the other obvious case, just as problematical) but perhaps that Freud, in the very resistance he provokes in Derrida, provides us with the means to think this very situation. Freud, who supposedly never thought through *his* relation with respect to metaphysics, would by that very fact have allowed Derrida to reflect *his* situation with respect to Freud, and thereby to reflect a more general situation of indebtedness with respect to metaphysics, i.e. the general *déjà* into the abyss of which Derrida's signature plunges. Derrida's debt to Freud is thus strictly *priceless*. Had he not resisted Freud, turned around him, had he not interminably carried out his circanalysis, Derrida would not have been able to think the structures of resistance to the call of metaphysics which define deconstruction in general, and, subscribing too quickly to the propositions of psychoanalysis, would thereby have signed nothing at all.

8

FOREVER FRIENDS

Should it, strictly speaking, be an act of friendship to discuss someone's work?[1] A traditional canon of academic objectivity would want to say not. On that view, even if a relation of friendship linked the author of a book and someone discussing it, that friendship *ought not* to obtrude, ought not to influence the discussion, should certainly not be its *raison d'être*, especially if that discussion has any pretension to the status of philosophy. I might, on this view, be rather *dis*inclined to discuss my friend's work, in public at least, in case that demand of academic objectivity drove me to be critical in a way that always might imperil our friendship. Or I might, on the contrary, be the *more* inclined to discuss that work, even if I were to be critical of it, lest my silence be construed by my friend as an index of my reservations about the work, and lest he then exaggerate those reservations in the infinite space for conjecture left by my silence, which I would then be taken to have signed. This structure, and the undecidability it brings, tells a certain truth about friendship in general, and can have enormous consequences: Jean-Jacques Rousseau, for example, can quite reasonably be said to have gone mad as a result of it.[2]

Within this structure, which opens up as soon as I rise to discuss my friend's work, as soon as I mention his name, as soon as I read the book he has sent me, lies a complex drama of *property* and *propriety*, proper names and their usurpation. When I discuss my friend's work, do I attempt the difficult act of friendship which consists in accepting his thought to such an extent that it becomes mine, to such an extent that I can speak it in my own voice, under my own name, with such familiarity, or with such a claim to familiarity, that it always might look as though I have simply appropriated that thought as my own, ghosting it or parroting it? Or, on the contrary, do I maintain a respectful distance, *quoting* his thought *as* his thought, the thought of an other, that is not mine, above all not mine, running then the risk of appearing to be so exterior to it that I am disowning it? Can there be friendship (or at the very least intellectual or philosophical friendship) without these symmetrical risks and the dangerous zone between them? What happens when the book in question is all about just these questions? Does that make the situation easier or more difficult? Can I appropriate in friendship a thought which shows up the essential undecidabilities that notion harbours, the way friend and enemy, friendship and enmity, mingle in one structure? I shall try to suggest, in friendship, that it would be naive to expect a book on friendship to *answer* these questions, to subordinate its thought to the authority of a question or even of *the* question: and, having once at least before risked all friendship by not quoting at all,[3] here I shall be quoting a great deal, doing little more in fact than quoting, letting the friend's thought speak for itself, and speak for itself about, among other things, quoting or speaking in one's own voice or name.

I

Politics of Friendship is an unusual book for Derrida to have written. For thirty years, the standard pattern of Derrida's writing has been the more or less extended *essay*, sometimes gathered together to form a book (*Writing and Difference*, *Margins of Philosophy*, *Psyché*), sometimes published as (usually quite short) books in their own right (*Speech and Phenomena*, *Of Spirit*, *Aporias*, and so on). These essays most typically dwell on the work of one author, or come to focus on the work of one author as a way of discussing questions which are of much broader metaphysical scope, and are often divided into units we would be tempted to call *Sections* rather than *Chapters*. *Of Grammatology*, which *is* explicitly divided into chapters, is most obviously seen as a collection of essays of uneven length, culminating in a very long one on Rousseau. And even *Glas*, which stretches the form of the book to a certain limit, can always be read, and in a sense *must* also be read, rather prosaically, as two quite long, and relatively independent, essays on Hegel and Genet.

    Politics of Friendship looks like no other Derrida book from this point of view. Although it is presented in the *avant-propos* as an essay (the first sentence says 'Cet essai ressemble à une longue préface' (PA, 11 [vii]), or more precisely as a sort of monstrous and multifarious distension of a single seminar session, its length and superficial organisation (divided into ten chapters with titles) make it look much more like, well, a *book*, no longer centred on the work of one author (there are detailed readings of Aristotle, Kant, Montaigne, Nietzsche, Plato and Schmitt at least, with the long appendix on Heidegger in the French version too), but following a sinuous course it is difficult to summarise (not chronological, not thematic in any obvious sense of that word) and would be difficult to represent schematically. Derrida talks apologetically in the *avant-propos* of the 'inchoate form of his remarks' (PA, 11 [vii]). What's happening in this elusive work? What's it all about? Out of respect for the at least minimal friendship that reading entails, let's not presume to reduce its strangeness too rapidly, for this is a book which will, by its end, have unsettled so radically any comfortable sense one might have had of what 'politics' and 'friendship' mean, that any quick remarks about it are likely to appear unworthy. I'll be making a few fragmentary observations based on some very specific moments in the book

II

Let me begin by characterising the structure of friendship rather baldly and provisionally. Friendship, unlike love, does not tend towards a fusion of the parties to it. If I love you, I want to become one with you, or so the traditional concept would have it, to fuse with you to the point of death, but if I am your friend, such a clear *telos* is absent, or at least the *telos* is not really clear. The *point* of loving seems clear enough, even if we might think it absurd, irrational or unhealthy, but the point of friendship is harder to grasp, and perhaps that makes it more attractive still. Love is something we can't do much about, it takes us over and sweeps us on and away, maybe into disaster: friendship seems cooler, more calculated, involves a salutary distance that, in principle at least, prevents it being such a mess. We all hope that love can resolve into friendship, or be converted into friendship, because friendship looks more plausible in the context of forever: when I'm in love, part of that in-love-ness is that I *assume* or *declare* that I will love for ever,[4] even if I know I won't: insofar as love leaves any room for reflexion, I hope – though I don't really believe it – that it might be transmutable into friendship sooner or later.

As Jacques Derrida shows abundantly in *Politics of Friendship*, this structure generates a paradox whereby the distance, what I've called the coolness, involved in friendship, can always make it look as though the best friendship is the *most* distant. If the exemplarity of the friendship of Montaigne and La Boétie depends in part on the singularity of each party to it ('parce que c'était lui, parce que c'était moi'), and therefore their continuing identity as *lui* and *moi*, then it might follow that the friendship is partly about *lui* and *moi* remaining just that. I am my friend's friend to the extent that I do *not* try to become one with him, but also in that I am infinitely respectful of what he is, of the irreducible *lui*-ness or singularity that he is. My friendship for him is devoted to the maintenance of that *lui*-ness, and his for me to the maintenance of my *moi*-ness. We might then think that the best way for me to do that is to withdraw absolutely from all contact with him, to leave him be, to push the distance that friendship entails to a maximum and leave him alone. The risk of what Aristotle calls *aprosegoria*, the etiolation of friendship through lack of contact, is on this view constitutive of friendship, which always involves finding the *right distance*, which always might be quite distant. My best friend is still my best friend even though we hardly see each other: but also, and perhaps more accurately, because we hardly see each other. My friendship flourishes when I hardly know my friend. 'We didn't see much of each other, it's true, especially the last few years ... '

This contrast means too that love and friendship have quite different relationships with death and finitude. Love projects an infinity and a mutuality of death – we might even say that love just is the fantasy of dying *with* someone, rather than dying alone. But in friendship, the non-coincidence of the parties to it which is an essential part of its concept means, as Jacques Derrida was already pointing out in *Mémoires: For Paul de Man*, that friendship is marked by the knowledge that we will *not* die together, that one of us will survive the other, will *see the other die*, and will live on in mourning and memory of the other. And this structure would be constitutive of anything like a self. Here's Derrida in *Mémoires*:

> If death happens to the other and happens through the other, the friend is then only *in us, among us*. In himself, by himself, of himself, he is no longer, no longer anything. He lives only in us. But *we* are never *ourselves*, and between ourselves, a 'self' is never in itself, identical to itself, this specular reflexion never closes on itself, does not appear *before* this *possibility* of mourning ... The strange situation I am describing here, for example that of my friendship with Paul de Man, would have allowed me to say what I am saying *before* his death. It suffices that I know him to be mortal, that he know me to be mortal – and there is no friendship before this knowledge of finitude.
>
> (MEM, 49–50 [28–9])

So where love promises the illusory overcoming of the *jemeinigkeit* of each Dasein in its solitary relation to its death, friendship reminds us of that structure, recalls us to it. If friendship can be thought to lead to any sort of community, which we might think is a condition of its taking on a properly political import, then it would seem to be a community of shared finitudes, the thought of exposed singularities brought out most saliently by Jean-Luc Nancy in *The Inoperative Community*.[5]

III

I'd like to pursue this question of community, or this reference to community, this *word* 'community', which haunts *Politics of Friendship*, and especially its references to Bataille, Blanchot, Lévinas and Nancy. It is no accident that this should be the case, I think, in that it looks as though a thought of community should follow from the structure of friendship I have just outlined as, precisely, its politics. A

politics of friendship looks as though it would have to be a politics of a community marked by the interrupted teleology that defines friendship itself, saving us
from fusional fantasies but allowing some thought of gathering nonetheless. I
imagine that the immense and powerful appeal of Nancy's *The Inoperative
Community* for thinking about politics today is based on that sense that it lucidly
shows up the illusions and dangers of identificatory models of community, while
retrieving *some* value of community to reassure us still. It is this retrieved value,
still under the sign of *fraternity*, that Derrida will question, and question *out of
friendship* (I mean that the question is asked from a position of declared friendship
for the authors in question, but, by the fact of its publication, does not just *address*
those friends, or keep the question *among* friends: publishing critical remarks
about those one declares one's friends, however respectful those remarks remain,
is not a simple gesture in the politics of friendship.) Early on in the book, in a
long footnote referring to these authors explicitly as friends ('the friends I have
just cited or named' (PA, 57 [47 n. 15])), Derrida begins to question the value of
fraternity which has been the traditional model of friendship, and especially of
political friendship, insofar as it contributes to what Blanchot and Nancy mean by
'community':

> There is still perhaps some fraternity in Bataille, Blanchot and Nancy,
> and I wonder, from the depths of my admiring friendship, whether it
> doesn't merit some loosening [*déprise*] and if it should still orient the
> thought of community, even if it be a community without community, or
> a fraternity without fraternity. 'The heart of fraternity', for example,
> which in the final words of 'The negative community' [Blanchot], still
> lays down the law: ' … not by chance, but as the heart of fraternity, the
> heart of the law'. I'm thinking too, without really knowing what to
> make of it, of all the 'brothers' gathered, the 'men gathered' in 'fraterni-
> ties', in *The Inoperative Community*, when we come onto 'myth
> interrupted' (pp. 109, 111, 112). Should not the interruption of this
> mythical scene, through some supplementary question as to what
> happens 'before the law', at the mythical moment of the murder of the
> father (from Freud to Kafka), also affect the figure of the brothers?
>
> (PA, 57, n. 1 [47–8 n. 15])

At the very end of *Politiques de l'amitié*, this suspicion of fraternity returns more
pointedly around the concept or value of community itself, still radicalising
Blanchot to the point of suggesting that friendship conceived of as a *call* to a
'dying in common by separation' ought to disrupt *all* values of community which
still remain attached to it in Blanchot's work: the call of friendship which makes
me the friend of *this* or *that* friend (and not of everybody) would on this sugges-

tion have nothing to do with any reference to community at all (be that community presented as positive, negative or neutral) (AP, 331 [297–8]). Why not? Because

> Be they affirmed, denied or neutralised, these 'communitarian' values always run the risk of making a brother come back [to haunt us]. Perhaps we must take note of this risk so that the question of the 'who?' [who is my friend?] can no longer allow itself to be politically forced via the schema of being-common or being-in-common (even a neutralised being-common or being-in-common) into a question of identity (individual, subjective, ethnic, national, State, etc.)
>
> (PA, 331 [298–9])

And just a little later, under pressure from a remark of Blanchot's about Judaism, in which Blanchot says that it was Nazi persecution that made 'us' realise that '*the jews were our brothers* and that Judaism was more than a culture and even more than a religion, but the foundation of our relations with the other [*autrui*]', Derrida asks again (accepting only provisionally this characterisation of Judaism):

> What does 'brothers' mean here? Why should the other be above all a brother? And above all why '*our* brothers'? whose brothers? Who are *we* in that case? Who is this 'we'?
>
> (PA, 338 [305])

And then immediately goes into a curious paragraph entirely enclosed in parentheses (this is quite a common device in the book, which is structured as a series of complex interlocking parentheses), a sort of semi-autobiographical (or auto-graphi-graphical) remark, reflecting both on writing past and on the book of which this is, right at the end, a part, a sort of inside pocket of the book in which its generating secret might be both kept and finally revealed as a *worry* about this constellation of friendship, Judaism, community and fraternity, a sort of semi-confidential murmuring, a doubt or a concern one might confide to a friend about another friend, or the way one might confide in a total stranger one's more general difficulties with one's friends. Derrida lowers his voice, then, from the level of public pronouncement, and quietly tells us this:

> (Reading this sentence [from Blanchot], and still from the depths of the admiring and grateful friendship that binds me to its author, I secretly [*à part moi*[6]] wondered, among other questions (more than one question): why could I never have written that, nor subscribed to it, when, if I relied on other criteria, this declaration might be easier for me to make

115

than for some others [presumably implying: easier for Derrida as a Jew than it is for Blanchot, the non-Jew]? In the wake of the same question, I wondered why – if I can put it like this – I have never been able to write this word 'community' (avowable or unavowable, inoperative or not), on my own account, in my name [*à mon compte, en mon nom* – I'll be coming on to the problems raised by these formulas]. Why? Whence this reticence of mine? And is it not at bottom the worry [*l'inquiétude*] which has inspired this very book? Is this reserve, in the light of the abovementioned definition of Judaism [i.e. as the foundation of our relation to the other] insufficiently Jewish? Or on the contrary, Jewish to the point of hyperbole, more than Jewish? Once again, what does 'Judaism' mean in this case? I add that the language of fraternity appears to me to be just as problematical when, reciprocally, Lévinas has recourse to it to extend humanity to the Christian, in the event the abbé Pierre [referring to]: 'the fraternal humanity of the *homme de confiance* of the *stalag* who, by everything he did, restored in us the consciousness of our dignity.')

(PA, 338 [304–5])

One of the many things that is striking about this confidential or revelatory aside is that it appears to be struck by an instance of amnesia, which, as if by chance, also, if a little more indirectly, involves Lévinas and the question of Judaism. Derrida confides in us here that he has never been able to write the word 'community' in his own name, never been able to subscribe to it, and it looks as though this worry about the value of community and the value of fraternity it harbours has something to do with Judaism. If we now turn back thirty years, and open *Writing and Difference* at the second paragraph of the essay 'Violence and Metaphysics', following a long opening paragraph raising questions about the death of philosophy and the future of thought, we find Derrida writing the following:

Perhaps even these questions [about the birth, death, and future of philosophy] are not *philosophical*, are no longer *of philosophy*. They should nonetheless be the only ones able to ground today the *community* of what, in the world, are still called philosophers by a memory, at least, that we should have to question without ceasing, and in spite of the diaspora of institutes or languages, publications and techniques which pull each other along, self-generate themselves and grow like capital or poverty. *Community* of the question, then, in this fragile instance where the question is not yet determined enough for the hypocrisy of a reply to be already invited under the mask of the question, for its voice to have already been allowed to articulate itself fraudulently in the very syntax of the question. *Community* of decision, of initiative, of absolute, but

116

threatened, initiality, in which the question has not yet found the language it has decided to seek, has not yet reassured itself in it as to its own possibility. *Community* of the question as to the possibility of the question. It isn't much – almost nothing – but in it today an unbreachable dignity and duty of decision take refuge and sum themselves up. An unbreachable responsibility.

(ED, 118 [79–80]; my emphasis each time on 'community')

Had Derrida simply *forgotten* this passage when writing the remark from *Politics of Friendship* I have just quoted? Is he not here, quite solemnly, in his own name, on his own account, writing the *word* 'community', and subscribing to just that *concept* of community repudiated in the later work? Would this mean that the later doubts about the concept of community undermine the assertions of this earlier work? Or does it perhaps mean that there is something *sui generis* about the *sort* of community invoked so insistently here in 'Violence and Metaphysics', as opposed to the more obviously 'political' communities discussed and questioned in the friendship book? If so, if the oh so fragile 'community of the question' is a community of what is still called philosophy or what are still called philosophers, does that mean that philosophers form (or could form) a sort of community which is essentially different from political communities (or politics thought in terms of communities, with the attendant suspect value of fraternity), that the friendship involved in philosophical communities (or the philosophical community) is therefore different, marking perhaps the *philein* of the philo-sopher, the friend of wisdom, as different from all other friendships? If that were so, then we might suspect that lurking here, in this apparently forgotten invocation of the community of 'Violence and Metaphysics' we might find the resources with which to develop the difficulty around community announced in the *Politics of Friendship*. And we might also be moved to ask an apparently more anecdotal or trivial question: who are Derrida's friends? What are the politics of friendship *around* the book called *Politics of Friendship*, for example here and now in this gathering today and tomorrow, this pseudo-community 'we' are forming around that book or around its author, 'we' on stage and 'we' all together in this place? Are we really all friends here? What is friendship in these terms?

'Violence and Metaphysics' is not in fact entirely forgotten in *Politics of Friendship*: Derrida refers explicitly to it in a footnote to Chapter 9, in the context of a discussion of alterity and responsibility which also goes to the root of the book as a whole, and which, through an invagination of the very issue at stake here, is all to do with what it might mean to speak or write *in one's own name* or *on one's own account*. The opening of the chapter shows how, even *quoting* the already quoted or misquoted declaration attributed to Aristotle ('Oh my friends, there is no friend') I am in some sense still responsible:

... even if I have still said nothing determinate *in my name* when I began by saying, with no preparatory protocol, 'Oh my friends there is no friend', one is *justified* [on est *en droit*] (but what is this right?) to suppose that nonetheless *I am speaking in my own name.*

So it is a matter of the name borne [*porté*], the *portage* or the *support* of the name — and of the *rapport* with the name. The *portée* [bearing, scope] of the name, that's a question that has not ceased to weigh here. Indeed it belongs to the name to be able to survive the bearer of the name, and thus to open, from the first nomination, that space of epitaph in which we have recognised the very place of the *great* discourses on friendship.

(PA, 255 [228–9])

This, like the 'forgotten' passage from 'Violence and Metaphysics', is based on a thought of *responsibility*: even if I am only quoting, 'mentioning' statements about friendship, it seems reasonable for you to hold me responsible, just by virtue of the fact of my speaking at all, for the words that come out of my mouth. Now, says Derrida (through a complex sequence I am abbreviating here, for which abbreviation I must of course take full responsibility, even though I am saying nothing on my own account, in my own name): supposing that I am to be held responsible, by the simple fact of speaking, for what I say, even if I am not yet saying anything in my own name, then that supposition *cannot not* presuppose some relation to the other, to whom I am *already* responding, in relation to whom the question of responsibility can arise at all. And this question of responsibility — of the responsibility taken or given as to what it means to say something in one's own name or to subscribe to something said by another, or indeed by oneself — this question engages the whole problematic of the entire book and leads to one of several passages that might be taken to represent the book as a whole, a *mise-en-abyme*, a part representing the whole, a part bigger than the whole, as Derrida used to say. It is in the middle of this sequence that the footnote to 'Violence and Metaphysics' appears, called up perhaps by a reference to violence a little earlier in the passage I will now quote at length, with a few elisions, engaging thereby (in the fact of quoting, and in the fact of eliding) in the very scene of responsibility the quote already, abyssally, lays out:

... before even posing the question of responsibility, of 'speaking in one's own name', of countersigning such and such an affirmation, etc., we are all caught up in a sort of heteronomic and dissymmetrical curvature of social space, more precisely of the relation to the other: before any organised *socius*, before any *politeia*, before any determined 'government', *before* any 'law' ...

118

Let us be clear: before any *determinate* law, as natural or positive law, but not before the law *in general*. For the heteronomic and dissymmetrical curvature of a law of originary sociality is also a law, perhaps the very essence of law. What is unfolding at this moment, the disturbing experience we are having, is perhaps only the silent deployment of that strange violence that has always already insinuated itself into the origin of the most innocent experiences of friendship or justice. We have begun to *respond*. We are already caught, surprised in a certain responsibility, and the most ineluctable responsibility – as if it were possible to think a responsibility without freedom. We are invested with an undeniable responsibility from the moment we begin to signify something. But where does that start? Does it ever start? We see this responsibility which assigns us our freedom *without leaving it with us*, if we can say that – we see this responsibility come to us from the other. It is assigned to us by the other, from the other, even before any hope of reappropriation allows us to assume this responsibility, to assume it, as they say, *in the name, in one's own name* [*en son nom propre*, in one's proper name], in the space of *autonomy*, where the law one gives oneself and the name one receives conspire together. In the course of this experience, the other appears *as such*, i.e. it appears as a being whose appearance appears without appearing [this is where a friendly footnote refers us to 'Violence and Metaphysics', although an even friendlier one might have referred us to *Speech and Phenomena*], without submitting to the phenomenological law of originary intuitive data which rules all other appearances, every other phenomenality *as such*, every other phenomenality of the *as such*. The entirely other, *and every other is entirely other* [*tout autre est tout autre*], comes along here to disturb the order of phenomenology.

[...]

... it is a question of a 'political' translation ... of suggesting that a democracy to come, still not given, not thought, or even suppressed or repressed [*réprimée ou refoulée*], not only would not contradict this dissymmetrical curvature and this infinite heterogeneity, but in truth would be demanded by them ... of thinking an alterity without hierarchical difference at the root of democracy ... this democracy would liberate a certain interpretation of *equality*, withdrawing it from the phallogocentric schema of *fraternity* ...

Questions, then: in what sense could one still speak of equality, or even of symmetry in the dissymetry and without measure of infinite alterity? With what right still speak of politics, right and democracy? Must these words completely change their meaning? Allow themselves to be translated? And what then will be the rule of translation?

(PA, 258–60 [231–3])

This long digression, and the long quotation on responsibility I have just taken responsibility for, were called for by the need to situate the fact that 'Violence and Metaphysics' as a whole is *not* forgotten in *Politics of Friendship*, that Derrida refers to that essay here, not just anywhere, but at a place of extreme condensation, summary or *mise-en-abyme* of the most insistent themes of the whole book – and yet seems to forget it in that closing autographical or confidential parenthesis which is *also*, in a different way, a moment of condensation or of *mise-en-abyme* of the book as a whole.

Our long detour through that other moment was also, you will remember, justified or overdetermined by the reference to *responsibility*, and to what it means to write something (for example, the word 'community') in one's own name. Derrida says in his confidential aside that he has never been able to write that word in his own name, but the paragraph I quoted from 'Violence and Metaphysics' seems to show him doing just that, and doing so, what is more, in the context of an appeal to a solemn and unbreachable responsibility. But this reference is *further* overdetermined by the *sort* of community in question in this opening to 'Violence and Metaphysics': the long passage I just quoted about responsibility from *Politics of Friendship* ended with an explicitly marked series of *questions*. Now the community invoked at the beginning of 'Violence and Metaphysics' is a community *of the question*, precisely. This makes its apparent forgetting in *Politics of Friendship* the more intriguing, in that if that book is clearly worrying away at the value of *community*, because of that concept's links with the phallogocentric value of fraternity, it *also* worries away at the value of the *question*, in a way that it is tempting to place in a history of Derrida's thought. On this construal, the apparent forgetting of the passage from 'Violence and Metaphysics' would be *doubly* motivated: once because of the appeal to community, and a second time because of the appeal to that community as community *of the question*.

The history-of-Derrida's-thought I just mentioned would point to an apparent progression from the 'forgotten' moment in 'Violence and Metaphysics', where 'the question' appears to be the determining feature of philosophical thought and indeed of thought in general, of which 'philosophy' would be only a more or less local figure, through the book *Of Spirit: Heidegger and the Question*, and more specifically to a curious, monstrous, footnote in that book (apparently added after the fact of the text, after the text had taken the shape it was to take, seeming *itself* to be repairing an oversight or an act of forgetting of certain texts of Heidegger's that the note suggests were drawn to Derrida's attention after the fact by Françoise Dastur)[7] and yet adding to the text as a whole a decisive move, as it tracks Heidegger's shift from the pre-eminence granted to the motif of the question in *Being and Time* and up to at least the *Question Concerning Technology* (where questioning is still described as 'the piety of thought'), to a later thought about something preceding the question, something of the order of a promise, an engagement or an affirmation, and which is obviously to be linked, in Derrida's texts of the same period, to his own promotion of a thought of affirmation, double affirmation, promise, and so on.[8] Now it is hard to resist the idea that *Politics of Friendship* comes along as a *third* moment in this putative history of Derrida's thought, in that it suggests, via a reading of Nietzsche, an 'earlier' priority still, namely the priority, even over that affirmation, of a *transcendental perhaps*, giving the book as a whole another of its most insistent motifs, and one which in fact already sketches out the possibility of the sort of history-of-Derrida's-thought I have mentioned:

Derrida has just asked a difficult question about Nietzsche's apparently anti-democratic pronouncements, and continues in parentheses:

(Let's leave that question suspended, it breathes the *perhaps*; and the *perhaps* which is coming will always have preceded the question. At the moment it is formed, a *perhaps* will have opened it. It will forever forbid it from closing, perhaps, at the very place where it forms. No response, no responsibility would ever abolish the *perhaps*. That a *perhaps* open and forever precede the question, that it suspend in advance, not to neutralise them or inhibit them but to make them possible, all the determinate and determining orders which depend on *questioning* (research, knowledge, science and philosophy, logic, law, politics and ethics, language itself and in general), that's a necessity to which we try to do justice in several ways.

For example:

1. In recalling that acquiescence (*Zusage*) which is more originary than the question and which, without saying *yes* to anything positive, can only affirm the possibility of the future by opening itself to determinability, therefore in welcoming what remains still indeterminate and indeterminable. This is indeed a *perhaps* which cannot yet be determined as dubitative or sceptical [there's a footnote reference here to *Of Spirit*], the perhaps of what *remains to* be thought, to do, to live (unto death). Now this *perhaps* does not only come 'before' the question (enquiry, research, knowledge, theory, philosophy); it would come, in order to make it possible, 'before' the originary acquiescence which engages in

121

advance the question with the other [*auprès de l'autre*, in the other's company].

(PA, 58–9 [38])

But *Politics of Friendship* goes further still in this outflanking of the question (which does not of course invalidate the form of questioning as an essential way of proceeding, and Derrida, as we have already had occasion to verify, proceeds in the book essentially by asking questions, including in the confidential aside we are still turning around here, where he repeatedly says 'je me suis demandé', I asked myself. Showing that the question is not perhaps originary does not imply we have to *give up* asking in favour of affirming, promising, or saying 'perhaps'.) This further outflanking or questioning of the question happens in the context of the reading of Carl Schmitt.

Schmitt makes the distinction between friend and enemy definitive of the political as such, and part of the drift of *Politics of Friendship* is to question the possibility of making that distinction once a certain complex co-implication of friendship and enmity (what I started off referring to as 'coolness') is recognised. But Schmitt's increasingly difficult attempts to define the enemy bring him, after the war, in prison, to link explicitly the enemy and the question. Schmitt comes to the thought that no longer is it simply a matter of answering the question, 'who is my enemy?', because the question *itself* is *already* my enemy insofar as it places me in question. And this is also an important moment in the question Derrida is putting to the concept of fraternity:

There would apparently be no question of the enemy – or of the brother. The brother or the enemy, the *frère ennemi*, is the question, the questioning form of the question, this question that *I* pose because it is first posed to me. I pose it only from the moment it bears down on me mercilessly, on the offensive, offensively. In crime and grievance. The question wounds me, it is a wound in me. I only pose this question, I only really pose it where *it places me in question*. Aggression, traumatism, war. The enemy is the question, and through the brother, the *frère ennemi*, it originarily resembles, it indiscernibly resembles the friend, the original friend as friend of alliance, sworn brother ... The question is armed. It is the army [the armed one] – friend enemy [*Elle est l'armée – amie ennemie*].

It would be easy to show, let's not spend too long on it, that the history of the question, from the question of Being, like the whole history it has ordered (*philosophia*, *episteme*, *istoria*, research, enquiry, request, inquisition, requisition, etc.) could not have proceeded without polemical violence, without strategy and without arms technology. One must know this, one can know this without for all that concluding that one must disarm the question – or ask only disarmed questions. But without giving up on any question, therefore any knowledge, and to enquire again vigilantly, *before and outside any war*, as to what makes possible a deployment of that question that Heidegger said one day was 'the piety of thought', perhaps we must once more – and this would *perhaps* be the friendship of the *perhaps*, of the *perhaps* 'before' the question, before even the affirmation that opens it and that we were speaking of earlier – climb back up the question, climb the whole length of the question, higher than it, with it and without it, with it before it, *at least before it takes shape*, when the friend and the enemy pass into each other via the figure of the brother. Before any question, before the question mark, one would thus have to hear an exclamation mark. We should have to hear again this double clamour addressed to the friend who is no longer or who is not yet ('O my friends, there is no friend!') as to the enemy who is no longer or who is not yet ('O enemies, there is no enemy!').

(PA, 173 [150])

And, a little later, this same passage in Schmitt is used to show that this *recognition* of the enemy in the question which places me in question not only strikes the distinction between friend and enemy with undecidability, but means that I become my own enemy, that the enemy takes on all the values of proximity and propinquity traditionally associated with the friend.

IV

Where does this leave the paragraph from 'Violence and Metaphysics' I suggested Derrida had forgotten in his parenthetical, confidential aside at the end of his book? Is the appeal to the community of the question, and what we must assume to be the associated value of the fraternity of philosophers as brothers in the question, simply now forgotten because it could not survive being remembered in the context of *Politics of Friendship*? Would this then have been a moment of youthful and even naive enthusiasm subsequently overcome by the increasing sophistication of argument and reference through the aforementioned 'history of Derrida's thought'? Would this type of invocation of community and question now have become anathema, the enemy itself, the enemy who overlooks this complex imbrication of enmity in the very form of the question supposed to gather the brothers into their community?

It would not be at all implausible to answer 'yes' to these questions. On one construal, it is the very condition of a philosophical career that it involve development and reconsiderations, even repentance and disavowal or repudiation. It is true that, to my knowledge, no-one has ever been able to show that Derrida has *ever* needed to renounce or repudiate *any* substantive argument from earlier work, and one of the many strange features of 'Derrida's work' is just that, its resistance to organisation into the shape of a career or a history, its extraordinary and paradoxical *consistency* or *constancy* it would be nice one day for a biographer to track back to a moment of originary insight about the non-originarity of origins and originary insights, about an irreducible originary complexity. On this view, we might then reasonably want to claim some modest credit for making a *discovery*, something to inscribe in the archives of 'Derrida scholarship', indubitable proof that he not only might sometimes *forget* an earlier assertion, but that that forgetting might be motivated by the need to forget, that he would have good reasons to forget this earlier enthusiastic pronouncement about community and question.

But there are a number of reasons for resisting this way of looking at it. For a start, the way the position of the question is described in this early text, it is clear that it is trembling on the brink of no longer being describable as a question at all. A pure question or questioning that has not yet given itself any assurance as to an answer or the possibility of an answer, a question as to the possibility of the question, is already not quite or no longer describable entirely by the traditional concept of the question. And then, the development of the point soon discovers, already before the question, an injunction or a commandment, namely that the question must be guarded *as* a question (ED, 119 [80]). I think it would not be hard on the basis of these observations to show that the way the question is determined here can already be read, with the help of the later work, as marked by affirmation, and even by the 'transcendental perhaps', that we have noted in *Politics of Friendship*.

What of the value of community, though, which was after all the object of the amnesia we thought we had detected in the confidential parenthesis from the end of *Politics of Friendship*? The 'community of the question' announced here is nothing as concrete or socio-historically identifiable as a given 'community' of philosophers, but retains a privileged relationship with philosophy which I think Derrida would not want to renounce today. But if that community still quite confidently named in 'Violence and Metaphysics' is put through the test of the remarks about community in *Politics of Friendship*, we would then be justified in asking a question nowhere explicitly raised in the later book, i.e. the question of *philosophical friendship*. Not the philosophical concept of friendship, nor even the sort of friendship or *philia* that defines philosophy as such (recalled in *Politics of Friendship* through a reading of Heidegger's *Was ist das — die Philosophie?* in chapter 9, where Derrida is happy to associate the *Zusage* with the pre-philosophical *philein* which gives rise to philosophy) but the (specific) sort of friendship, and the (specific) sort of *politics* of friendship that holds among philosophers.

Do philosophers have friends? Not friends in the sense of personal friendships with individuals who might or might not be other philosophers, but *philosophical friends*. Not all my friends are philosophers, thank goodness, but not all my friends who happen to be philosophers are my *philosophical friends*; and some of my philosophical friends I do not know at all, except perhaps through having read their work. The point here would be to define a notion of philosophical friendship which respected the logic of the concept of friendship, including its political radicalisation by, or through, Carl Schmitt. Such a radicalisation ought to leave open the possibility that I do not really like my philosophical friend at all, and indeed that the best chance for my philosophical friendship is that I do not really like my philosophical friend, once we recognise the paradoxology of friendship itself.

My question in conclusion then is just this: who are Jacques Derrida's friends? And my suggestion, which I make to cut short all the preliminary clarifications such a question would require, is that his best friends (his best philosophical friends) might be found not at all where we might be tempted to look. My aim in conclusion is to clear some ground towards formulating the following question: who are Jacques Derrida's philosophical friends? I do not mean by this, what is the intersection of the set of philosophers and the set of Jacques Derrida's friends, nor something like 'which philosophers does Jacques Derrida *like*', but, with the 'political' moment in place: which philosophers are Derrida's friends?

This question needs refining further. Not only does it not mean: which friends of Derrida's are philosophers, it does not even mean, 'which philosophers have expressed philosophical friendship for Derrida?'. A test case here might be that of Richard Rorty. I do not know if he and Derrida are friends, but I do know that Rorty has expressed for Derrida something it might seem reasonable to call philosophical friendship (though I'm not aware of the reciprocal being true). Rorty *likes* Derrida. But I would not want to say that Rorty was Derrida's philosophical friend, not just because his direct expository attempts with Derrida are demonstrably wrong, but because the drift of Rorty's own thinking appears inimical to the drift of Derrida's. Although we might imagine many situations in which Rorty and Derrida were in agreement, and even in political agreement, it seems to me that they are not philosophical friends, or at least not a very strong case of philosophical friendship. Indeed, it is at least possible to envisage that other English-language philosophers who have never read or cared to read Derrida might in fact be much more – and much more durably – his friends than Rorty ever could. It is at least possible that Derrida and Donald Davidson, for example (who have probably never read each others' work) are much better friends in this sense than Derrida and Rorty.

But this further refinement would also need to look carefully at cases where friendship seems obvious. I know that Philippe Lacoue-Labarthe and Jean-Luc

Nancy, for example, are Derrida's friends in almost all the senses I have elaborated so far. But I want to suggest that here the concept of friendship runs up against something more problematical, perhaps something more akin to the 'love' I began by separating from friendship. Without wanting to suggest that the work of Lacoue-Labarthe and Nancy is merely that of *acolytes* of Derrida (nor indeed wanting to suggest any very close connection between their two very different bodies of work), I suspect that the friendship here is not strictly, or simply, of a philosophical nature.

So let's entertain that possibility that Derrida's best philosophical friends always might be philosophers who are, or have been, more or less violently critical of him, or of whom he has been more or less violently critical. In the past, I think the way I have characterised the relationship between Derrida and Lyotard would answer to this notion of philosophical friendship. I want to argue that Lyotard and Derrida are philosophical friends, not in the very crude and general way in which they are often perceived as belonging to a movement of thought called poststructuralism or postmodernism, the way in which they would obviously enough be 'on the same side' against certain sorts of criticisms or attacks, but in a more refined and interesting way. We might have to say here that they are better friends than they know, that the more or less explicit criticisms each has made of the other's work do not prevent this friendship from flourishing.[9]

But I'd like to conclude by suggesting another name too which seems to me to fall neither into the Rorty camp of merely apparent friendship, nor into the Nancy and Lacoue-Labarthe camp of close collaboration. What would it mean, for example, to suggest that Derrida's best philosophical friend might be, or might have been, Gilles Deleuze? Pending further development of this thought, I'll simply end by quoting from something Derrida wrote in the newspaper *Libération* after Deleuze's death:

> Deleuze remains no doubt, in spite of so many dissimilarities, the one to whom I have always judged myself to be closest among all those of that 'generation'. I have never felt the slightest 'objection' well up in me [*s'annoncer en moi*], even virtually, against anything he said [*aucun de ses discours*], even if I did on occasion mutter about this or that proposition in the *Anti-Oedipus* (...) or perhaps against the idea that philosophy consists in 'creating' concepts. I would like to try one day to say something about such an accord on the philosophical 'content' when this same accord never excludes all those distances that I still do not know how to name or situate. (...) I only know that these differences never left room between us for anything but friendship. To my knowledge, no shadow, no sign ever suggested the contrary. This is rare enough in the milieu that was ours for me to want to note it here and now. This friend-

ship did not only depend on the (significant) fact that we shared the same enemies. We didn't see much of each other, it's true, especially the last few years ... .[10]

9

IS IT TIME?

'The time has come,' the Walrus said,
'To talk of many things:
Of shoes – and ships – and sealing-wax –
Of cabbages – and kings –
And why the sea is boiling hot –
And whether pigs have wings.'[1]

No *différance* without alterity, no alterity without singularity, no singularity without here and now.[2]

Blessed *is* he that readeth, and they that hear the words of this prophecy, and keep those things which are written therein: for the time *is* at hand.[3]

Is it time?[4] It's *about* time. Just a moment. Any moment now. But the moment or the time in the sense I shall be discussing it has a curious and difficult relation to time in general. In English at least, it is difficult to separate questions about time in general in all its complexity (cosmological time, psychological time, the phenomenology of internal time-consciousness and so on) from questions about *the* time, the time that might have come, the right time, the moment as appropriate moment, not the moment as just *now* or as *present*, but as the *right* moment, *le bon moment*, the moment as *kairos* rather than as *nun*. This thought of the moment as the *right* moment, the moment whose moment has come, for which the time is ripe, the time whose time it is, the time that must accordingly be grasped or seized[5] before it has gone, the time as opportunity not to be missed, is, or so it would appear, *itself* a thought whose time has come. The time has come to talk of many things, but among those many things the thing whose time has *most* come is, apparently, blame the millennium, the thought *of* the time's having come. And the proof of that is given among many other signs (including a flurry of recent French philosophical interest in St Paul, messianism and eschatology)[6] by the fact of the conference for which this paper was written, which could not but invite the reflection that it had been organised at the right moment, that this is indeed the moment to talk about the moment. And it seems that any attempt to think about the moment as right or appropriate moment has to accept this reflexive paradox from the start. Whatever I talk about, I implicitly claim that it is the right moment to talk about it – *any* speech act, however mistakenly or apologetically, lays claim, usually tacitly, to its own timeliness: and a speech act concerning the question of the moment, the time, or timeliness in general leads to a potentially paradoxical reflection of that structure. Any talk about the moment suggests that it really is the right moment to talk about the right moment, that its time has come – and explicit claims to untimeliness or intempestivity are, one might suspect, no more than a further twist of this structure. For there's nothing for which the time has come so much as for the very thing no-one is now talking about, nothing hopes to be more timely than meditations which proudly claim to be untimely. The proud or apologetic claim to untimeliness is just a claim that the timeliness of what is being presented as untimely is not obvious or widely perceived, and it thereby adds a supplement of timeliness to the untimely. Fashion, which will return as a question in a moment, is a helpful way of thinking about this link of the timely and the untimely: timing in fashion is all about the timeliness of the untimely, choosing the right moment to go against the present moment, and apparently modest claims to be unfashionable, to be refusing fashion, quite common in academic discourse, always hope to set the trend again.

But if the untimely can in this way always claim to be the most timely, the gesture that reverses appearances and renders the fashionable dated and instantaneously makes the unfashionable into the *dernier cri*, then the apparent reflexivity of the relation of the right moment to itself is disturbed in some way. If the most apparently untimely *always might* be the most timely, then the timeliness of the timely is no longer so secure. The untimely can turn out to be timely only to the extent that there is at least the suspicion of a non-coincidence between the time that has come and the time *in* which it comes, between the moment as container and the moment as arrival. If I need to say or to announce that the time has come to talk of shoes or ships or sealing-wax, then I imply that in some way that necessity, the having-come of the time that has come, is not so obvious, not so present. If I need to tell you that the time has come, then this implies that you hadn't noticed, or might not have noticed, if I hadn't told you. The arrival of the right moment is in this sense always at least potentially not synchronised with the time in which that moment arrives: it is time *only when* in some sense it is untimely. Nietzsche's *Untimely Meditations* of course present themselves as arriving at just the wrong – and therefore right – time,[7] and the same can be said for Derrida's book on Marx — *just because* everything suggests that the time is wrong, then maybe in truth it is right. The time is *always* ripe just for the untimely. The chance of the right moment's really being the right moment is given only by its discordance with the time in which it arrives. The moment in its arrival, its event, has to arrive in a moment of time; the *kairos* has to present itself as a *nun*, so that it can, 'by extension' according to the dictionary, signify also just 'the present time' or 'the times'. But the possibility of the moment's being the right moment depends on an at least possible (and in fact necessary) dissonance between the moment as event and the moment as the time of its arrival: and this dissonance then opens the possibility that *any* moment could be the moment, that the question 'is it time' can be asked of *any* time. We might speculate that the experience of time is always the experience of the more or less muted expectation that any moment be *the* moment, and that the various fantasies we may have as to just what any moment might be the moment for are secondary to this fundamental structure of the relation between time and event. If I am right that this is just an analytical consequence of the concept of *kairos*, then we could link it rapidly to the famous Benjaminian notion of the *Jeztzeit*, the thought, itself as timely as it is untimely, with which, according to Benjamin, historical materialism 'cuts through' historicism (*kairos*, from the verb *keirein*, to cut or shear). The chance of a moment's being the right moment, given by its interruptive untimeliness with respect to the present, generates in Benjamin the thought of messianic time (which is famously also a cessation or interruption of time, a revolutionary moment), whereby, in the Jewish tradition on which Benjamin is drawing, 'every second of time [is] the strait gate through which the Messiah might enter'.[8]

* * *

I want to suggest that it is time today, the right moment, to think about two broad ways of dealing with this situation. The first, which is massively dominant in the metaphysical tradition (and especially perhaps the Christian tradition) attempts to map the apparent untimeliness of the time in its arrival onto a truer timeliness, giving rise (or birth) to a metaphorics of ripeness and fruition, pregnancy and childbirth. The second, traces of which can be found no doubt throughout that same tradition, but which might be seen more obviously in, say, Stendhal, Kierkegaard or Benjamin, accentuates the irruptive or interruptive temporality of the moment in its intempestive arrival.[9] I want to suggest that the function of the first type of view is, to state it rather bluntly, to resolve contradiction: if there is a time for every purpose under heaven, as Ecclesiastes affirms, then the various contradictory activities the passage goes on to list are no longer contradictory: war and peace, for example, each has its right moment or right moments, and this rightness is the sign of the overall prospect of the resolution of contradictory predicates in the mind of God: no one *in the world* [i.e. 'under the heaven' (3:1); 'under the sun' (3:16)] can 'find out the work that God maketh from the beginning to the end' (3:11). The temporal world unfolds puzzling contradictions, but the puzzle is not insurmountable if it is thought that each element is right for its time, its *appointed* time, even if the detail of that appointment remains a mystery to us. Of course not all biblical texts encourage the type of languid contemplative acceptance of this structure that this passage from Ecclesiastes might seem to promote: St Paul, famously the thinker of the *kairos* in a more urgent sense,[10] thinks of it more as a moment of awakening from the type of slumber Ecclesiastes might be taken to encourage: 'And that, knowing the time [*ton kairon*], that now it *is* high time [*ede hora*] to awake out of sleep: for now [*nun*] is our salvation nearer than when we believed' (Romans 13:11): but this awakening still, of course, brings a promise of reconciliation and redemption (I Corinthians 4:5: 'Therefore judge nothing before the time [*pro kairou*], until the Lord come, who both will bring to light the hidden things of darkness, and will make manifest the counsels of the hearts: and then shall every man have praise of God.', or II Corinthians 6:2: 'Behold, now is the acceptable time [*nun kairos euprosdektos*]; now is the day of salvation').[11] And this urgency brings out another feature of the thought of the time as the right time – it is, typically, referred to the question of *judgement*, the moment of separation of the good from the bad, the moment at which all becomes clear, at which the temporal resolves into the eternal. On this view, the right moment not only cuts into the flow of time, but it is the *end* of time – time as such will be revealed on the day of Judgement to have been only for the sake of that day of Judgement: the whole of time is the ripening of the *kairos*, the *point* of time, which will put time to an end in a definitive moment of judgement and redemption.[12] My further unresolved question today will be that of whether it is possible to think the interruptive force of messianic time without being committed to the thought of a rebirth, or the thought of the end of time, of time having an end in *parousia* or epiphany, the thought of *telos* or *eskhaton*; and, relatedly, whether it is possible to think of a judgement that is not more or less surreptitiously mortgaged to a thought of the Last Judgement.

* * *

In order to keep things relatively simple, I shall concentrate for this first type of thinking about the moment on Hegel,[13] and for the second on Derrida. It will rapidly become clear that I do not think that the relationship between these two types of thought is simply oppositional or contradictory, nor indeed that there is, under heaven, a time for one and a time for the other. With luck, *si ça tombe*, we may hope to understand a little more clearly how and why deconstruction, as deconstruction of *presence*, is also and thereby affirmative of the here and now.[14]

In a very famous passage in the *Introduction* to the *Philosophy of History*, Hegel is discussing 'world-historical individuals'.[15] History is the sphere in which collisions between existing ethical systems (States as ethical totalities) appear as contingencies which disrupt and unsettle such systems. Only such disruptive contingencies (most typically in the form of war, that agent of ethical health for the State) prevent States from achieving the somnolent repetitive permanence that would otherwise be their goal (and simultaneously their collapse back first into the merely worldly concerns of civil society, and ultimately into nature), and world-historical individuals are the agents of such contingencies – contingencies which are, of course, according to the general rule of Hegelian thought, to be grasped as necessities at a different level of description.[16] For that to be possible, the contingencies in question cannot be simply random or irrational, and it is to a version of the thought of the *kairos* that Hegel will appeal, as to a 'general principle' (p. 29) to operate the required conversion of contingency into necessity. It is a crucial feature of Hegel's account that such individuals (Caesar being his prime example) are not *conscious* of pursuing any goal other than an essentially particular, passionate and even selfish one – Caesar acts against the established legality of the Roman constitution and turns it in his own interests into an autocracy, but that shift was, says Hegel,

> an independently necessary feature in the history of Rome and of the world. It was not, then, his private gain merely, but an unconscious impulse that occasioned the accomplishment of that for which the time was ripe. Such are all great historical men – whose own particular aims involve those large issues which are the will of the World-Spirit.
>
> (p. 30)

The temporality of this 'ripeness' is complex. According to the paradoxical structure I sketched out at the beginning, the timeliness of the world-historical individual's action depends, at least in part, on the *untimeliness* of the action, as measured by the time in which it takes place. Hegel says:

> Such individuals had no consciousness of the general Idea they were unfolding, while prosecuting those aims of theirs; on the contrary, they were practical, political men. But at the same time they were thinking men, who had an insight into the requirements of the time – *what was ripe for development*. This was the very Truth for their age, for their world; the species next in order, so to speak, and which was already formed in the womb of time. It was theirs to know this nascent principle; the

necessary, directly sequent step in progress, which the world was to take; to make this their aim, and to expend their energy in promoting it.

(*ibid.*)

That for which the time is ripe, on this description, is precisely not what is coincident with the time in which the actions take place, but what disrupts and disturbs that time. The time *in* which the world-historical individual acts is the time of the tendential permanence of the State: the act itself cuts into and disrupts that time, and if it is nonetheless *time for* this other, disruptive, time, it is time for it in that the *proper* time for that time (the time in which the action in question will in some way coincide with itself) is still to come. The time is ripe, but its ripeness is not a self-coincidence – ripeness here is rather an anticipation on such a coincidence. This anticipatory gesture is itself complex: the event anticipates on a time in which it will turn out to be right or appropriate, it will drag the time in which it occurs along to the stage which it already represents, ahead of its time; but it also anticipates on a time in which it will be possible to see that it *always was* going to turn out to be appropriate, that the next stage already was 'formed in the womb of time', as its very appearance will have proved. The metaphorics of ripeness or of pregnancy mean that the appearance of the fruit or the child is an event the absoluteness of which is immediately compromised by its necessary earlier preparation or anticipation.[17] This way of thinking the moment gathers up past, present and future in a way that is entirely consistent through the tradition: in the same chapter of Ecclesiastes as I was quoting before, for example, the 'time' or 'season' for every purpose *under* heaven is guaranteed by a divine time in which 'That which hath been is now; and that which is to be hath already been' (3:15).[18] The adventurous and passionate unconsciousness of the world-historical individual achieves its rational character from the point of view of Spirit having come to knowledge of itself as a result of the sequence of ripe times in which the world-historical individuals played their part. And just this is the operation of reason as essentially cunning, that is dialectical.

Which seems to confirm that the very thought of a right moment or a *kairos* entails some thought of a temporal dislocation or non-coincidence. The *kairos* is always *another time* appearing in *the present* time: its *own* time is never that of the present, and to that extent is arguably not 'in' time at all. The rightness of that other time is asserted through an anticipation of the knowledge of its past: the right moment *will have been* right because, its structure implies, we will be able to see that it was always going to (have) be(en) right. Figures of ripeness, maturation and especially childbirth carry this complex recognition and denial of the otherness of the moment: the appearance of the new is thereby retrospectively presented as, if not exactly always *planned*, then at least explicable by the retrospective assumption of a causal sequence with its own laws.

It is, then, perhaps not surprising to find Derrida himself making a curious and displaced use of this figure of childbirth in one of his earliest essays. In 'Structure Sign and Play in the Discourse of the Human Sciences' (1966), in the context of the famous explanation of why the 'two interpretations of interpretation' cannot be the object of a *choice*, we find this:

> And because this is a type of question [i.e. a question as to the common ground of those two irreducibly different interpretations of interpreta-tion] – let's call it historical still – whose *conception, formation, gestation, labour*, we can today only glimpse. And I say these words with my eyes turned, certainly, towards the operations of childbirth; but turned too towards those who, in a society from which I do not exclude myself, are still turning them away before the still unnameable which is looming [*qui s'annonce*[19]] and which can only do so, as is necessary every time a birth is at work, in the species of the non-species, the formless, mute, infant and terrifying form of monstrosity.
>
> (ED, 428)[20]

This rather less reassuring view of the figure of childbirth as giving rise to the terrifying and the monstrous is, or so it seems to me, announcing already in Derrida the theme of the 'out-of-jointness' of time which is arguably already the central point of his early analyses of phenomenology, but which becomes explic-itly formulated – and is explicitly given the ethico-political resonance the notion of the *right* moment cannot fail to provoke[21] – only much more recently, most notably at the beginning of *Spectres of Marx*, where a certain 'non-contemporaneity of the living present with itself' (SM, 16 [xix]) is presented as a condition of possibility of responsibility and justice (see too SM, 44 [19–20] and 55–6 [27–8]). And, as is quite often the case in Derrida, such a non-contemporaneity is explicitly presented as non-dialectical:

> To hold together what does not hang together, and the disparity itself, the same disparity, can only be thought – we shall ceaselessly return to this as to the spectrality of the spectre – in a dislocated present time [or tense], at the jointing of a radically dis-joined time, with no assured conjunction. Not a time whose jointings would be denied, broken, ill-treated, dysfunctioning, ill-fitting, according to a *dys* of negative opposition and dialectical disjunction, but a time without *assured* jointing nor *determinable* conjunction. What is said here of time also goes, conse-quently or concurrently [*du même coup*] for history, even if this latter can consist in repairing, in conjunctural effects, temporal disjuncture: 'The time is out of joint', the time is *disarticulated*, put out, unhinged,

dislocated, the time is unbalanced, hunted down and unbalanced [*traqué et détraqué*], both broken and crazy.

(41–2 [17–18])

Our exegetical problem will be to understand this out-of-jointness in its non-oppositional difference from the dialectic understanding of the moment we have briefly seen in Hegel; and the challenge it will lay down to us will be that of seeing how this non-dialectical disjointing is in fact already at work *in* Hegel's understanding of the moment, as an 'earlier' and more powerful quasi-temporal dispensation.

Derrida himself first discusses this motif of the time being 'out of joint' in the context of discussing the difficulty of translating that idiom into French: the translations are *themselves*, he says, out of joint, depending on their understanding of the word 'time' here as meaning temporality in general, the times in which we live, or the world itself in its actuality. [This difficulty of translation is of course rendered even more serious when Derrida's work is translated back into English: Derrida says that the translations, in their irreducible inadequacy, can only aggravate or confirm the inaccessibility of the other language. When all of this is translated back into that other language, the effect is less to render familiar the Shakespearean idiom and more or less laughable the French versions rendered back into 'the language of Shakespeare', where their unavoidable inadequacy shows up all the more starkly just because of the still ready availability of the idiom Shakespeare actually used, so that the need for the English translator to avoid it in rendering the different French versions makes them look curiously blind or perverse – less that, than to open up the out-of-jointness of English itself with respect to itself, so that these retranslated translations stand for and provoke different possibilities of reading the English (even if we are reading in English as competent anglophones), the expression 'out of joint' *itself* thereby out of joint with itself. A little later I'll be suggesting that the constitutive (and still temporal) out-of-jointness of reading is a promising way of understanding the structure of the moment we are trying to unpack, and a good way of attacking its relation to Hegel.]

We might in any case wonder if it is by chance that Derrida goes on from his remarks about the dislocation of time from itself to an incisive reflection on the timeliness or untimeliness of his reading of Marx. (And indeed the blurb on the back cover, which I would imagine was written by Derrida himself, brings this out quite explicitly: 'Distinguishing between justice and right, crossing the themes of inheritance and messianism, *Spectres of Marx* is above all the gage – or the untimely wager – of a position taken up: here, now, tomorrow.') That (un)timeliness depends on an attempted cutting intervention into what is seen as a 'fashion[22] or coquetry' that 'one feels coming', namely the fashion for now treating Marx as a mere object for scholarship, a philosopher among others, in other words for treating Marx as fundamentally non-political, as having no bearing on the urgency that the dislocation of the present generates in the thought of the here and now. That dislocation should also bear on the way in which we have seen past, present and future being knotted together in the Christian-Hegelian version of the *kairos*. Derrida is commenting on a 1959 text of Blanchot on the end of philosophy:

> *We do not know* if expectation prepares the coming of the to-come or if it recalls the repetition of the same, of the thing itself as ghost ... This non-knowledge is not a lacuna. No progress of knowledge could saturate an opening which must have nothing to do with knowledge. And therefore not with ignorance either. This opening must preserve this heterogeneity as the only chance of a future affirmed or rather re-affirmed. It is the future itself, it comes from the future. The future is its memory. In the experience of the end, in its insistent, instant coming, always imminently eschatological, at the extremity of the extreme today would be announced in this way the future of what is coming. More than ever, for the to-come can only be announced as such and in its purity from a *past end*: beyond, *if it is possible*, the last extremity. If it is possible, *if there is any*, future, but how to suspend such a question or deprive oneself of such a reserve without *concluding in advance*, without reducing in advance both the future and its chance? Without totalising in advance? We must here discern between eschatology and teleology, even if the stake of such a difference constantly risks being erased in the most fragile or the slightest inconsistency – and will in some sense always and necessarily be deprived of an assurance against this risk. Is there not a messianic extremity, an *eskhaton* whose ultimate event (immediate rupture, unheard-of interruption, untimeliness of infinite surprise, heterogeneity without accomplishment) can exceed, *at each moment*, the final term of a *physis*, and the labour, production and *telos* of any history?
>
> (SM, 68–9 [36–7])

This affirmation of untimeliness, out-of-jointness of time, involves, then, a certain eschatological affirmation against its teleological recovery. This is a refined distinction in view of a more general 'post-structural' (and indeed earlier Derridean) tendency to identify the eschatological and the teleological, or at least to treat them as in some way equivalent metaphysical closures. This eschatological affirmation is what Derrida also calls a 'messianic without messianism', or a *formal* messianicity which cannot project any content or specificity whatsoever into the advent or coming it nonetheless affirms. So where Benjamin in the *Theses on the*

Philosophy of History invokes the Judaic thought whereby 'every second of time was the strait gate through which the Messiah might enter' (XVIIIB), Derrida's attempt to radicalise this[23] involves the affirmative maintenance of the strictly messianic *moment* not only short of any predictive *when* (for that is already the case with the Judaic construal to which Benjamin refers), but of any content and axiological determination whatsoever. The event of the coming of the other is 'properly' (i.e. formally) eschatological to the extent that its *what* is radically indeterminable, and so cannot confidently be called the Messiah, for example. (In *Spectres de Marx*,[24] Derrida points out that this would already make his version of the messianic unacceptable to any messianism whatsoever, depriving it of what it would have to think of as the essential point, i.e. the Messiah himself whose coming is promised. The Messiah is the first casualty of this construal of the messianic, which is why the word 'messianic' can seem a risky or unduly provocative term for Derrida to use in these contexts, a perhaps extreme form of the familiar deconstructive strategy of paleonymy, the use of old names.) Derrida's point, then, is to radicalise the messianic motif beyond the tendency of messianism to map it onto a teleological schema – and just this is what we were seeing in the biblical and Hegelian passages we were considering earlier. The moment the moment is figured as occurring *on time*, in due time, at the right time, in the ripeness or fullness of time, then we can conclude that the radically disruptive thought of the event as absolutely unpredictable arrival of the other, for which no amount of preparation could prepare, in other words the thought of the future as such, has been written back down into a teleological structure, which is most clearly evidenced by the figures of ripeness or pregnancy that we have picked out. The here and now which allows for the thought of singularity as alterity in its arrival requires a thought of the moment that is not only not simply present to itself in the presence of the present, but which is not recoverable as the *telos* of any natural or institutional process whatsoever, an *eskhaton* without salvation or redemption.

* * *

I would like to conclude by trying to relate this structure, from which Derrida's thinking about what is traditionally called 'ethics' and/or 'politics' explicitly flows, to the question of reading. The point of doing this is not to fold back this complex thinking about time onto a 'merely literary' problematic, but to try to show how it must be presupposed by all attempts to refute it. I want to say that Derrida's affirmation of the messianic without messianism is also an affirmation of reading, and that the metaphysics of presence, dominated by the interpretation of time as deriving from the presence of the present moment, necessarily entails the foreclosure of the moment of reading. I would like to suggest, for example, that the experience of reading is a salient and familiar experience of the non-coincidence of the present with itself. The simplest way to argue this is simply to point out that reading is necessarily in a relation of *delay* with respect to the text read: however minimal that delay, reading always *comes after* the writing it reads. But that irreducible belatedness goes along with a sort of internal dislocation whereby reading is always remembering and anticipating on reading in order to function. My reading can never coincide with the present moments of its activity (can never simply read one word after another, one at a time, for example), but must recall and anticipate other reading moments at every moment. As Derrida points out at the beginning of *Glas*, we cannot form the project of reading Hegel *in order*, from the first word of the first text onwards, because at the very least we should have to 'anticipate, if only the end of the first sentence of the first text'.

In that context, Derrida goes on as follows:

Genealogy cannot begin with the father.

Anticipation or precipitation (risk of precipice and fall) is an irreducible structure of reading. And teleology does only or always have the appeasing character people wish to give it.

(GL, 12a [6a])

If this is so, then it is because teleology cannot ever quite reduce the moment we are calling, on the basis of *Spectres de Marx*, the messianic, and to that extent can never quite be teleological, so that the programmed ends do not quite come out at the appointed time, so that it is never quite time. It is no accident that Hegel should appear as a test case for this type of argument (though it is certainly possible to run it through the teleology of Kant too, not to speak of Aristotle), both in the earlier account I gave of the moment, and in Derrida's remarks here about reading, because Hegel represents the most complete and thorough attempt to reduce reading altogether. One description of Hegel's writing is just that it is an attempt to be its own reading, or to read itself so exhaustively that there is no opening for reading left, and therefore no chance of that text's having a future other than one of confirmatory coincidence, on the part of competent readers, with the reading the text is already dictating to them. Hegel's text is calculated to account for and include within itself all the readings to which it might be open, including bad ones, as Derrida also discusses in *Glas*.[25] Which is why reading Hegel turns one into a Hegelian. But in order to be read at all, Hegel's text, like any other, must in principle be *open* to reading, and thereby open to a reading it cannot entirely predict and dictate in advance. It would not be hard to show that any reading worthy of its name *must depart from* the text it reads, meaning both that it must begin with it, but also that it cannot just stay with it – if Hegel is to be read rather than simply repeated, then the *chance* of a radically unpredictable reading must be left open even in this text which is entirely written in order to *prévenir* [forestall] any such reading.[26] And once we have shown that reading must in principle be subject to a pre-teleological principle in this way, to a moment of 'pure reading' prior to, and making possible, any subsequent issue about correct or incorrect reading, respectful or disrespectful reading, then we have *already* dislocated reading's moments beyond the grasp of a teleology read merely respectfully (i.e. not read at all). To this extent, *any reading of Hegel* is already, as I suggested at the start, in a relation of structural disagreement with the text read, and the most Hegelian reading must somewhere and somehow be marked by this non-Hegelian moment.

And just this is the point of Derrida's remarks in *Spectres de Marx* about inheritance. Inheritance as a relation of indebtedness to the traditionality which makes it possible to speak and think at all must involve, if it is to be worth its name, a moment of possible infidelity with respect to what it inherits. An inheritance that was always completely faithful would not inherit from the earlier moment, but would merely be a causal outcome of it. According to a familiar form of Derridean argument, the *necessary possibility* of infidelity to the tradition is a positive condition of the chance of being faithful to it – implying that fidelity is always marked by, or tormented by, infidelity. This is a general structure of Derrida's thought, and part of what it has become common to call the 'quasi-transcendental': what might look like a negative contingency which might affect or compromise the ideal purity of an event is integrated into the description of that event as a condition of possibility which is simultaneously the condition of the *a priori* impossibility of the event's ever achieving that ideal purity. And this structure of inheritance is insistent in *Spectres of Marx*:

> Let us consider first the radical and necessary *heterogeneity* of an inheritance, the difference without opposition that must mark it, a 'disparateness' and a quasi-juxtaposition without dialectic (the very plural of what further on we shall call Marx's spirits). An inheritance is never gathered, it is never one with itself. Its presumed unity, if there is one, can only consist in the *injunction* to *reaffirm by choosing*. *You must* [il faut] means you must filter, select, criticise, you must sort out among several of the possibilities which inhabit the same injunction. And inhabit it in contradictory fashion around a secret. If the legibility of a legacy were given, natural, transparent, univocal, if it did not simultaneously call for and defy interpretation, one would never have to inherit from it. One would be affected by it as by a cause – natural or genetic. One always inherits a secret, which says 'Read me, will you ever be up to it?'
>
> (SM, 40 [16])

And, a little later:

> Inheritance is never a given, it is always a task. It remains before us, as incontestably as the fact that, before even wanting it or refusing it, we are inheritors, and inheritors in mourning, like all inheritors. In particular for what is called Marxism. *To be* ... means ... *to inherit*. All questions about being or what one is to be (or not to be) are questions of inheritance. There is no backward-looking fervour involved in recalling this fact, no traditionalist flavour. Reaction, reactionary or reactive are only interpretations of the structure of inheritance. We *are* inheritors, which does not mean that we *have* or that we *receive* this or that, that a given inheritance enriches us one day with this or that, but that the *being* we are *is* first of all inheritance, like it or not, know it or not.
>
> (SM, 94 [54])

This scene suggests a rather different gathering of past, present and future to the one we noted in the biblical construal of the *kairos*. The structure of inheritance commits us to a view of the here and now as a moment when the past always still remains before us as an endless task. The chance of the moment is that it is never a moment of Last Judgement (in which the eschatology is gathered up by a teleology), but a moment of judgement in the radical absence of last judgement, an eschatology without end. This would mean that we could never really know – even after the event – whether or not the time was ripe for this or that, just because any judgement to that effect would itself be subject to the same structure of uncertainty. The absence of a Last Judgement liberates judgement from its traditional status as a provisional anticipation of a Last Judgement to come. The out-of-jointness of the time dislocates it across its responsibility towards the past in the form of the inheritance it cannot simply accept and the concomitant futural task which, however, commits it here and now.

Is it time? It is now. It's time.

10

ALMOST THE END

Genealogy cannot begin with the father.

Anticipation or precipitation (risk of precipice and fall) is an irreducible structure of reading. And teleology does not only or always have the appeasing character one might wish to give it. It can be questioned, denounced as a lure or an effect, but its threat cannot be reduced.

(Glas)

There are very many things that deconstruction is not.[1] According to Derrida, critique is one of these very many things. In the 'Letter to a Japanese Friend', for example (a text which says, almost at its end, 'What deconstruction is not? Everything!' (PSY, 392 [LJF, 275])), Derrida spends some time discussing the historical context of his early uses of the word 'deconstruction', and is especially concerned to minimise the negative connotations of the word: ' ... to undo, decompose, desediment structures, a more historical movement in a certain sense than the "structuralist" movement, which found itself thereby placed in question – this was not a negative operation' (PSY, 390 [LJF, 272]), although he recognises the tenacity of that negativity in the grammar of the word itself, and gives some credence to the albeit hasty invocation of negative theology that ensued.

It may, then, seem curious, in the context of this reservation about negativity (which is something that could be traced throughout Derrida's work: deconstruction, he claims more than once, is affirmative and creative or it is not – if we try not to be negative about deconstruction and what it is, if we try to be affirmative about it, we end up affirming affirmation, affirming that deconstruction is affirmative, the affirmation of affirmation) – it may seem curious in this context that Derrida should himself remain so resolutely on the *via negativa* in his characterisation of deconstruction.[2] The next paragraph of the 'Letter' proceeds as follows:

In any case, in spite of appearances,[3] deconstruction is neither an *analysis* nor a *critique*, and the translation ought to take account of this. It is not an analysis, in particular because the dismantling of a structure is not a regression to the *simple element*, to an *undecomposable origin*. These values, like that of analysis, are themselves philosophemes subject to deconstruction. Nor is it a critique, in either a general sense or a Kantian sense. The instance of the *krinein* or the *krisis* (decision, choice, judgement, discernment) is itself, as indeed is the whole apparatus of transcendental critique, one of the essential 'themes' or 'objects' of deconstruction.

(ibid.)

It looks, then, as though, among the very many things deconstruction is not, critique, along with analysis, has a certain privilege or precedence. Critique is not just one thing among many that deconstruction is not, but something that deconstruction *especially* is not, and especially is not *in spite of appearances*. Deconstruction is especially not analysis or critique just because appearances suggest that it just is analysis or critique. In a familiarly disconcerting topology of proximity and distance, deconstruction can look as close as can be to analysis or critique just when (and perhaps just because) it is at the furthest remove from it.[4] Now one of the reasons for choosing the theme of 'Critique and Deconstruction' for this conference (the idea was Paul Davies's) was the suspicion that there is still work to be done to elucidate this 'especially is not' in the case of *critique*, and rather more so in that case than in the case of analysis, the other prime suspect for mistaken identity with deconstruction in this description (the next one Derrida comes on to in the 'Letter' is *method*: deconstruction is not a method). For on the one hand, Derrida has recently devoted a quite extensive and explicit discussion to this motif of analysis, and more especially to its inflection in psychoanalysis. This involves careful attention to the 'twin motifs' of analysis, namely what Derrida calls the 'archaeological' or 'anagogic' motif of regression to principles, origins, to the simple and elementary, and the 'lythic' motif of decomposing, untying, dissolving or absolving.[5] And on the other hand, more straightforwardly, as is clear from the passage I've been quoting from 'Letter to a Japanese Friend', the primary reason given why deconstruction is not analysis seems intuitively quite clear and relatively easy to grasp: we all know that deconstruction is a thinking which casts doubt on the thought of simple, elementary or atomic origins, and to the extent that the motif of analysis entails confidence in at least the possibility of arriving at such origins, then it is clear that deconstruction cannot simply be analysis.

But the case of critique seems more complex, and it seems much harder to achieve an intuitive grasp of why deconstruction is not, is especially not, critique. It seems far harder to produce a quick argument in this case, and indeed Derrida does not do so in the passage I have just been quoting: it seems to be one thing to say that the immediate components of the concept of analysis are subjected or submitted to deconstruction, and another to say that the apparatus of transcendental critique is one of the essential 'themes' or 'objects' of deconstruction. And I imagine that most of us would find it much harder to give a quick compelling account of the deconstructive take on the values of *krinein* or *krisis* (glossed here, you will remember, as 'decision, choice, judgement, discernment') than in the case of analysis.

If analysis and critique, then, are the two things that, in spite of appearances, deconstruction most importantly or most especially is not (and this pairing seems to be confirmed in *Résistances*, where Derrida begins his discussion of the relation of deconstruction and analysis with the concession that 'deconstruction undeniably obeys an *analytical* demand, both critical and analytical' (RES, 41)), the suspicion to which this conference is devoted is that critique, more mysteriously and perhaps more urgently than analysis, is what deconstruction is not. One of the ways this added mystery shows up in the 'Letter to a Japanese Friend' is that Derrida needs to gloss the term 'critique' in a more complicated and careful way than appears necessary with 'analysis': here it seems to divide into a 'general' and a 'Kantian' sense, but exactly *what* divides into these two senses, the presumed unity of the motif of critique in 'the instance of *krinein* or of *krisis*', seems to be, allusively but unmistakably, referred to Husserl. What I'd like to do is on the one hand to try to bring out some of the ways in which some of these terms and references (to Kant, to Husserl, to the transcendental and so on) are articulated, especially in some of Derrida's earliest writings. I shall try to show that, where the point about analysis involved an investigation of origins and their non-simplicity, a movement determined as *archaeological*, the point about critique will be essentially referred, via the transcendental, and more especially via the 'Idea in the Kantian sense', to an investigation of *teleology*.[6] I want to suggest that the reason why deconstruction is not, especially not, critique is that critique is bound up with a teleological structure. And on the other hand, I shall sketch a very partial reading of Kant, and more especially of part of the *Critique of Teleological Judgement*, to test out the thought that, although deconstruction is not, especially not, critique, critique in the eminently Kantian sense that seems to be developed in the third *Critique* just might be, and especially might be, deconstruction. The basis for this suggestion will be the proposal that there is a sort of internal falling short of teleology inscribed within its concept (at least as Kant works that concept out in the very difficult latter parts of the third *Critique*), a sort of necessary self-interruption of teleology which makes it simultaneously non-teleological, or a teleology without telos, something like what Derrida, in his most recent essay on Lévinas, describes as an 'interruption of self by self as other'.[7] And the suspicion would be that if this is the case, then this would have an effect on our understanding of critique itself: the *Critique of Judgement* seems to propose a more radically critical sense of critique than either of the first two *Critiques* (if only because the critique of judgement explicitly does not look forward to, or is not teleologically determined by, the formulation of a corresponding doctrine: the Introduction to the third *Critique* explicitly states that judgement has no place in a doctrine in which there is room for only two sorts of concepts: concepts of nature and concepts of freedom).

* * *

Derrida's first explicit engagements with the notion of critique come not in relation to Kant, but via the motif of *krisis* in Husserl, and they always associate this motif with problems of the transcendental, with the 'Idea in the Kantian sense' as Husserl wields that concept (or that Idea, for we shall see in a moment that, at least on Derrida's reading of Husserl's use of this motif, the 'Idea in the Kantian sense' is itself an Idea), and with teleology. For example, in the very early Master's thesis on the problem of genesis in Husserl (a thesis which is still happy to propose what it is doing as a 'radical critique' of Husserl (GEN, 275)), the final section is entitled 'teleology' and develops thoughts which, after the event, it is not difficult to recognise as those developed in later work.[8] (The fact that in making that claim I am still relying on an archaeo-teleological schema is, of course, part of the problem, and I shall return to it in conclusion.)

But it is at the end of the 'Introduction' to his translation of Husserl's *Origin of Geometry* that Derrida analyses most fully this motif. Husserl identifies in the origin of geometry a moment of 'infinitisation' which prescribes to humanity an endless task of scientific or rational endeavour. The move from the type of ideality involved in the pre-scientific concept of 'something round' to the concept of the circle is a move from the finite to the infinite: no finite sensory intuition is adequate to the concept of the circle, the discovery of which throws humanity forward in an infinite anticipation of truth that will never be fulfilled. Husserl appeals (in fact in a rather un-Kantian or ultra-Kantian way) to the concept of the 'Idea in the Kantian sense' to describe this situation (*Ideas*, I, §74). Now the peculiarity of this appeal in Husserl, as Derrida analyses it, lies just in the fact that, by definition, the 'Idea in the Kantian sense' describes a situation where the fundamental watchword of phenomenology is inoperative – the Idea comes into play just where the 'thing itself' *cannot* be given 'in person' to intuition, just because the Idea comes into play to refer to a possibility of infinite progress beyond any given experience of intuition.[9] As Derrida says,

> It is no accident if there is no phenomenology of the Idea. The Idea
> cannot be given in person, it cannot be determined in a self-evidence,

for it is merely the possibility of evidence and the opening of the 'seeing' itself; it is merely *determinability* as horizon of every intuition in general, invisible *milieu* of seeing …

(OG, 151–2 [138])

Derrida draws a number of features from this position of the Idea as Husserl takes it from Kant. First of all, he characterises it as 'the ethico-teleological prescription of the infinite task', and later, in a note, claims that this Idea 'is the common root of the theoretical and the ethical' (OG, 149 n. 1 [136 n. 162]). Later he will say that the Idea, escaping the sphere of the visible, which it nonetheless in some sense opens, can only be *heard*, as a *call*:

The Idea is that on the basis of which a phenomenology is instigated to accomplish the final intention of philosophy [remember this expression 'final intention']. That a phenomenological determination of the Idea itself be, thereafter, radically impossible, signifies perhaps that phenomenology cannot reflect itself in a phenomenology of phenomenology, and that its *Logos* can never appear as such, never give itself to a philosophy of seeing, but only, like all Speech, give itself to be heard through the visible.

(OG, 155 [141])[10]

Derrida goes on to suggest that this grounds phenomenology in something it can never directly address, something that is, then, of the order of a radical *responsibility* taken up by a necessarily finite philosopher in the very constitution of a transcendental historicity and a transcendental intersubjectivity. Derrida ends this, the penultimate chapter of the 'Introduction', with the suggestion that 'this does not seem to be literally the case with Kantian critique' [*Cela ne semble pas être le cas avec la critique kantienne considérée dans sa lettre*]. It is the latter claim that I want to pursue a little, in the hope of clarifying a little further the relation between what Derrida is not yet calling 'deconstruction' at the time of the *Origin of Geometry* text, and 'critique' in its more specifically Kantian sense. It seems at any rate as though the configurations brought out in these early texts between transcendentality and the Idea in the Kantian sense, and the teleological determination of reason in its necessary historicity that ensues, also provides the insight behind that famous and still difficult slogan from the end of *Speech and Phenomena*, where Derrida claims that 'Infinite différance is finite' (VP, 114 [102]). One of my aims or ends today is to try (again) to understand that slogan a little better, and to show how the means to do so can be provided by Kant himself.

* * *

Towards the end of the second preface to the *Critique of Pure Reason*, Kant reflects on the changes he has been led to make compared with the first edition of the work. He is confident of not having changed (of not needing to change) anything substantive, and this is not just because he meditated long and hard before publishing the first edition, but because pure reason has a true structure [*Gliederbau*: 'build' or 'frame' in the anatomical sense]. Saying that it has a structure here means that it is *organised* in the sense of being *organic*: that is, that it is made up of interconnecting parts or organs such that, as Kant puts it, 'everything is there for the sake of each member, and each individual member is there for the sake of all' (Bxxxvii). This sort of arrangement we may here reasonably call *teleological*, in the sense that, as the third critique will develop, it is organised *in view of* something, of some purpose, aim, or end. That something comes out when Kant explains by what experiment one can test the unchangeable state of the structure of pure reason, and this will, in passing, confirm our sense that there is a solidarity between the analytical motif and the critical, those two primary things that deconstruction most especially is not:

> I hope, moreover, that this system will continue to maintain itself in this unchangeable state. What entitles me to this confidence is not self-conceit, but merely the fact that this [unchangeable state of the system] is evident from the following experiment: We obtain the same result whether we proceed from the minutest elements all the way to the whole of pure reason, or proceed backward to each part when starting from the whole (for this whole also is given by itself, through reason's final aim in the practical sphere).
>
> (Bxxxviii)

Reason as a whole is given, then, as an organic whole, as an essentially teleological structure, by or from its *telos*. That *telos* is not theoretical but practical, and Kant calls it reason's 'final aim'. 'Final aim' here translates *Endabsicht*, final intention or design, final project. And this thought is picked up again some 800 pages further on, almost at the end of the first *Critique*, in the first section of the 'Canon of Pure Reason': reason cannot help but press on beyond the bounds of experience in its demand for the unconditioned: in the speculative sphere this leads only to humiliation as no theoretical, objective, knowledge is there possible – the only positive use of reason in this regard must be practical. Now the unity of reason demands that its purposive structure cohere around a *single* final end or aim, which here Kant is still calling its *Endabsicht*. Teleology is only properly rational to the extent that it cannot remain with a plurality of scattered ends or purposes, but must finalise those purposes again until one final end is thought. Reason thinks itself beyond itself in its singular end. This final purpose or end of reason means that *Reason is itself an Idea of reason* in Kant's thought, perpetually beyond its own reach, and only this gives the practical its pre-eminent position in the Kantian system (and shows up the error of the various epistemologising neo-Kantianisms); it is to the aporias generated by this thought of a teleology with a final purpose or end that I shall be devoting most of the rest of my discussion today: put crudely, I shall try to show that Kant's account of ends ends, *almost at the end* of the third (and final) *Critique*, in an idea of a sort of self-interrupting teleology, or of a teleology as in some ways a self-interrupting structure which goes some way towards suggesting a characterisation of critique which would make it look rather more like the deconstruction which is especially not that.

I can give a quick characterisation of this self-interrupting teleology, or of teleology as self-interrupting, on the basis of Kant's political writings. Kant's view of politics (and analogically of philosophy itself) is teleologically determined by the notion of perpetual peace. But as perpetual peace is synonymous with death (the peace of cemeteries), peace has a chance only if it holds itself this side of perpetuity, perpetually deferring its perpetuity, if you like. And this interruption of what looks at first like a straightforward teleological structure has important consequences for Kant's political thinking around cosmopolitanism, and in fact it is just this structure which generates the complex business of hospitality which has interested Derrida recently.[11] Cosmopolitanism has to be *limited*, or limit itself, to rights of hospitality, says Kant, just because a cosmopolitanism that fulfilled itself in the form of an internationalism or world-state would catastrophically fall into just the sort of violence and oppression that the whole teleological setup was supposed to overcome. I want to suggest that this structure of falling short is intrinsic to teleology more generally, at least as Kant understands it.

The *Critique of Teleological Judgement*[12] begins from the thought that nature contains certain objects (most notably organisms) which are inexplicable in the mechanically causal terms that the understanding, as developed in the first *Critique*, prescribes for nature in general as a law-bound sphere of necessity. Such objects remain radically *contingent* in terms of such an explanation, and seem to require treatment in terms of teleology, i.e. they have to be judged as being determined by an end or aim or intention, or, more precisely, *as though they were* determined by an end or aim or intention. We cannot but judge such natural objects as though they were the products of an intentional technical production, what Kant calls a *technic* as opposed to a *mechanics* of nature. What Kant calls the *antinomy* of teleological judgement results from a possible conflict between the maxim that tells me always to judge nature in terms of mechanical necessity, and the fact that such a maxim appears no longer to work when faced with natural objects such as organisms, where it gives way to the maxim that tells me that at least sometimes I must judge in terms of teleological or purposive causality. This antinomy initially appears quite anodine, and at least once (§71) Kant himself

147

suggests it is merely apparent, and disappears so long as we remember that these two possible approaches to nature are simply expressed as *maxims*, and therefore as merely subjective guides to how nature is best approached, rather than taken as objective principles of nature – in which case there would indeed be a conflict of reason with itself, in that there would obviously be a contradiction between any *objective* claims to know that nature was organised on the one hand mechanically, and on the other purposively. All seems well, however, so long as we stick to the mechanical maxim *as long as possible*, and only resort to the teleological one when we must – and this seems perfectly possible so long as our purpose is the concrete investigation of nature in a scientific spirit.

As the antinomy progresses, however, Kant slowly and carefully reverses the apparent hierarchy or priority this implies. Suppose we wish to judge, not this or that object of nature, but nature as a whole. This 'speculative' question might not trouble our scientific investigations of nature in detail (scientists need not bother with it so long as they are doing science), but cannot fail to arise for the philosopher: for if *some* natural products remain contingent with respect to mechanical explanation, then it follows that nature *as a whole* remains contingent with respect to mechanism, and requires the appeal to a different sort of explanation. In which case, Kant argues, we must prefer the teleological to the mechanical: the individual details *within* nature which call for teleological judgement (i.e. those elements which are *contingent* with respect to mechanical explanation) hint at the need for a teleological judgement of nature as a whole. The rather startling consequence of which would be that a certain contingency of nature as a whole would be necessary for the judgement of necessity which we typically and rightly want to make when dealing with nature in detail. This apparent reversal in the hierarchy of the mechanical and the technical, of the necessary and the contingent, brings with it a reversal of all the major Kantian conceptual pairs, so that determinative, dogmatic, 'objective' judgements will now be subordinated to reflective, problematic and 'subjective' ones, constitutive principles to regulative ones, and so on.

This shift has some startling effects. For example, in a section (§76) in which Kant runs through some paradoxical 'examples' (showing that it is *possible* for us to imagine an intelligence for which the modality of possibility could not hold, for whom there would be no difference between possibility and actuality (or between contingency and necessity), so that the modality of possibility is maintained in the perspective of its own demise, its end – it's possible for us to imagine the end of possibility; and showing similarly that we can imagine an intelligence for whom the distinction between free and mechanically necessary causality would not hold, for whom there would be no distinction between is and ought, so that we *ought* to imagine an end to the ought as a way of thinking it, so that the end of morality would be the end of morality) – Kant comes, via the further imagination that for such an intelligence there would be no difference between mechanical and teleological causality, to the claim that as the particular is always in some sense contingent for us, the concept of purposive causality becomes for us *as necessary as necessity*, or even more necessary than necessity, in that our determinative judgements of objective necessity would have no sense if they were not guided by the regulative ('subjective') principle of teleology.

* * *

We must, then, view nature as a whole teleologically. But it can only be so viewed if the local purposes we begin from (in a given organism, for example) are themselves finalised by higher purposes. Teleology makes sense only if the whole system is teleological, i.e. if it is determined by *one* end, an end to end all ends. But this end turns out in fact to be split in two: what Kant calls the *letzter Zweck* on the one hand (translated as 'ultimate purpose' by Pluhar: the *letzter Zweck* is something like the last aim among a collection of aims), and the *Endzweck* ('final purpose': something like the aim of all aims) on the other. The relationship between these is rather complicated, but it is here that we can see the logic according to which the *telos* of teleology is cut from it (so in a sense arguably not its *telos* at all, in which case the teleology stops being really teleological, or can be thought of teleologically only in the radical inaccessibility of its *telos*). Kant, perhaps unsurprisingly, makes mankind the 'ultimate purpose' of nature, but just this position generates the paradox of teleology.

Man is, then, the ultimate purpose of nature, but he is so only to the extent that he is 'the only being on earth who can form a concept of purposes' (§82). So the ultimate purpose would be the possibility that there be purposes, post-ultimate purposes, the purpose that there be further purposes, the end that there be further ends. What comes at the end is the possibility of seeing that there must be an end, and that that end is the possibility of setting (oneself) further ends. Now, it is clear that it will not do in this context to say that the ultimate purpose is man *himself*, for man, in part at least, forms part of nature as mechanism.[13] So we have here a paradox: as ultimate end *of nature*, man, insofar as he is *of nature*, is not the ultimate end (for he would then remain in nature-as-mechanism). If man as natural being were the end of nature, nature would not even be a teleological system, but pure mechanism, and would therefore have no ultimate purpose at all. For man to be the ultimate end of nature as teleological system of ends (and he must be, for without this nature would have no end, would be mere mechanism, without end or meaning even for scientific exploration), what in man constitutes this end must be a capacity for going beyond nature as such: what man must do to be the ultimate purpose of nature is to project another end *beyond* nature, and that end is no longer *in* nature as its ultimate purpose, but outside nature as its final purpose (as *Endzweck*, then, rather than *letzte Zweck*). So man is the ultimate purpose of nature only to the extent that he can give himself purposes which will no longer be *of nature*. Man is the ultimate end only by dint of his ability to give himself ends that come *after the last end*, and this can only happen through *culture*, i.e. the cultivation of the capacity for ends in a rational being. Properly speaking, then, the ultimate purpose of nature is not mankind, but culture as such (culture being a situation Kant describes as being one of 'brilliant distress'), and the purpose of culture (as nature's ultimate purpose) is to promote an end quite beyond nature. Nature has its end in culture, which has its end outside nature.

This frontier between nature and culture ('man' is one rather confusing name for it, and 'politics' might be another) is the place of the interruption I am interested in. For the natural teleology can here maintain itself as teleological only by the paradox of finding its end in something which is radically cut from it. Nature can only be saved as ultimately teleological for us, according to the 'subjective' necessity that is more necessary than objective necessity, by being assigned an end which has nothing to do with it, from which it is to be radically cut. And this is what Kant explicitly says at the beginning of §84: *Endzweck ist derjenige Zweck, der keines andern als Bedingung seiner Möglichkeit bedarf.* 'A *final purpose* is a purpose that requires no other purpose as a condition of its possibility.' The final end has no need of that of which it is the end, to be its end. And reciprocally, that of which this end is the end (nature) cannot bring this end about, for in that case the end would flow from, and be conditioned by, the very thing (nature) in which nothing unconditioned is to be found. Everything in nature is conditioned, so the final end cannot be in it.

Kant still holds this end to be human, in the sense that man is the only natural being who acts according to a purposive causality while *representing* to himself the final purposiveness of that purposiveness as being necessary, unconditioned, and therefore outside nature. But the humanity thus identified is still divided, for if, on the one hand, we can say that man is the final purpose *of nature*, to the extent that natural beings need such an end if they are not to fall back into the blind contingency or necessity of natural mechanism, on the other we must say that precisely insofar as he is the final purpose, man is cut from all teleology and all nature.

> That being is man, but man considered as noumenon. Man is the only natural being in whom we can nonetheless cognize, as part of his own constitution, a supersensible ability (*freedom*), and even cognize the law and the object of this causality, the object that this being can set before itself as its highest purpose (the highest good in the world).
>
> Now about man, as a moral being (and so about any other rational being in the world), we cannot go on to ask: For what [end] (*quem in finem*) does he exist? His existence itself has the highest purpose within it; and to this purpose he can subject all of nature as far as he is able, or

at least he must not consider himself subjected to any influence of nature
in opposition to that purpose.

(§84)

So nature as a whole is teleologically subordinated to a natural ultimate purpose
(mankind), and again to a non-natural final purpose (mankind again). But as an
end cut from that the end of which he is, as purpose without purposiveness, then,
man (as noumenon, of course), is no longer entirely human. Just as the end of
nature in nature is not natural, so the end of man in man is not human. Teleology
arrives at its end only by cutting itself from the end to which it is, however,
constitutively tending.

* * *

If, then, teleology as such requires the thought of a final end or single *telos* in
order to remain teleological, we can see easily enough why deconstruction might
be suspicious of it. Here we would have something like a mirror image of its
suspicion of the archaeological motif of analysis: the convergent movement of
teleology implies a gathering and unification of all partial purposes under the
authority of a supreme purpose which may be infinitely removed and in principle
unattainable, but which would, according to Kant, be the *sine qua non* of the ratio-
nality of reason itself. That teleology end in a theology is in this way no surprise,
and to the extent that critique depends on this over-arching teleological structure, then we can see why deconstruction is not critique, to the extent that it
projects no unifying *telos* at all, but rather sketches a dispersive, pluralising or
scattering movement that Kant would find an unacceptably depressing prospect,
and indeed an unthinkable contradiction within reason itself (and for which
Epicurus is consistently the reminder in Kant's work). But on the other hand, we
have seen Kant, through the very radicality of the critical gesture, arrive at a
thought of a teleology which can subsist only in the absolute separation of its *telos*.
Teleology as such turns out to be disrupted by something of the order of an interruption or a falling short of its *telos*, and this seems to confirm the logic of the
perpetual peace argument. But this self-interrupting structure, which just is that
according to which Derrida was able to say that 'infinite *différance* is finite'
perhaps cannot adequately be thought in terms of interruption.[14] The figure of
interruption is itself probably still too teleological, to the extent that its purpose
is to disrupt or frustrate purposiveness. If we want to take the logic of the teleological judgement seriously, it would seem that we have to interrupt teleology
so radically that its interruption cannot even be gathered up in the figure of interruption. The temptation here is to look to figures of scattering and dispersion, of
chaos and randomness, to what Kant regularly dismisses as absurd Epicurean

materialism, and to oppose that supposedly deconstructive gesture to the still-all-too-teleological critical one. And it seems to me that such a temptation is not simply to be resisted, if it is true that deconstruction is not critique because critique is intrinsically bound up with teleology. The difficult thing about it, however, is that such a gesture falls back into a sort of negative teleology of absolute dispersion, which the quasi-concept of *différance* is explicitly written to avoid. For it can only be a teleological gesture to take the interruptive structure of teleology to its end, *jusqu'au bout*. Even though that structure has effects *throughout* the teleology, from the start (and indeed just this is the same principle that disrupts the simplicity of origins on the archaeological side, so that deconstruction is not analysis or critique *for the same reason*), it seems important for its intelligibility to recognise that that interruption nonetheless happens *almost at the end*, not *right at the end*, *and* that, paradoxically enough, the less teleological gesture is the one which allows the teleology to develop its own interruption, rather than the one which, in purist style, tries to prevent it even getting started. Only this can explain why deconstruction is *especially* not critique, importantly not critique, rather than just *anything but* critique; and only this can explain why deconstruction remains critical *up to a point*, that point being the unpredictable point at which the auto-interruptive moment occurs. That such an auto-interruptive moment occurs *in critique itself* would then be the confirmation both of an almost absolute proximity (so that we might want to say that the transcendental *just is* the quasi-transcendental, and, by extension, that Derrida *just is* Kant (or Plato, or indeed anyone else)), and of an almost absolute distinction (so that the quasi-transcendental is the *ruin* of the transcendental, and Derrida is absolutely not Kant (or Plato, or anyone else). Deconstruction is not quite the end of critique, neither its outcome nor its demise, but rather its almost-the-endness, its structural interminability, the (a-)teleological principle of its teleologies.

This is exactly the structure Derrida brings out almost at the end of *Speech and Phenomena*: the teleological system of 'essential distinctions' in Husserl depends on its non-fulfilment. The distinction between fact and principle depends on the fact of facticity (which thereby becomes a principle of principles), and would disappear if the *telos* were ever to be reached. The infinite is only ever announced or promised in the finite. The end is the end only to the extent that we don't reach the end. The end would be the end of the end. But to the extent that we don't reach the end, and must therefore each time begin again, then we can't really ever begin at the beginning, but always somewhere in the middle (GR, 233 [162]).

This is the end.

Part III

PHILOPOLEMICS

11

GENUINE GASCHÉ (PERHAPS)

The Tain of the Mirror established Rodolphe Gasché as the undisputed moral consciousness (or let's say the super-ego) of all Derrideans (and maybe even of Derrida himself).[1] There was something inexorable and unavoidable about the book, probably because in almost every detail it was so clearly *right*. Any temptation we, or some of us, may have had to get playful or, especially, 'literary' about Derrida, was sternly put in its place as irresponsible, because philosophically ill-informed, and this judgement could be felt, immediately and a little dispiritingly, stretching into all our Derridean futures, condemning us to at least Kant, Hegel and Heidegger if we wanted to earn the right to keep following the master. The book was essentially, explicitly and unashamedly a *rephilosophising* of Derrida, the beginning of a systematic and potentially exhaustive[2] transcription of Derrida's work back into something more 'properly' philosophical than Derrida's work itself seemed always to be. Derrida did deconstruction, and Gasché was doing the philosophy of deconstruction. Derrida, the book seemed to imply, *always might* be seducing us, leading us astray, especially if we were 'literary' people, because the *apparently* literary feel of some of his work *always might* hide its *true or genuine* philosophical import. Gasché offered no such prospects of seduction and wandering, keeping us firmly away from temptation, on a rather puritanical straight and narrow that looked as though it would require constant vigilance, lots of honest hard work, and a good deal of self-denial. The gesture of the book was one of reclaiming rightful property from irresponsible tenants or borrowers, or of rescuing Derrida from being misused or even abused outside the home of philosophical tradition.

Inventions of Difference, which Gasché describes as a 'companion volume of sorts' (p. 2) to *The Tain of the Mirror*, has no qualms whatsoever about pursuing this project. Not only does Gasché repeat and indeed reinforce the fundamental gesture of the earlier book by maintaining the view that Derrida's work is formalisable as a set of 'infrastructures' (ignoring any explicit attempts that have been made to show that this is, both conceptually and philologically, an extremely unhappy term to use in the way he uses it),[3] but he tells us repeatedly that even Derrida's 'later', reputedly more 'playful' texts (largely left to one side in the earlier book, and maybe still, or so we might have thought, a refuge for the literary) 'belong to philosophy'.[4]

This 'belonging to philosophy' is, as in the earlier book, still essentially argued against the possibility of a possible rival 'belonging to literature', although Gasché does also make more traditional philosophical gestures, separating the properly philosophical from the 'merely empirical', or the domain of the human sciences.[5] He also spends several pages in his introduction refuting Rorty's view of Derrida's later work as giving up on the public and the philosophical in favour of the private and ironical, and does indeed refute it convincingly, but Rorty makes an easy target in this respect (if only because he has, along with many other professional philosophers, such a philosophical idea of the non-philosophical and its supposed joys or advantages), and there are much more 'serious' ways of trying to talk about the relationship of Derrida and philosophy than Rorty's. It is easy to argue that Derrida 'belongs to philosophy' if the only other possibility is to lose him to the sort of alternative Rorty describes, or to some soft and non-specific 'literary criticism'. But the point here is to claim that 'philosophy' (and this is just what Derrida will have helped us to understand) is, in its permanent efforts to secure belongings in general, properties, proprieties, adequacies, authenticities and genuinenesses, also the permanent witness to the 'logic' of impropriety that makes those efforts both possible and necessary, and necessarily endless. Gasché's particular insistence on Derrida's 'belonging to philosophy' paradoxically does more (helpful) damage to *philosophical* appropriations or criticisms of Derrida as non- or anti-philosophical (Habermas, Marion, Rorty, Taylor, Vattimo, Zizek[6] all fare more or less badly at Gasché's hands) than to the vaguely invoked 'literary' commentators whom Gasché clearly thinks he has put in their place once and for all in the 1979 essay 'Deconstruction as Criticism', reprinted here as Chapter 1, and whom he tends not to deign to name. But being very philosophical like this, *more* philosophical about Derrida than other philosophers, however admirable and necessary that is – and it is admirable and necessary – involves an inevitable reap-propriative limitation of what in Derrida is *ultra*-philosophical: Derrida's work, as I have tried to argue elsewhere, is both the most and the least philosophical discourse imaginable, at one and the same time: Gasché is thus paradoxically enough oh so philosophical, but *not philosophical enough* to traverse philosophy in the non-belonging way that Derrida does explicitly, and has done at least since *La voix et le phénomène* and the *Grammatology* (VP, 98 [88]; GR, 90 [61]). This point also has institutional and professional implications for the 'ownership' of philos-ophy by 'philosophers': Derrida's work may annoy philosophers by being so disciplinarily promiscuous, so *available*, despite its very real difficulty, to readers of all sorts – including literary ones – but dealing with that annoyance by making a claim for proper ownership is always likely to be reactively metaphysical. It also leaves open the possibility that some less professionally philosophical readings of Derrida might well be *more* philosophical than Gasché's, *opening philosophy up* (in the sense both of democratic accessibility and anatomical dissection) in ways he cannot.

This problematic of 'belonging', and all that it implies, communicates more or less explicitly with an insistence on the *proper*,[7] the *genuine*[8] and the adequate[9] which underpins all of Gasché's discussions as their ultimate appeal and guarantee. A familiar if subterranean Germanic thread of words in *eigen*[10] links a concern to establish what is philosophy's property with what is proper in general, it just being proper to philosophy – and this is inseparable from its concern with truth[11] – to worry as to what is proper to everything and especially to itself.[12] Gasché cannot but invoke the genuine once he has made his claim to (proper) property over Derrida's work. What has to be genuine or adequate here is a *response* (or an encounter with alterity), and here that problem separates into two aspects: (1) Derrida's 'response' to metaphysics; (2) 'our' (Gasché's) 'response' to Derrida. (The problem of 'our' [my] response to Gasché does not appear in the book as *Gasché's* problem, but it is clearly enough *our* problem.)

The problem of Derrida's response to metaphysics justifies the tenor and approach of Gasché's (re-)philosophising of his work. Derrida's work, for Gasché, *just is* a response to metaphysics in its most challenging and difficult aspects (especially Hegel and Heidegger). So, for example, the motif of difference so prevalent in recent criticism must be understood, according to 'The Eclipse of Difference' (Chapter 3), via Heidegger's meditations on the ontico-ontological difference; the motif of infinity or interminability in Derrida, according to 'Structural Infinity' (Chapter 5), must be read as a response to Hegel's account of 'good' and 'bad' infinity; Derrida's stress on affirmation as reading the Hegelian speculative 'yes' ('Yes Absolutely', Chapter 8). Let us spend a moment on this last example and its extension in the following chapter ('Responding Responsibly'), for it is here that Gasché most clearly and helpfully thematises the issues of response and responsibility, which have indeed been given extensive treatment in some of Derrida's recent work.[13] A 'genuine response', he tells us in three descriptions on page 199, is sudden, unexpected, unpredictable and spontaneous: that is, it has the character of an *event*. In Hegel, the 'yes' that appears in religious consciousness then moves on to the sublation of its own finite irruption in the 'absolute yes' of the Notion, setting a problem for reading which Gasché unpacks admirably as follows:

> How is one to respond to Hegel's all-inclusive *yes*, which, by sublating up
> to the finite event of its eruption, has also forgone its nature as a
> response [insofar as a response, or at least a genuine response, is marked

by just that irruptive finitude]? More precisely, how does one relate to a *yes* that not only is all-encompassing but that by virtue of its all-inclusive-ness consists in his having attempted to demonstrate that all finitude sublates *itself*, and that the reconciling *yes*, the *yes* between the extremes erupts into a relation of Otherness to self? Evidently, whatever such a response may prove to be, in order to be that response – both responsive and responsible – it must respond to the absolute *yes*. Yet, to make such a response, one must first read and hear Hegel to the end – to the erup-tion of the resounding *yes*. There can be no responsible debate with Hegel without the recognition that all the Hegelian developments take place in view of, and are always already predetermined by, the telos of absolute knowing, or the Notion, that is, by the thought of a figureless and nonrepresentational thinking in which thought can say *yes* to itself in a mode in which even saying is no longer different from what is said. In other words, any genuine response to Hegel must say *yes* – and not in the mode of parrotlike repetitive affirmation – to the call of the Other by the speculative *yes* itself, which, as the event of the positive assimilation of all Otherness, addresses itself as a whole to the Other. The *yes* of genuine response is, at its most elementary, a *yes* to it in its all-embracing affirmation of self and Other in absolute identity. But such a response, precisely because it is presupposed, requested by the *yes* of Hegel's thought, falls out of its range and power. While the responding yes comes to meet the demand for recognition, it necessarily escapes what it thus lets come into its own: the speculative *yes*. Indeed, any genuine response to the Hegelian *Yes* implies not only that it be formulated in its most powerful and demanding articulation – that of the end of *Phenomenology of Spirit* and the *Greater Logic* – rather than in disembodied or decapitated versions, but also that it resist *corresponding* to the demand and the call of the all-encompassing yes. Although the *yes* must stand up to the demand to respond to the speculative yes it must fail to keep the appointment. Only thus is it a genuine response.

(pp. 201–2)

The – difficult – logic of this passage is exemplary of the positions Gasché espouses in his book, but also, or so I shall try to show, of the unthought aporia that underlies his whole project of reclaiming Derrida for philosophy. If Derrida is to respond 'genuinely' to metaphysics (of whom Hegel is here the exemplary representative), he must take the measure of its most powerful and resourceful articulations, read them according to their own programme (insofar as every text programmes something of its own reading, and philosophy in its metaphysical guise attempts to programme that reading as the only possible or appropriate reading – Hegel's system being at the limit an interminable reading of itself), in order then to do something different. If a genuine response is to be a surprise, as Gasché says it must be, then it cannot simply be the response called for by that to which it responds.

The 'genuineness' of the genuine response, then, involves a measure of infidelity to the text to which the response is made. Gasché makes this clear at the end of the chapter:

> Without the possibility of slippage, no response to the call to say *Yes to yes* is thinkable to begin with. In addition, genuine response to the call to say *yes to yes*, and thus to a mode of thinking that is both encyclopedic and self-inclusive, is genuine only if it remains different ... The *yes* of response must be a *yes* that can always be denied. Its singularity is constituted both by the possibility that it might not occur and by the possibility that if it does, its response recedes out of the reach of that to which it consents.
>
> (p. 226)

This is what Gasché explains under the head of responsibility at the beginning of the following chapter, 'On Responding Responsibly' (Ch. 9). Responsibility cannot responsibly be thought of as following a programme of ethical (or political) correctness: responsibility can be taken only when such programmes are exceeded or surprised by the event of the advent of the other. Responsibility occurs on the occasion of a singular event which escapes prior normative preparations. Responsibility is responsibility to the other, but is also *of* the other: the responsive decision I must take is not mine, but a measure of 'my' originary depropriation in the advent of the other and the other other. The other, we might say, signs my responsibility for me and only thus might I take a responsibility upon myself *as* other.

Gasché's response to this structure is to displace it into the 'demanding *question of* responsibility' (p. 227, my emphasis).[14] He wants to 'speak responsibly about responsibility' (*ibid.*), to say responsibly what responsible responsibility is. As he quite rightly shows, this commits him on the one hand to an investigation of the inherited concept of responsibility, and, on the other, to some unpredictable break with that concept. There is, then, an essential risk that, *through its very responsibility*, the responsible response to the question of responsibility will appear irresponsible. It cannot but 'lead to something anethical' (non-ethical or violent opening of ethics, as Derrida's 'early' work already said (ED, 188 [128–9]; GR, 202 [139–40])) that, 'because it does not coincide with a given ethics, will invariably be called anti-ethical' (p. 228). Whence the need to assert responsibility 'in the mode of a "perhaps"', marking 'an essential lack of dogmatic certitude' (*ibid.*).[15]

This 'mode of a perhaps' is the most difficult challenge posed by someone responding to Gasché's response, and articulation of the logic of response. The last thing it implies is the false or feeble – irresponsible – modesty of saying 'perhaps he's right (but then again perhaps he isn't)'. We *know* (can demonstrate) that Gasché is right about almost everything he says in his book (there's room for a small amount of scholarly murmuring here and there, the odd complaint about lack of clarity or clumsy prose): the 'perhaps' affects not that, nor even the tone of the writing which can seem at times overbearing. Let's imagine that there were no such problems. How can we hear a 'perhaps' in Gasché now? Where is the 'invention' here? Or, how can we register the *event* of Gasché's book (if it 'is' one)? Not of course, by simply looking in it for something 'opaque, silent or immediate in a nondialectical sense' (p. 14).[16] But this, perhaps: Gasché's book asserts a *perhaps* with such a clear, serious honesty, such an admirable sense of responsibility, such a willing acceptance of pedagogical burdens, that the perhaps 'itself' escapes, perhaps in the call, here so generously transcribed and transmitted, to *reading*. Reading as such *always* engages a radical perhaps – and thereby a responsibility – insofar as it must *open* the book to get started. Gasché's rigorous insistence on philosophy as the true home of Derrida's work, his immeasurably helpful precision around the tradition Derrida reads, curiously refers us in its interstices to that 'perhaps'. A *certain* silence in Gasché calls irresistibly for our further unrepentant inventions of a still unread Derrida to come.

One way of elaborating this problem is to concentrate on the question of the tradition itself. In 'Deconstruction and the Philosophers' I complained about Gasché's historicising of Derrida's work on the grounds that Derrida's thinking of historicity and traditionality exceeded all historicist determination, making it very difficult to situate deconstruction 'in' history, for example as coming 'after' Heidegger. 'Plato's Pharmacy', for example, showed deconstruction happening in fifth-century BC Athens at least as much as in '70s Paris. In 'The Law of Tradition' (Chapter 2), Gasché picks up this point, arguing now that the impossibility of situating deconstruction in a history of ideas does not mean that it does not need to be related to tradition as a 'whole', or to the traditionality of tradition (p. 62).[17] This is in fact an analytic consequence of what Derrida calls the 'déjà', that we are always *already* in a language that we neither create nor initiate. Oddly enough, however, and this is where Gasché does not go, this means not that we are therefore forever condemned to re-working that tradition, but that Derrida's loving and meticulous readings of texts from the tradition partially liberate indebtedness to Heidegger (but also Plato, Hegel, Marx or Blanchot), and this does not so much indebt us in our turn to those same texts, as in part (whence our gratitude and indebtedness to Derrida 'himself', who is, however, just this

liberatory reading machine) open us to other, always different debts and engagements. It is precisely Derrida's endless negotiation of the tradition that generates
the possibility of reading Derrida *outside* the law of tradition he thus formulates,
for example as a sort of 'system' whose permanent debt to tradition is already
inscribed within it and is thereby in part already paid off on our account. This
inscription is such that, for example, the Hegel column in *Glas* is at one and the
same time utterly dependent ('parasitic') on Hegel, and radically free from
Hegel, to the extent that 'Hegel' becomes something like a fictional character in
Derrida's work, someone whom we read in reading Derrida.[18] Gasché thinks we
ought to read Hegel and Heidegger to read Derrida, and thereby locate his singularity with respect to them: but we, who have read Derrida, have *thereby* read a
Hegel and a Heidegger to whom we would not otherwise have access (not least,
but not only, in that Derrida's own pedagogical generosity makes them *easier*), and
who are henceforth *part of* the singularity of 'Derrida'. This does not at all *exclude*
our continuing to read Hegel, Heidegger, or anybody else, and in fact encourages
it by lifting from that reading certain academic taboos, but enables a reading that
could not have *preceded* Derrida. By giving us to read the traditionality of the
tradition of metaphysics, Derrida simultaneously frees up a non-traditional and
essentially non-academic relation to tradition and its traditionality that is the
chance of tradition's no longer determining what futures are now to come, and
therefore also the chance of responsibility and invention. The 'perhaps' in
Derrida, the moment of risk at which the best and the worst are always possible,
is also the mark of this strictly *unprecedented* (non-traditional) relation to tradition,
which is as far as can be from the Heideggerian thinking of tradition to which
Gasché brings it so close. This liberatory (not liberationist) 'perhaps', which is not
the mere lack of dogmatic certainty that Gasché thematises, is opened every time
a book – including a book of philosophy – is opened for *reading*, and philosophy,
which is committed – that's tradition – to the *reduction* of reading, cannot have
any thematic grasp of it, and cannot fail to be professionally unsettled by it.
Traditionality is allergic to reading – its own condition. The vertiginous perspective this opens up (one that is, as such, radically indifferent to academic or
editorial guarantees, shot through with ambivalence, desire and duplicity, more
originary than truth) cannot possibly 'belong' to philosophy, and is just the sort of
thing Gasché cannot but anathematise as 'literary', though it cannot possibly
'belong' to literature or literary criticism either. Anyone can understand this –
perhaps.

12

EMERGENCIES

τεχνε can only go to meet φυσις, hasten recovery more or less; as τεχνε it can never replace φυσις and become on its own and in its place the αρχε of *health* as such. That would only be the case if life as such became a work that could be fabricated 'technically'; but then there would be no health either – nor birth, nor death. Sometimes one is tempted to say that modern humanity is driving towards this goal: *that man should produce himself technically*; if this were to succeed, man would have made himself (*i.e. his being as subjectivity*), explode into the air – the air in which all that is valid as 'meaning' is the absolute absence of meaning, and where the maintenance of this validity appears to be the 'domination' of man over the earth. It is not thus that 'subjectivity' is overcome; it is only 'calmed' in the 'eternal progress' of a Chinese-style 'constancy'; which is the most extreme counterfeit [*Unwesen*: inversion] of the ουσια φυσις.[1]

La réaction à la machine est aussi automatique (et donc machinale) que la vie même.

(FS, 61)

I

A sense of urgency does not come easily to philosophy.[2] Of all disciplines, philosophy ought to be the one most protected from the need to hurry. Philosophers may on occasion be in a hurry, like Kant in his old age pressing on from critique towards doctrine,[3] but philosophy, it seems, has – or at least demands – in principle all the time in the world. Urgency is difficult to think as a quality of philosophical problems, and, if philosophy were to make urgency *itself* one of its problems, it would no doubt have to do so at leisure. Philosophy, in its traditional – philosophical – concept, takes the time that it takes, and quite rightly is suspicious of calls to hurry up, seeing in them the sign of a quite unphilosophical impatience and intolerance of thought. Where other disciplines press more or less dynamically on, the gesture of philosophy consists in an admonishing and inhibitory 'Not so fast ... Wait a moment ... Just a minute ... Hold on there'. Philosophy, Owl of Minerva, always late on the scene, after the event, doesn't suffer emergencies gladly.

But philosophy, making a demand for all the time in the world, never has that much time. The desire for wisdom is not wisdom, and to that extent is struck by finitude and, thereby, by a time that is intrinsically, if indefinitely, limited. And this limitation is as much a positive condition of philosophy as a restriction on it. Given all the time in the world, philosophy would never even get started, but would remain dumbstruck or stupefied in the *thaumazein* that may be a condition of philosophy,[4] but only on condition that we shake ourselves out of it and say something, always late, but always too soon, never considered enough, never really thought through. However slowly and carefully it goes, philosophy is to this extent always the passion of its own urgent and unjustified precipitation.[5] Urgent, emergent. Urgency is emergency.

Once philosophy is caught up in temporal negotiations like this – from the start, then, always – it is already involved in a sort of discursive politics, if we can use 'politics' as a general term for strategic calculation or negotiation.[6] No philosophy can avoid some relation of this sort with the time available to it, once that time is finite, however indefinitely, and this negotiation is from the start a negotiation too with other things and other demands. Philosophy's urgency is, like any urgency, *one among others*, one urgency in an economy of urgencies, for urgency is thinkable only where nothing is *absolutely* urgent. Even (or especially) Hegel recognises this, for example in the Preface to the Second Edition of the *Greater Logic*: having said that the need to occupy oneself with pure thought is 'the need of the already satisfied need for the necessities to which it must have attained, the need of a condition free from needs, of abstraction from the material of intuition, imagination, and so on, of the concrete interests of desire, instinct, will, in which material the determinations of thought are veiled and hidden', he concludes the Preface with the following:

> Anyone who labours at presenting anew an independent structure of philosophical science may, when referring to the Platonic exposition, be reminded of the story that Plato revised his *Republic* seven times over. The remembrance of this, the comparison, so far as such may seem to be implied in it, should only urge one all the more to wish that for a work which, as belonging to the modern world, is confronted by a profounder principle, a more difficult subject matter, and a material richer in compass, leisure had been afforded to revise it seven and seventy times.

However, the author, in face of the magnitude of the task, has had to content himself with what it was possible to achieve in circumstances of external necessity, of the inevitable distractions caused by the magnitude and many-sidedness of contemporary affairs, even under the doubt whether the noisy clamour of current affairs and the deafening chatter of a conceit which prides itself on confining itself to such matters leave any room for participation in the passionless calm of a knowledge which is in the element of pure thought alone.[7]

Reckoning with the lack of time to do philosophy properly is part of doing philosophy properly: it is always urgent for philosophy to negotiate its urgency in the context of the urgencies of distraction, clamour and chatter. Philosophy cannot help (and must therefore affirm) its own being carried away by its resistance to being carried away, it must engage with distraction, clamour and chatter and to that extent at least must *itself* distract, clamour and chatter, and part of that chatter in philosophy is its constitutive inability to decide as to the priority of contemplation and action, *theoria* and *praxis*, metaphysics and politics.[8]

If it is difficult to avoid the sense that this ineluctability of urgency, even though it is originary, is becoming more and more urgent, that the pressures of distraction, clamour and chatter have increased exponentially since Hegel wrote his Preface – so that, paradoxically enough, the increasing liberation of the need of thought from material needs has also increased the compromise of thought with urgency, and therefore increased the urgency of urgency – then it is difficult to avoid the thought that one index of that increase of urgency is provided by the changes that go under the obscure heading of 'technology'. If technology were to be the name for this becoming-urgent of urgency in thought, then nothing could be more urgent than to think technology: and it is this thought that gives its impetus – its urgency – to Bernard Stiegler's book, and which Richard Beardsworth carries over into a more specific study of Derrida and politics.[9]

* * *

As nothing is more urgent than urgency itself, according to a reflexive capitalisation the point it is to resist and thereby think, and as urgency is what these two works are, in their very different ways, trying to think, then it is perhaps not surprising that both on occasion give in to just the sort of strident clamour – and a concomitant hectoring tone, for urgency generates a sense that someone has to give orders if all is not to be lost – just the rushing out of control they are also trying to think and hold off. Stiegler is so urgent in urging the urgency of the problem of technics on us that the opening of his preface all but closes his book before it has got started:

The object of this work is technics apprehended as the horizon of every future possibility and every possibility of a future.

This question still seemed secondary when I sketched out its first formulations ten years ago. Today, it cuts through all questioning and its enormity is clear to all. This calls for a work the urgency of which has scarcely been measured in spite of the liveliness of the stakes and the worries it provokes, a long drawn out task that is as exciting as it must be patient and will be difficult, shot through with a dull, necessary and dangerous impatience. I want here to warn the reader of this difficulty and its necessity: at its very origin and right up to the present, philosophy has *repressed* technics as an object of thought. Technics is *the unthought*.

(p. 11 [ix])

But, according to a paradox that just is that of philosophy itself, what is urgent is to hold up against urgency so as to think it, to be patient enough with the emergency to do its urgency justice by not just running with it: the thinking of urgency will, then, also be a thinking of the resistance to urgency:

The *reactions* – immediate or mediate and mediatised, gut or calculated, provoked by the extraordinary changes for which our age is the stage, and of which technics constitutes the most powerful dynamic factor, must be *imperatively overcome*. The present time is carried away in the whirlwind of a dull process of decision (*krisis*), the mechanisms and tendencies of which remain obscure, and which we must strive to render *intelligible* at the cost of a considerable effort of *anamnesis* as much as of meticulous attention to *what is happening* [ce qui arrive: what is coming]: the results presented here are still only an attempt as *groping* as it is *resolute*: groping (and the hand that makes it possible) is the very object of this reflexion ... That a radical change of point of view and attitude be required gives rise to all the more reactivity for being ineluctable.

(p. 11 [ix-x])

The strength of Stiegler's work will be the consistency with which it maintains itself in this paradoxical movement: the urgency it wants to communicate will thus depend in part on its patience, on its taking its time (10 years' work or more, three volumes expected,[10] pushing 1000 pages), and its patience will consist in the rigour with which it can establish that the urgency indexed by technics is of the order of the always already: it is urgent for 'us' (the identity of that 'us', as always, poses a question to which I shall return) to think the urgency of technics because that urgency has always already begun, and indeed is the condition for our thinking anything at all. What's new here is in part that this is nothing new.

* * *

Epimetheus (brother and double of Prometheus) is the figure of this situation of technics, and gives Stiegler's first volume its subtitle. According to the myth recounted by Protagoras in Plato's dialogue of that name, the gods, creating 'the mortal races', give Prometheus and Epimetheus the task of giving each race its qualities [*dynameis*: the word is heavy with implications for Stiegler's argument, as we shall see]. Epimetheus convinces Prometheus to let him do the job on his own, and duly distributes various capacities to the different animals, so that they all have equal chances of survival – so some are given speed to compensate for a lack of strength, some strength without speed, and so on. Having given out all the *dynameis*, he realises he has forgotten mankind, who remains naked and exposed. This is the context in which Prometheus, checking the distribution and realising his brother's blunder, famously steals fire (and by extension the wisdom of *tekhnè*) from the gods so that mankind shall not go without all capacity. Epimetheus, forgotten figure of a forgetting at the origin, becomes the emblem for Stiegler's whole project:

> Epimetheus is not only *the forgetful one*, the figure of the essential absent-mindedness in which consists *experience* (as *what happens* [arrive], what *passes* [se passe], and which, once past, must be ruminated), he is also the *forgotten one*. The forgotten one of metaphysics. Of thought. And the forgotten one of forgetting when thought thinks itself *as* forgotten. Every time people speak of Prometheus, they forget this figure of forgetting who is like its truth arriving always already too late: Epimetheus. It is stupefying that this figure of the *après-coup*, of the return from the fall of experience, of that *epimetheia* that gives its name to thought itself [*epimetheia* in Greek means reflecting afterwards, ruminating, and *epimethes* means wise or prudent], should not only not be at the centre of the phenomenological thought of finitude, but should be quite simply excluded from it.
>
> The figure of Prometheus alone (to be found, for example, in the *Rectorship Address*) is meaningless. It consists only in its doubling by the figure of Epimetheus, which itself doubles up as 1) committing the fault, absent-mindedness, imbecility, idiocy, forgetting, and ... 2) ... meditating it, always too late, reflexivity, knowledge, wisdom, and a *quite different figure of rememoration*: that of *experience*. The common Greek

language roots reflexive knowledge in *epimetheia*, i.e. in the essential technicity that finitude is. The inexistence of these figures in Heidegger's existential analytic cannot fail to strike us violently while seeming obviously necessary, because

1) the intertwining of the two figures of *prometheia* and *epimetheia* delivers up very precisely the major elements of the structure described as being-towards-the-end, and

2) the originary and impassable rooting of this relation in the technicity signified by these two figures absolutely contradicts the possibility of opposing authentic time on the one hand, and time of calculation and preoccupation on the other.

(pp. 194–5 [186–7])

This 'stupefaction',[11] and the *animus* against Heidegger that appears to go along with it, is curious, but sets up an agonistic scene that is already announced by Stiegler's title. *Technics and Time* does not have an entirely modest relationship with *Being and Time*. Thinking thinking as forgetting, Heidegger has forgotten the one who began by forgetting. What Epimetheus forgot was to provide man with a specific *dynamis*, and Prometheus's cover-up replaced that lack, or repaired that fault, by providing man with the means to procure, prosthetically, *any dynamis* at all: fire, figure of dynamism itself, replaces any lacking dynamic by being the source of an endlessly supplementary *dynamis*. The dynamic of technicity will thus be the dynamic of the prosthetic – and thereby the human as non-proper supplementarity – in general. Everyone has forgotten Epimetheus just because his original enabling forgetting was supplemented by the spectacular Promethean cover-up, but Heidegger has *exemplarily* forgotten him because Heidegger, of all people, really should have remembered the one who forgot. Heidegger's forgetting of the original forgetting seems to give rise to a generalising *epimetheia*: Heidegger's 'fault' repeats that of Epimetheus, but also strikes Stiegler with a stupefaction that always might resemble the idiocy characteristic of his emblem. Conversely, if Stiegler is concerned to rehabilitate Epimetheus as in some sense the truth of Prometheus, and if Heidegger in some sense stands in the place of Epimetheus, then all Stiegler's efforts to indict Heidegger for his fault are likely to end up rehabilitating him. All the paradoxes of urgency and patience centre on this emblematic figure, and more especially on the concept of *dynamis* itself. As we shall see, Stiegler has a certain *faith* in *dynamis* itself as a sufficient operator for thinking technicity (whereas his presentation of Epimetheus should in fact commit him to the view that *dynamis* is intrinsically *lacking*), and this commitment will dictate from afar what I attempt to show are misreadings of Derrida, (and of Heidegger himself).

However this may turn out, the structure of the argument about urgency clearly *owes* something to Heidegger (through and beyond whom Stiegler argues that the history of Being just is Being's 'inscription in technicity' (p. 18: the more detailed reading of Heidegger occupies the last 60 pages of *La faute d'Epiméthée*)), and more to Derrida, and a similar paradox of urgency could no doubt be derived from the latter's opening to the *Grammatology* in 1967.[12] Both Derrida and Stiegler share a sense (in both cases derived in part from a reading of Rousseau, oddly enough) that the most apparently irruptive or catastrophic newness is the more irruptive or catastrophic for being originarily prepared since ever: as I shall try to show, however, Stiegler differs from Derrida in that he thinks that technics is the *proper name* for the newness already there at the origin (for the emergency) – as we shall see, this leads him to a principled and argued difference of opinion with Derrida which, however, commits Stiegler (and Beardsworth beyond him, as we shall see) to a positivism (about techno-science) and a humanism (about 'us') which loses the very urgency it urges, and loses it through the very fact of urging it on a totalised 'us' as the totalisation of urgency itself.

What is it that philosophy has failed to think in failing to think technics? Stiegler has an apparently straightforward answer: *organised inorganic entities*. These are, he says, situated *between* the inorganic beings described by the physical sciences, and the organised (organic) beings studied by biology,[13] and they have a dynamic proper to them (so that technical objects are in a sense *self*-organising inorganic matter (58 n. 1; 85 [281 n. 7; 71])) that has never been thought through, though Stiegler will draw on the work of Gille, Simondon and Leroi-Gourhan to develop that thinking. The major moves in Stiegler's argumentation are as follows: (1) establish an ontic specificity of technical objects; (2) establish that such objects form a *system* with a quasi-intentional dynamic proper to it; (3) show that this dynamic is inseparable from the process of 'hominisation' as such. Technicity, metaphysically thought of as a mere supplement or prosthesis[14] of what is properly human, turns out to be the 'origin' of humanity,[15] which is thus marked by an originary 'defect' or 'lack' that technics tries to make good. Man is in this sense *essentially* technical, defined by an originary prostheticity (p. 64 [50]).

It is at this point (the emergence or emergency of the human) that Stiegler makes a discreet but ambitious displacement with respect to Derrida's arguments in the *Grammatology*.

Discussing Leroi-Gourhan himself, Derrida elaborates (*in that context*) a description of *différance* as 'the history of life ... as history of the gramme'. Within this history, the emergence of 'intentional consciousness' is an emergence that 'makes the gramme appear as such', and in so doing, 'no doubt makes possible the appearance of systems of writing in the narrow sense'. Stiegler has two questions to ask of Derrida, or after Derrida, and they are quite different in their tenor and scope. The first, based on an acceptance of these descriptions, suggests that, accepting that 'intentional consciousness' is the emergence of the gramme as such in this way, there is a further question to be asked. Stiegler again makes extensive use of italics to underline the urgency here:

> *The fact remains that it is a matter of determining what are the conditions of such an emergence of the 'gramme as such', and what are the consequences of this for the general history of life and/or of the gramme. This will be our question.* The history of the gramme is also that of electronic filing-systems and reading machines: a *history of technics* – the invention of man is technics. As object as well as subject. Technics inventing man, man inventing technics. Technics inventing as well as invented. Hypothesis ruining the traditional thought of technics, from Plato to Heidegger and beyond.
>
> (p. 148 [137])

Thus far, then, Stiegler is taking over from Derrida a certain generalised structure (which the latter calls the gramme *in this context*, but which is not different from what he elsewhere calls the trace) which he is on the one hand appropriating (by calling that structure by the name 'technics' as though that were the proper, or at any rate the better, name), and on the other focussing on a certain moment marked by the 'appearing *as such*' of the gramme,[16] i.e. on a moment identified with the appearance of something traditionally called 'man'. Stiegler calls this an 'articulation' or a 'stage' of *différance*, the point (if it is one) of the passage from the genetic to the non-genetic and thereby from the animal to the human. 'If there should be no question now of grounding the *anthropos* in a pure origin of himself, there remains to be said whence emerges his type' (p. 149 [138]).

This first question, then, already pushes the Derridean analysis towards a certain internal distinction or rupture: in the history of life in general (i.e. *différance*), Stiegler wants to say that *one* moment is privileged, and that moment is that of the emergence of 'man'. This focus motivates Stiegler's *second question* to Derrida, which looks more like a criticism than the first. Quoting from the essay 'Différance' where Derrida is glossing the double sense of the French verb 'différer' to motivate his neologism for a certain originary articulation of space and time, spatialisation and temporalisation, Stiegler incautiously assimilates this 'logical' description of *différance* to the more local remark he has just quoted from the *Grammatology* assimilating *différance* to 'life in general', and goes on with a passage worth quoting in full, if only because it illustrates how a certain phenomenological heritage can skew the understanding of Derrida even in the hands of a reader as acute as Stiegler:

> All of this [i.e. the description of the sense of the verb 'différer' in the essay 'Différance'] designates above all life in general [but this is not in

169

fact true of the passage from 'Différance']: there is time as soon as there is life, whereas Derrida also wrote, before the passage where he cites Leroi-Gourhan [i.e. back in the *Grammatology* again], that '*the trace is différance opening appearing* and signification [articulating] the living on the non-living in general, [which is at the] origin of all repetition'. Is to articulate the living on the non-living in general to already have crossed beyond the break, to no longer be in pure *physis*? There is as it were an indecision about *différance*: it is the history of life in general, but that gives (itself) only as (dating) from *after* the break, whereas that break is, if not nothing, at least much less than what is meant by the classical distinction between humanity and animality. The whole problem is the economy of life in general, and the meaning of death as economy of life once the break has happened: life is, *after* the break, the economy of death. The question of *différance* is death. This *after* is [and now quoting again from 'Différance']:

culture as nature differing-deferring/differed-deferred; all the others of *physis* – *tekhnè, nomos, thésis*, society, liberty, history, spirit, etc. – as *physis* differed/deferred and as *physis* differing/deferring. *Physis in différance*.

Now *physis* as life was already *différance*. There is an indecision, a passage *remaining* to be thought. The question is the specificity of the temporality of life when life is inscription in the non-living, spacing, temporalisation, differentiation and deferment by, of and in the non-living, in the dead. To think the articulation is also to think the relation to time that we call existing, is to think anticipation.

(p. 150 [139–40])

Where is the hesitation in Derrida's thinking of *différance* supposed to lie? In the fact that *différance* is on the one hand presented as *physis itself* (understood quite problematically by Stiegler as meaning 'life'), and on the other as the articulation of *physis* and (all) its others (but especially – for Stiegler, given his focus on life – death). The first presentation has *différance* before the 'break' (between *physis* and its others); the second must have it coming after, in that it is the articulation of the before (*physis*) *and* the after (its others). This is Derrida's 'hesitation' according to Stiegler, which he later develops into a *différance* of *différance*, or a 'differed-deferred *différance*' (p. 186), which Derrida himself supposedly cannot think within his grammatological setup.[17]

It is not difficult to see that this argument with Derrida is based on a mirage.[18] Stiegler sees a problem in Derrida's account by (1) assuming that the description of *différance* as the 'history of life in general' in a particular context of argument is

a general *definition*; (2) identifying life with *physis*; (3) assuming that the emergence of 'intentional consciousness' as the appearing of an 'as such' of the gramme
must be thought of as a *break*; (4) being surprised to find *différance* on both sides of
such a presumed break. These arguments only have any purchase if one is somewhere assuming, in phenomenological style, that *physis* is or could be a pure
presence *subsequently* affected by *différance*. But the 'logical' presentation of
différance should be sufficient to show that *no* concept can attain to the value of
'presence', and that this situation is (logically) originary. To that extent, however
interesting palaeontological work may be to deconstruction, and however
pressing (urgent) the question of the emergence of 'intentional consciousness'
may be to deconstruction or any other philosophy, it can never in principle enter
directly into this problematic of the trace, as Stiegler attempts to make it so enter
through his claims about a double *différance*. The possibility of the 'appearing as
such' of the gramme is built in to the description of the trace quite independently
of the factual history of the emergence of mankind or any other species. In a
gesture which also informs his readings of Heidegger, Stiegler wants to force the
whole philosophical argumentation of Derrida through the 'passage' of the emergence of mankind: the fact that he *then* goes on to characterise that 'passage' in
terms of an originary technicity which is very close to Derrida's own thinking
does not alter the fact that his first gesture commits him to a certain positivism
about difference, and this leads to his confident identification of 'technics' as *the*
name for a problem which he *also* recognises goes far beyond any traditional
determination of that concept. The curious effect of this, which means that the
reader of Stiegler's book is called upon constantly to exercise a vigilance that the
text does not always facilitate, is that a compelling, and at times brilliant account
of originary *technicity* is presented in tandem with a set of claims about *technics*
and even *techno-science* as though all these claims happened at the same level. This
mechanism makes of Stiegler's book perhaps the most refined example to date of
the confusion of the *quasi-transcendental* (originary technicity) and *transcendental
contraband* (technics), whereby Stiegler constantly reinstates all the oppositions
(summarised here in the *physis/tekhnè* opposition) his analysis is also acute enough
to criticise and deconstruct. The upshot is that, in contrast to a Rodolphe Gasché,
who writes a *philosophy* of deconstruction which he thinks just is deconstruction,
Stiegler writes a *phenomenological anthropology* of deconstruction which he thinks
just is deconstruction. The 'emergency' of the book arises because the deconstructive refinement that nevertheless informs the work shows relentlessly that
the *anthropos* grounding the whole analysis is, from the start, vanishing into the
generalised *tekhnè* which, because of the anthropological perspective itself, can
then only appear as a threat to 'us' humans.

* * *

Urgency is also the dominant tone of Richard Beardsworth's dense, incisive and quite excellent account of *Derrida and the Political*. This is arguably the most authoritative account of Derrida yet written in English, and the confidence and reliability of its understanding makes a welcome change from the more or less grossly reductive work which has been the norm. Beardsworth knows and understands many aspects of Derrida's thought (such as the idea that deconstruction is an 'experience of the impossible', or the relation between undecidability and decision) that most Anglo-American commentators would be quite unable to explicate accurately. Despite its modest title, this book deserves to become a standard (though difficult and rather uncompromising) guide to Derrida's thought more generally, and exhibits hardly any of the more or less gross misunderstandings and misrepresentations that can be found in almost all other such books. Let there be no doubt that this is a major and innovative contribution to our understanding of Derrida's work. As I shall suggest, though, the security the reader may begin to feel is bought at the price of a number of powerful but reductive decisions Beardsworth has taken about Derrida: these decisions allow a writing of great authority, but which can at times verge on the authoritarian.

For it is indeed still urgency, rather than any exegetical complacency, that gives the book its main tonal character, and is often given an explicitly and rather disconcerting millenarian inflexion: 'It is my purpose, however, to redress the misunderstandings of Derrida's thinking on the political which have themselves proved unhelpful to the task of thought and practice which lies ahead of all those who are involved in political reflection today: namely, the reinvention of political concepts to measure up to the technicization and globalisation of political communities in the next century' (p. xi).[19] It is tempting to speculate that this is of a piece with what is arguably Beardsworth's most powerfully reductive gesture in his reading of Derrida, which consists in presenting deconstruction as essentially a way of thinking about *time*. Beardsworth's understanding is that Derrida takes 'metaphysics' to be to do with a 'disavowal' of time (he uses the term within mild scare-quotes at first, but soon stops that and never thinks through the difficult implications there may be in relying on a psychoanalytically determined concept to describe this situation), and that he, Derrida, recalls thinking *to* time, or to the passage of time, by formulating what Beardsworth repeatedly calls, in a strong singularising gesture, '*the* aporia of time' (my emphasis). Now it takes only a moment's reflexion on Derrida's most schematic presentations of the thought of *différance* or the trace to realise that this must be, from the start, a partial and inaccurate presentation, insofar as *différance* is very precisely and explicitly to do with thinking, not just time, but 'spacing' as the common root of space and time, the 'becoming time of space and the becoming space of time', as the *Grammatology* has it (GR, 99 [68]). However important Derrida's meditations on time may be, it is a bold reader (but Beardsworth is nothing if not bold) who takes as his central concept for the explication of deconstruction something which Derrida himself says is irreducibly metaphysical. If, as 'Ousia and Grammè' famously claims, but as Beardsworth does not see fit to recall, there can be no non-metaphysical concept of time,[20] then making *just that concept* the centre of one's account is already quite a statement, but also a sign that something is being quietly simplified. Given the complexity of much of Beardsworth's argumentation, this may seem a churlish complaint, so I shall try to justify it a little in what follows.

Beardsworth very rapidly and helpfully sets up a scene which will guide all his concerns, and gives him a powerful way of understanding the dominant strands of the reception of Derrida until now:

> On the one hand, Derrida wishes to show that it is impossible to domi-
> nate philosophical concepts from *outside* philosophy, since the attempt
> meets an essential limit in the very philosophical nature of the terms
> being used to dominate it (terms, for example, of propriety embedded
> in the discourses of anthropology, linguistics, literary studies and
> psychoanalysis). [So far, then, following the logic of 'transcendental
> contraband' whereby discourses in the human sciences cannot help but
> put up as a principle of explanation a transcendental term they cannot
> understand: this might seem to invite the type of triumphant philosoph-
> ical correction administered by Gasché, but Beardsworth is also able to
> formulate the 'quasi-transcendental' side of the matter:] On the other
> hand, and for the same reason, philosophy is incapable of dominating the
> 'empiricity' or 'facticity' of these same discourses (what I will later call
> their 'inscription') since this empiricity and facticity inform its very
> gestures when it is least aware of it ... The consequent negotiation
> between the discourse of philosophy and the human sciences enacts a
> displacement and reorganisation of the 'metaphysical' opposition
> between the transcendental and the empirical, opening up an aporetic
> and uncontrollable 'position', neither in philosophy (as it is traditionally
> organized) nor outside it, one from which the future of thinking and
> practice is thought.
>
> (pp. 4–5)

This enables Beardsworth to hold tight to the thought that

> Thinking this necessity means thinking the inescapability of inscription
> in general – which would include the instances of history, the body,
> technics, politics – but it means thinking it *without* losing the inescapable
> gesture of the transcendental in order to do so.
>
> (p. 5)

... and to derive from this situation the major themes of his book:

> An aporia demands decision, one cannot remain within it; at the same
> time its essential irreducibility to the cut of a decision makes the deci-
> sion which one makes contingent, to be made again. The promise of the
> future (that there is a future) is located in this contingency. In this
> contingency of time resides the possiblity of justice. In other words, the
> aporia of thinking which emerges from within Derrida's play between
> philosophy and the human sciences inaugurates a philosophy of *judgement*
> and a thinking of *justice* in relation to *time*. I shall argue that the ethico-
> political dimension of deconstruction resides in this relation between
> aporia and judgement.
>
> (*ibid.*)

The rest of the book is in many ways simply (though it is in fact very far from
simple) an unpacking of this initial set-up, with important considerations of
Derrida's relation to Kant, Hegel, Heidegger and Lévinas along the way, and
indeed many valuable and powerfully synthesising insights into the work of those
authors considered in their own right. The essential upshot of Derrida's complication of the relation between the transcendental and the empirical is that it opens a
space that might reasonably be called 'political' insofar as it makes judgement
necessary while disallowing any full cognitive grasp or possible programming of
that judgement, against a 'technical' sense of politics which would strive for just
such a cognitive grasp or ability to programme. Judgement (and therefore politics) emerges as a result of the impossibility of knowledge transcendentalising the
singular out of existence, or as the loop whereby all transcendentalising gestures
(which begin at least as soon as anything gets said) rise only to fall back into their
contingent *milieu*, like Adami's fish back into the water.[21] Philosophy would traditionally like to get the fish right out and keep it there, stuffed and mounted; the
'human sciences' would like to keep it right in, and probably get in with it –
deconstruction as a thought of the irreducibility of 'politics' insists on the rhythm
of its leap and falling back.

I cannot here unpack all the implications of this deceptively simple picture.
One, on which Beardsworth is particularly strong, is that all thinking gives rise
more or less violently – but always violently – to *institutions* of thought which,
just because of this rhythm of the quasi-transcendental, remain more or less
violently unstable and subject to destabilisation and collapse.[22] Rather than track
the admirable analyses that Beardsworth devotes to this issue at a number of decisive moments in his book, I want to follow on the one hand the thought that the
trenchancy and incisiveness of Beardsworth's analyses are bought at the price of a
simplification of the quasi-transcendental into a question essentially about *time* (so

that 'time' itself emerges as the specific transcendental contraband of Beardsworth's book),[23] and that this determines the way in which the general opening of the space of 'the political' gets reduced to the urgent and even sometimes strident millenarian claims about politics, themselves further reduced, partly no doubt under the influence of Stiegler (whose understanding of Derrida is in fact rather less refined than Beardsworth's), to issues of technics and techno-science. For Beardsworth, Derrida gives us *the* aporia of time, in the singular, and this singularising gesture, operating on what Derrida will *always* make plural, dictates a certain number of consequences for Beardsworth's thought.

Time emerges as an issue in these analyses, let us remember, because of the structure of the quasi-transcendental itself: the judgement or decision that necessarily supervenes in the situation of undecidability or aporia is, to the extent that it is not programmed by the past, an irruptive cutting of temporal continuity which, as we are here starting by talking time, it seems natural to refer to the future. But this futurity has two aspects: (1) the future is the future (and not just a future present) to the extent that it is radically unpredictable ('formless' or even 'monstrous', as Derrida famously puts it in a couple of early texts, and as Beardsworth recalls by placing one of them as an epigraph to his book[24]) and is therefore what 'appears' (though never as such) in the arriving of any event whatsoever. (2) But in that arriving *from* the future (the structure of which implies that judgements are not made by subjects, but befall 'subjects': 'I' do not judge in my judgements, it is always the other who judges in my place), judgement also opens in return a *promissory* dimension *towards* the future, or *back to* the future, if you like. My judgement, insofar as it *is* a judgement and not just the administrative application of a prior rule, comes to me from the future, and returns to the future a promise of what is to come. The question of justice arises not when I know the law and apply it to the case at hand, but when the case irrupting from the formless future calls for a judgement for which no law is yet in place: and the judgement thus essayed or risked – and in these circumstances judgement is always a risk – promises a justice to come which will certainly never *arrive* in a present, but will remain a promise. It is a constitutive element of that promise that it always might not be fulfilled (a promise is not worth its name if it does not involve the necessary risk of not being kept: just as a letter always might not arrive at its destination – and that's its only chance of arriving – so a promise is made in the knowledge that it always might not be realised, and that's its only chance of promising).

It is easy to see that this notion of the future is not straightforwardly temporal at all: time, that irreducibly metaphysical concept, relies on the centring of the present, and the determination of past and future as mere modifications of it. If, as Derrida claims, the only concept of time is 'vulgar', and if therefore Heidegger himself does not escape that vulgarity in prioritising the futural *ekstasis* of temporality, then it looks as though the type of radical 'futurity' implied here bears a relation to 'time' that is at best 'strategic'. One indication of this is the ease with which this thought of a radical futurity converts into a thought of an 'absolute past', as Beardsworth admirably shows through a reading of Lévinas (pp. 125–9). But what this implies is that 'time' stops having any particular privilege in this situation (though it's helpful to set the question up in this way, as always through the retention of 'old words' more or less explicitly crossed through), and cannot communicate as straightforwardly as Beardsworth needs it to with that future he habitually and portentously calls 'the twenty-first century'. The complex arrival of the event in its non-presence is always in some sense an emergency, but cannot be thought of in terms of urgency: the very radicality of the 'future' means that deciding what is urgent is already to enter the very games of prediction and pre-determination the analysis was designed to avoid, and which are themselves essentially technical. This in no sense implies that complacency rather than urgency is the appropriate pathos for writing about these matters, but that the urging of urgency maintains a relation to complacency that is not here thought through, just because of the urgency of the argument.

This extremely refined blind spot has at least two consequences for Beardsworth's presentation of Derrida. One is that it is still, and in spite of itself, unduly historicist (in terms of 'modernity' at least), and runs the risk of implying in authoritarian pedagogical fashion that it is impossible to understand Derrida without first understanding Kant and Hegel (at least), whereas a necessary and paradoxical consequence of Derrida's analyses of traditionality and its irreducibility is that this is simply not the case – as I have argued elsewhere, Derrida, just because of his loving and careful readings of the texts of the tradition, also liberates us from some of these traditional pedagogical pressures. Another, more important consequence is that Beardsworth, like Stiegler, is pushed by this singularising gesture into the desire to articulate the thought of deconstruction onto a positivistically understood notion of technics or techno-science, for one of Beardsworth's most insistent claims is that it just is this which is increasingly determining, and will increasingly determine, our experience of time. This is why, entirely consistently with his analysis, Beardsworth arrives at a number of reservations or 'hesitations' about deconstruction, the matrix of which is stated at the end of Chapter 2 on 'The Political Limit of Logic':

> By returning logic to the aporia of time which this logic first disavows to constitute itself as such, does not Derrida run the risk of leaving the historico-material determinations *of* time too 'undetermined', and, in so doing, of leaving these very relations between time and matter too undeveloped for *their invention* to take form? Now, without the very

development of these relations, it could be argued that the political domain will collapse.

And this is what is developed in the Conclusion, where Beardsworth convincingly shows how Derrida provides a way of thinking an originary technicity contaminating the 'human', and, in the context of general claims about the impact of technics on the human experience of time, goes on to suggest that 'Derrida is nevertheless avoiding something in the above type of analysis of technical finitude' (p. 150), and, so the claim goes, increasingly disavowing his earlier insight into the originary technicity of the human (the originary articulation of human and non-human) in favour of a view of the promissory structure more suited to the analysis of religion or the religious organisation of time.

The fundamental doubt Beardsworth is voicing here is that Derrida is still too tied to the metaphysics he is deconstructing: or at least that that's the way it *looks*:

> The 'promise' ends up ... *appearing* too formal, freezing Derrida's deconstructions into a finite, but open set of 'quasi-transcendental' logics which turn the relation between the human and the technical into a 'logic' of supplementarity without history (the technical determinations of temporalization). Quasi-transcendental analysis remains the other of the logics which it deconstructs, thereby remaining itself logical. Derrida's mobilization of the aporia of time, as irreducible to the logical and the technical, is a logic! It refuses to lose itself in matter, in technics!
>
> (p. 154)

This 'appearance' derives from what Beardsworth claims is a shift in Derrida's thinking: earlier work stressed the contamination of 'originary technicity': later work stresses the originarity of the promise, and implicitly makes the promise *more* originary than technicity without explicating that fact nor elaborating on the relation between these two emphases:

> There are, consequently, 'two' instances of 'radical alterity' here which need articulation and whose relation demands to be developed: the radical alterity of the promise and the radical alterity of the other prior to the ego of which one modality (and increasingly so in the coming years) is the technical other.
>
> (p. 155)

Beardsworth wants to allow that these two instances are inseparable but not on the same ontological level: Derrida, on this reading, has surreptitiously dropped

177

originary technicity in favour of a 'more' originary promise without saying anything about it. An urgent task, then, for Beardsworth, would be to do that articulation for him, or to 'immerse philosophy in the techno-sciences for the promise to appear *through* the relation between the human and the nonhuman' (p. 156).

These concluding statements, and the 'loose speculation' that follows them,[25] are rather mysterious. Given everything Beardsworth has helped us to understand in Derrida's understanding of alterity, it simply cannot be true that there are two such massive ways of thinking it, and nor can it be true, as he claims, that they are 'not on the same ontological level', nor that 'both these instances cannot be originary, without making the concept "originary" nonsensical' (p. 156: of course 'making the concept "originary" nonsensical' is one, slightly bluff, way of characterising just what Derrida is doing, in for example the elaboration of the 'originary trace' in the *Grammatology*). But originary alterity as thought in *différance* necessarily precedes the distinction between, for example, the religious and the technical in their established senses, even if the only handle we could ever have on that alterity is provided by the 'old names' bequeathed by the traditions that carry our possibility of thinking anything at all, and of which 'religion' and 'technology' are only two among many others. That originary complication means just that we could never decide on a priority of arche-promise over arche-technics, and therefore never securely prescribe a greater urgency of analysing technics in its factical forms than religion in its factical forms. Beardsworth's conclusion really says no more than that *he* is more interested in techno-science than in religion, and tries dogmatically to justify that interest, and its concomitant prescriptions, by claiming with Stiegler that techno-science (rather than religion) just is more important to 'our' experience of time. And one perverse side-effect of this is that Beardsworth returns to something more like a humanism about 'us' than he could possibly want to support.

One answer to this concluding confusion is to argue that, even in their most empirical forms, religion and techno-science are absolutely inseparable, and that it is impossible to analyse the one without analysing the other. By what may be more than a coincidence, Derrida's essay 'Foi et savoir', published while Beardsworth's book was in the press, puts just this argument, and other recent texts show a keen interest in thinking about 'new technologies' of one sort or another.[26] If, as seems to follow from these thoughts, 'religion' is just as open to analysis in terms of an originary technicity as is techno-science, and techno-science just as open to analysis in terms of the promise as is religion,[27] then the apparent duality Beardsworth ends up with evaporates (he himself says disingenuously that there is no choice to be made, having made the choice extremely clear) into a singular multiplicity which is not 'too philosophical' or 'too logical' just because it is *not* positivistically married to thinking about technics. This does not of course mean that it is uninteresting to think about technics, on the contrary, but that the satisfactions of urgency to be derived from calling us away from other thoughts to attend to just that one can be held off too. Techno-science *already* demands our attention or 'immersion' in a way 'we' might want to resist. The technically-inspired programming of emergency as urgency paradoxically enough runs the risk of closing off just the 'political' opening it was designed to promote, by directing us all, rather religiously, towards a prophet of doom's 'twenty-first century' the very religious-technological predictability of which is already blocking the arrivals it will also, necessarily, contingently, surprisingly enough bring.

13

AN IDEA OF SYNTAX

Marian Hobson's book brings off that rare feat of making its main point seem self-evident.[1] After reading *Opening Lines*, it is simply obvious, perhaps blindingly so, that she is right to insist on the importance of a certain *syntax* in Derrida's work. Previous commentators have habitually concentrated on the explication of individual 'lexemes' within the Derridean corpus (writing, *différance*, dissemination, deconstruction, etc.), but, as Hobson convincingly shows, nothing is less Derridean than a thinking based on, or organised round, individual words or names. As Derrida himself more than once explicitly affirms,[2] what *works* in texts is the more or less complex sequences of argument around words or concepts (what Hobson calls 'strings' or 'circuits of argument' (p. 3)), and not individual words or concepts having some magical inner virtue ideally independent of the contexts in which they appear. Our reading of Derrida, insofar as we have focused it on the lexematic view, has hitherto, then, been in thrall to a perfectly pre-Derridean and even logocentric understanding of textuality. One of the welcome effects of the insistence that, as Hobson puts it perhaps rather obscurely on page 1, 'writing in Derrida's work ... sometimes induces an organisation of ideas which affects their import', is that it becomes possible in retrospect to see anticipatory traces of this new understanding in previous commentators, as they struggle to unpack the lexemes that have indeed become the general academic shorthand for discussing Derrida. Hobson naturally does not think that the lexemes are unimportant, and indeed spends a fair amount of her time offering accounts of them that are perhaps not always the most perspicuous yet proposed, but gives too a broader analysis that in principle explains their proliferation according to two levels she calls 'circuits of argument' (or occasionally, with a provocative Adornian resonance, 'micrologies') and *syntax* itself. The relationship between these different levels (one of which seems to have more to do with the distribution of thoughts, the other with the distribution of words) is itself quite complex and hard to grasp, as we shall see.

To the extent that it explicitly makes this move from the lexematic to the syntactic, Hobson's book marks a real breakthrough or opening in the study of Derrida's work, and the general nature of that breakthrough ought to have a general effect on the ways in which Derrida is henceforth discussed. She ranges effortlessly across the whole Derridean corpus (foregrounding along the way a number of texts which have been little discussed in the Anglo-American context), and addresses a reader who is not obviously already 'in' deconstruction, but who has quite severe philosophical expectations and demands. She eschews any deconstructive coquetry or stylistic ambition in her own writing, and often prefers, perhaps strategically in view of the reader she is hoping for, the robust if unsatisfactory use of common-sense descriptions (philosophers express their ideas in words).[3] She also brings Derrida's work close to a number of more or less unexpected sources in analytic philosophy and mathematics which come as a welcome surprise to the 'continental reader' and would certainly not all be expected by the 'analytic' one. Shutters, then, are being opened. As is the way with such openings, the brightness of the light this one brings also generates its own difficulties of focus and orientation, and in some ways has led Marian Hobson to write a very difficult book indeed. I shall try to navigate through at least some of the difficulties she generates, and endeavour to show – in a way with which I think she would have to agree – that the various circuits or strings she identifies and unpacks can be organised around, or from, a particular understanding of Derrida's early interest in the 'Idea in the Kantian sense' as it appears as a motif in Husserl. But as we shall see, the very idea of the Idea turns out to give Hobson's discussion a focus or orientation that is not always quite Derridean, so that the Derrida that emerges from *Opening Lines* is interestingly and productively different from the Derrida that emerges from the texts he has written: the difficulty of the book, and this difference it thus opens from its object (as indeed it must if it is right to claim that the organisation of Derrida's 'ideas' is not itself one of Derrida's ideas) add up to a demand for re-reading which identifies the book as an undoubted *original*.

* * *

Hobson begins with what her Introduction might have led us to think would be the most difficult, namely the level of *syntax* itself. This level of organisation is defined as 'a repeated form of articulation of one element of Derrida's discourse, one philosophical problem, with another' (p. 3). Chapter 1 duly identifies such a general repeating pattern in 'the relation between genesis and structure (to borrow the title of one of his earlier articles), or between the empirical [...] and the transcendental [...].' (The elusive 'or' in this sentence already gives a sense of the difficulties of Hobson's own syntax: is this an 'or' of equivalence, or one of disjunction? *Aut* or *vel?*) In a complex way that is never quite thematised, Hobson is led to a broadly *genetic* account of this syntax of genesis and structure, but one which will quite properly have *structural* effects throughout her later discussions. Here is Hobson giving a further gloss to the still elusive notion of syntax:

> It is an example of what my introduction has called a Derridean 'syntax': a form of argument which is articulated by philosophical terms acting in relation to their distribution, that is, as functions rather than as lexemes, and which, as does syntax, conveys a form of meaning which is not lexical, but structural. The piece of 'syntax' studied in this chapter artic- ulates philosophy with history of philosophy; it articulates a set of problems considered as a system and separable from their historical circumstance, with history as a complex succession of interdependent effects, events, or moments; or [that 'or' again!] it sets off different values of 'transcendence' (...) against 'history'[...]

> [...] there is a constant way of articulating the questions he is concerned with in this earlier work which is not thematized as a conclu- sion in the work; it acts more as a load-bearing formation, a way of thinking the questions. It is for this reason that I have called it a 'syntax'.
>
> (p. 8)

This developing notion of syntax which Hobson is struggling to formulate, can *itself* find some (lexematic? – certainly *thematic*) support in Derrida's writing, and it happens that arguably the most obvious example, given here by Hobson herself, is a remark from 'The White Mythology' about the (syntactic) functioning of the (lexeme) 'idea' itself. Hobson claims that this moment in Derrida has been over- looked: 'these remarks have not hitherto been followed up; this piece of "syntax" itself is not especially salient, and has hitherto escaped notice' (p. 8).[4]

This moment in 'The White Mythology' is itself quite complex, and extends beyond the brief reference Hobson provides in her book.[5] Derrida has been pursuing his reading of Aristotle on metaphor into later rhetoricians, and the metaphors to which they resort to clarify metaphor itself, to give the 'idea' of metaphor. 'Idea' is caught in a complex set of terms that relates understanding to a non-literal clear sight (*theoria*) which we can understand only in some metaphorical or tropical relation to sensory sight. In Fontanier, for example, 'Idea' is supposed to be the pre-linguistic (and therefore pre-metaphorical) sense or meaning which only secondarily falls into language and rhetoric. This originary figurality of 'Idea' means that the supposedly pre-rhetorical is caught in a rhetoric it can neither escape nor understand. The paragraph from which Hobson quotes a few words now runs as follows:

The point of recalling here the history of the signifier 'idea' is not to give in to the etymologism we have refused above. While recognising the specific function of a term within its system, we must not for all that hold the signifier to be perfectly conventional. No doubt Hegel's Idea, for example, is not Plato's Idea; no doubt system-effects here are irreducible and must be read as such. But the word Idea is not an arbitrary X and it imports a traditional baggage which continues Plato's system in Hegel's system and must also be interrogated as such, following a stratified reading: neither pure etymology or origin, nor homogeneous continuum, nor absolute synchronism or simple interiority of a system to itself. This implies that one criticise *both* the model of the transcendental history of philosophy, and that of systematic structures perfectly closed in on their technical and synchronic organisation (which has only ever been recognised up until now in corpuses identified according to the 'proper name' of a signature).[6]

These assertions spawn a sequence of remarks later in the text which indeed explicitly invoke the notion of syntax. Aristotle's view of language reduces the syntactic by insisting on the nominal or nominalisable: is Bachelard's apparent sensitivity to the '*syntax*, the systematic logic of metaphorical productions, the "metaphors of metaphors" ultimately compatible with the concept of metaphor'? (*ibid.*, p. 317). But Bachelard re-unifies syntax around a thematic unity, thus reducing it in the very effort to do it justice.[7] The syntax or 'grammar'[8] of Descartes's conceptual terminology is no doubt specific to him in some sense, but 'as a metaphorics it belongs to a more general syntax, to a more extended system that constrains Platonism just as much ... ' (*ibid.*, p. 319): and the text ends on a famous affirmation of the plurality of metaphor which is inseparable from syntax: 'it is because metaphor is from the start plural that it does not escape syntax; and that it gives rise, in philosophy too, to a *text* which is not exhausted by the history of its meaning ... But it is also because metaphorics does not reduce syntax, but on the contrary works its deviations in it, that it carries itself off, can be itself only in erasing itself, indefinitely constructs its destruction' (*ibid.*, p. 320). The point is to motivate a way of reading that will resist the temptation to privilege *either* the specific – different, *signed* – syntax of the system in question, *or* the supposedly transhistorical or transcendental syntax of 'metaphysics'. 'Idea' in Hegel is and is not Platonic, is and is not metaphysical, and indeed is and is not metaphorical.[9]

Hobson's claim, then (in part authorised by this explicit and thematic reflection on syntax *in* Derrida), is that at least some of Derrida's work (and notably the early texts on phenomenology) are individuated or at least characterised by a non-explicit syntax of conceptual deployment which 'bears, structurally and tacitly, on what has appeared so far to readers to be the fully thematised and overt content of these works of Derrida' (pp. 8–9). Just as the concept of metaphor has committed philosophy and rhetoric to an attempted but impossible reduction of the syntactic in the interests of the semantic, and ultimately the supposed presence of a sense or Idea, so readers of Derrida have heretofore read Derrida metaphysically, accepting in traditional fashion that these works are to do with an essential content which is thematic and available in the mode of presence to the sufficiently perspicacious reader. Insofar as Hobson shows that this is not the case, but that Derrida's texts (even his most 'philosophical' texts) are *textual*, i.e. reliant on a syntactic armature they in principle cannot exhibit thematically (or perhaps that they *show* but cannot *say*), then she opens the prospect of the first genuinely *Derridean* reading of Derrida ever seriously attempted. This prospect is both powerfully reductive (in that it proposes a quite *specific* syntactic motif as organising a wide range of texts) and endlessly open (in that syntax thus understood just is a principle of multiplication and dispersion). Which means that in the first few pages of her book Marian Hobson has in principle already outflanked and displaced all previous accounts of Derrida's work, *and* Derrida's own account of his work – for on his logic, a Derridean reading of Derrida will always produce a Derrida different from himself, countersigning a Derrida different from the one who signs.

The *specific* syntax here identified in Chapter 1, and which I have just described as reductive, bears essentially on the relation between what metaphysics calls the empirical (historical) and the transcendental. Derrida (though, according to Hobson, not yet explicitly or thematically in these early texts) is attempting to think in a way that escapes both a historicist or empiricist determination of differences, and their absorption into transcendental sameness. Neither straightforward continuity nor radical rupture. And this is indeed the concern of his earliest texts, fuelled by the later Husserl's consternation about the historicity of idealities, and notably those of geometry.[10] This problem rapidly leads Derrida to formulate his famous remarks about the originary trace (i.e. an originary synthesis or complication, a non-simplicity at the beginning), the non-originary origin, and so on, and will later spawn a series of 'in the beginning' formulations which all say something about how in the beginning it was not the beginning.[11] In a famous and dense moment in *Of Grammatology*, this originary complexity is referred to as the common opening of 'temporalization, relation to the other, and language'.[12] While quite properly reminding the reader of the uncertainly transcendental status of this argument, Hobson nonetheless wants to refer to time, language and the other here as 'necessarily absent' and 'intentions of the infinite'. And it is around this issue that the difficult question of the Idea will re-emerge. In the earlier remarks about syntax we were quoting, following Hobson's lead, from 'The White Mythology', it happened that the example Derrida took was that of the concept (or idea) 'Idea', and it is around this concept or idea (though in a more specifically – never absolutely specifically – Husserlian-Kantian syntax than a Platonic or Hegelian one) that the issues emerging here are dealt with in these early texts.

Kant's concept of the Idea, to which Husserl makes constant appeal, is that it allows us to refer to 'objects' which, just because they are 'infinite', can never be the object of conceptually validating intuitions. I can *think* the infinite, I have an idea of it, but I cannot circumscribe it in intuition and thereby make it the object of a concept (in the narrower sense of what Kant calls the understanding). Reason allows me to think *beyond* what I know, but tempts me into 'transcendental illusion' by leading me to treat the objects of Ideas as though they were the objects of concepts. The correct use of the Ideas is regulative, i.e. they guide me by setting a *task*, suggesting the possibility of an infinite asymptotic approach to something which by definition I can never reach. Husserl, as Hobson usefully summarises it (pp. 45–7), takes up this dimension of the infinite task to describe the endless progress of, for example, geometry, but also of phenomenology and philosophy itself. In his 'Introduction' to Husserl's *Origin of Geometry*, Derrida picks up on this difficult status of the Idea in Husserl, showing how it both allows Husserl to think the transcendental as in some sense essentially historical ('transcendental historicity'), and yet itself escapes phenomenological analysis – for the watchword of phenomenology, 'to the things themselves', is inoperative in the case of the Idea in the Kantian sense, which works just where the 'thing itself' is by definition inaccessible to full intuition. The Idea-in-the-Kantian-sense, then, has a paradoxical status in these late Husserl texts, providing phenomenology with a vital resource for thinking the relation between the transcendental and the empirical, and yet itself perpetually escaping phenomenological grasp.[13]

Husserl's use of the Idea makes of it a *telos* which guarantees a certain coherence beyond what coherence is actually given. As Hobson stresses, this introduces a certain absence or hollowing out into the supposed plenitude of experience, which *would be* present if its infinitely coherent interconnectedness could be intuited, which it cannot. Intuition in general is hollowed out by an *intention* ('of the infinite', as Hobson has just said) which constantly outstrips *intuition*. And this dislocation of the so-called 'Living Present' from itself leads to some of Derrida's most difficult formulations, in for example *La voix et le phénomène*, about Husserl's distribution of the domains of fact and right, empirical and transcendental, and so on. These are admirably glossed by Hobson, who also provides excellent accounts of other philosophical and mathematical treatments of the paradoxes of infinity.

The question that this raises is that of knowing what relation 'Idea-in-the-Kantian-sense' (in the Husserlian sense) bears to those *Derridean* 'intentions of the infinite' Hobson is glossing. Is *différance*, for example, just a version of the Idea?[14] The answer to this question must be 'no', though Derrida's fascination with the Idea suggests an affinity that will be difficult to disentangle. And just this (dis)entanglement is the figure Hobson is referring to as a piece of syntax (she tracks it through many more texts and arguments than I am able to mention here). At first sight, it seems as though the point of difference between Derrida and Husserl comes down to the question of finitude. What Husserl supposedly neglects in his deployment of the Kantian Idea is *the finite nature of the empty intuition of the infinite*, and ultimately, the particular aspect of finitude signalled by death:

> In the account Derrida gives of Husserl's Living Present, the strange knot that is the Kantian Idea is presented even more fully. The absolute present of experience as given, that Husserl searched for, can only appear as such if it appears as indefinite, prolongable in a unity of possible meaning which is limitless though connectable with the Kantian Idea. But then, says Derrida of Husserl, the finite mode of appearance of the indefinite is neglected; human finitude is not built into the account. This is tantamount to making of death a fact, not a condition, and thus extrinsic to the process ...
>
> (p. 50)

Derrida does indeed often point out (in the wake, perhaps, of Heidegger's *Kantbuch*) the solidarity of the motifs of transcendentality and finitude.[15] But it is not sufficient simply to put a traditional or factical notion of 'death' back into the equation to solve the problem and to distinguish Husserl's Idea (-in-the-Kantian-sense) and Derrida's *différance*. Death is still a perfectly metaphysical motif unless it is patiently disengaged from the metaphysical syntax which even Heidegger inherits and cannot quite undo[16] – and a paradoxical property of Derrida's generalisation of the motif of death throughout his work (so that life is described famously as 'an economy of death' and 'I am' is shown to entail 'I am dead') is that death is radically de-dramatised and robbed of its traditional existential pathos. But what this operation does is to *scatter* the relation of finite and infinite across texts in a way which makes it difficult to organise them teleologically according to the 'Idea-in-the-Kantian-sense'. It is not, as in Husserl, that facticity is simply a sort of delay or drag on progress towards the infinite, but that it becomes impossible to imagine the infinite as the 'object' of regulated (albeit infinite) approach at all. One perhaps unfortunate effect of the 'deferral' component of *différance* is that it can so easily be construed as the measured deferral of the infinite idea, a sort of 'negative phenomenology' whereby the thing itself is always infinitely absent, but always still the object of an ordered approach. But it is just this tendency which the *other*, 'spatial' component of *différance* disrupts, dispersing the infinite across a ('syntactic') network which has no given historical or temporal orientation at all, and in which 'the infinite' is always ('finitely') promised here and now, 'to come' perhaps, as the recent texts on democracy have it, but not ever to be present, always to come *now*. To this extent, *différance* is *exactly* what *interrupts* the idea of the Idea, not just at a certain point in the progress to infinity, but from the start, before it can start *as* progress. And this means that it becomes difficult to accept the description of *différance* et al. as 'intentions of the infinite' at all, because these quasi-concepts are, rather, the deconstruction of the very opposition between finite and infinite.[17] Derrida's work with death does not simply call the transcendental adventure back to the stern reality of human finitude, but shows up the metaphysical solidarity of that adventure *and* its recall. And to the extent that 'Idea-in-the-Kantian-sense' is determined by a metaphysical sense of the infinite, then Derrida must be suspicious of it. Hobson admirably shows that this commits Derrida to the now-familiar paradoxical formulations about conditions of possibility and impossibility which characterise the 'quasi-transcendental' in general.

The 'syntactic' approach, then, allows Hobson to identify patterns of argument across a wide range of texts which do not always explicitly exhibit or thematise the same concepts. But there is still some obscurity in the explanation. 'Syntax' in this first chapter began as a matter of arguments about the historical and the transcendental, but shows up more saliently at the end in formulations involving possibility and impossibility. Hobson calls the second sort of formulation a 'further piece of "syntax", in operation at a more visible level … ' (p. 59), admits that it has been the object of extensive prior commentary, and now wants to argue that the problem is that 'in the good deal of critical attention it has attracted, it is often divorced both from its anchoring in Derrida's relation to the history of philosophy … , and from its point of origin in Derrida's reading of Husserl' (*ibid.*). 'Point of origin' cannot fail to sound odd here (as does 'anchoring'), and shows up the fact that 'syntax' may be doing too much work: for *on the one hand* it appears to be used in the explicitly Derridean sense picked out above (namely describing a conceptual organisation in its 'synchronic' axis, as it were, how 'Idea' works *in Hegel*, as opposed to its 'diachronic' axis of inheritance from Plato) – and this allows Hobson to 'leave aside for the present the fact that this occurs at a specific point in the history of philosophy as thought through by Derrida' (*ibid.*) – and *on the other* to refer to the very historicity or traditionality to which this first sense appeared to be opposed ('The previous chapter suggested that Derrida's "syntax" – the functioning induced on some of his arguments by patterns in the distribution of their elements – implicitly articulated a recent history of philosophy in terms of genesis and structure … ' (*ibid.*)). This tension now relaunches an investigation of Derrida's characteristic lexemes in the 'contexts of their proliferation' (p. 61), but is disconcerting for the reader – Hobson is keen to stress the importance of a sort of internal history of Derrida's work, and yet is happy to formulate an all-but transcendental logic of that work when she organises her second chapter with reference to that 'further piece of syntax' about possibility and impossibility.[18] For that further piece of syntax is organised in two ways, one of which is indeed drawn from the early work on Husserl (where the terms are placed in a paradoxical equation: 'Their possibility is their impossibility'), but the other of which jumps lightly to the '90s for a formulation drawn from the reading of Heidegger in *Aporias*, as 'the possibility of the impossibility' (and here Hobson does not follow the bewildering inversions and redoublings that Derrida operates on this Heideggerian motif of death as the 'possibility of the impossibility of *Dasein*').

Just this tension, in different guises, becomes the main 'theme', or syntactic signature, of Hobson's book. Put briefly, how do we understand the proliferation of Derridean lexemes on the one hand as producing a dispersion of singular terms in singular contexts, and on the other as having among themselves a connection which is not of the order of an essence or a common *eidos* (p. 67)? How can we grasp the relations between these terms without committing ourselves to the idea that they must all somehow name the same thing, which would then have to have a *proper* name – so that *différance*, for example (or any of the others) would become superordinate with respect to all the other terms, the real name for whatever Derrida is on about? In other words, can we think a dispersion without gathering it around a centre or a single origin point?[19] Just this is the work that the concept of syntax is being called upon to do, and the tension it induces will remain constant through Hobson's book (so that the 'logical' point about repetition allowing both the production of essence as repeatability-of-the-same and the non-identical doubling, mimicking or parodying that undermines the claim of essence is, Hobson insists, not just logical, but 'also a historical point. Derrida is anchoring his analysis in the history of philosophy, by relating it to Plato's cave, and Heidegger's account of Plato's cave' (p. 69): 'anchoring' again here looks a little strong). But what is most striking here is undoubtedly the logical side of this (still traditional) pairing: Hobson produces, essentially via the texts gathered in *Dissemination* and *Limited Inc.*, a quite brilliant account of how Derrida thinks through patterns of repetition and doubling, so that the unstable 'origin' or 'root' (archi-writing, archi-trace, dissemination, itself only ever nicknamed after the event of its splitting, doubling and re-application) splits to produce a 'stabilised systole' (on the side of essence, truth, presence, etc.), which opposes itself to a double of the 'originary' term, which double inherits the originary instability and continues splitting further, down a tree of non-identical pairings – this logical 'machine' generating the (no longer quite logical) possibility of history to which logic is opposed only in the sense of the unstable splittings thus described. It is this mechanism that allows Hobson to say that the Derridean lexemes are 'not just multiple [which could be no more than an empirical observation], but can be said to multiply' (p. 107).

However, the problem we have identified around Hobson's version of the Idea, and its relation to the infinite, will not go away so easily. Hobson wants to go on past what she has been able to formulate so wonderfully about the replicating and doubling structure of the 'lexemes'. This seems to relate to the distinction between the two sorts of relation of possibility and impossibility we have mentioned: the dynamic structure of doubling is what allows formulations *equating* possibility and impossibility: but a new development will try to account for the 'possibility *of* impossibility' relation we saw Hobson pull out from the very specific context of *Aporias*. She is prepared to argue here that *only one* 'lexeme' (*restance*, as used in *Limited Inc.* – but even if she is right about this – *concesso non dato* – this *only one* is *at least one*) points to this functioning, which she will endeavour to bring out from her 'circuits of argument' or *micrologies*, where it functions beyond the general ability of any lexeme to 'set in doubt what it labels' (p. 108), and has to be tracked 'at the level of the phrase, not the article or book' (p. 109, confirming that that was the level of analysis for the 'syntax' discussed thus far). The specificity of *restance*, and the patterns to be brought out, are related to a thinking of a *limit* which still involves 'a process of infinite approximation' (p. 108: Hobson perhaps unconsciously dramatises the process she is describing by an almost word-for-word repetition on p. 125 of the sentence from which this phrase is here quoted). But Hobson's ambition, as we have seen, is to bring out something that is happening within Derrida's texts but which those texts do not reflect on in the form of a lexeme at all – and this involves some very difficult thinking about time and singularity. By a leap which is certainly not self-evident, Hobson herself provides a name for this pattern ('strange attractors', drawn from so-called 'chaos theory'),[20] and motivates that choice of term by claiming (wrongly, I think) that this term is translated into French as 'singularité', singularity.

Hobson develops this thought across Derrida's readings of Barthes and Ponge, but might have illustrated it too from the earlier 'Freud and the Scene of Writing', or 'La parole soufflée', from *Glas*, the text on *Romeo and Juliet*, from *Circumfession*, or any number of texts. Derrida is interested in a structure whereby the radically singular or idiomatic is both constituted and betrayed by the trace-structure: the singular (i.e. a first time that is also a last time) *as such* would be radically inaccessible; for it to be perceived, recorded, registered, recognised *as* singular, indeed for it to have an 'as such' at all, its singularity must have been already betrayed by some possibility of recovery (it must have left a trace, i.e. some mark it cannot exhaustively re-absorb into itself). A signature marking the uniqueness of an event must be repeatable as the signature that it is in order validly to mark the singularity of the event that it marks. A similar argument is developed around dates in Derrida's text on Celan, and gives rise to the explicit thematic of spectres and ghosting which is implicit in the 'original' thought of the

trace, and which becomes a dominant motif in *Spectres de Marx*.[21] Bearing witness
to the singular, then, involves betraying it in the very effort to respect it: this is
the thought behind a good deal of Derrida's most recent work on ethics and politics (displacing the resources and frontiers of the philosophical domains of ethics
or politics, however), and has generated some new lexemes in '-bility': pervertibility would be an essential condition of ethics, for example.[22] And it is just this
necessarily compromising iterability that makes the 'same' (as always produced in
repetition) always also 'other', and produces a whole problematic around the law
that. I cannot unpack here. Singularity is always (of the) other. Hobson percep-
tively picks out from Derrida a use of terms such as 'response' and 'negotiation'
to describe this situation, and shows how it is complex (though as often her point
of comparison can seem just as difficult as what it is designed to elucidate):

> Like strange attractors, 'singularités' in French, where prolongations of
> certain apparently chaotic series subside within the limits of a certain
> form, they have a double self-construction. They are produced both by
> what is beyond approximation and works through the double bind,
> short-circuit or violent interruption; but they are also produced by the
> negotiation which involves constant approximation.
>
> (pp. 134–5)

The point, and increasing difficulty, of Hobson's book, is to think these two
aspects (interruption and approximation) together, and indeed as in some sense
the same. But this, it seems to me, also reduces somewhat the specificity Hobson
is claiming for this part of her account. I think that there is a reasonably straightforward continuity between the functioning of the more or less familiar 'lexemes'
in Derrida, and these so-called 'strange attractors' to which Hobson is concerned
to give a different, more 'shadowy' status. The difficult unity of approximation
and interruption, for example, is referred by Derrida himself, in a passage
Hobson quotes, to the lexeme *différance* (p. 145) – and indeed we could say the
same of *all* the lexemes: just as singularity is both given and lost in one and the
same moment, so the 'identity' of each lexeme is given and lost only by its relative dispersion in the syntax of its occurrences and its relation to the other
lexemes.[23] What Hobson is inclined to present as a 'strange attractor' always out
of reach looks as though it would have to be either pure syntax (pure relationality
without terms) or pure lexematicity (pure term without relation); but *différance*
and the rest are just bespeaking the becoming syntactic of all terms, their dissolution as terms into a syntax which also regularly secretes (or vomits out) such
quasi-terms, in a *rhythm* which is that of Derrida's writing.

The problem I am attempting to draw out from these extremely refined
descriptions becomes clearer in relation to the 'example' of justice as presented in

Force of Law, which Hobson mentions almost in passing at the end of her chapter (p. 145). Many readers have been struck and perhaps disturbed by Derrida's claim in that text that justice is the 'undeconstructible': 'justice itself seems to form what I have called a "strange attractor"' (p. 145). Derrida describes this situation as follows:

> In the structure I am describing in this way, right is essentially *decon-structible*, either because it is grounded, i.e. constructed on textual strata that are interpretable and transformable (and this is the history of right, the possible and necessary transformation, sometimes the improvement of right), or because its ultimate ground by definition is not grounded. That right be deconstructible is not a misfortune. One might even see in it the chance of all historical progress. But the paradox I would like to submit to discussion is the following: it is this deconstructible structure of right or, if you prefer, of justice-as-right which also ensures the possibility of deconstruction. Justice in itself, if some such thing exists, outside or beyond right, is not deconstructible. No more than deconstruction itself, if some such thing exists. *Deconstruction is justice* ... Whence these three propositions:
>
> The deconstructibility of right (for example) makes deconstruction possible.
>
> The undeconstructibility of justice also makes deconstruction possible, and is even indistinguishable from it.
>
> Consequence: deconstruction takes place in the interval separating the undeconstructibility of justice from the deconstructibility of right. It is possible as an experience of the impossible, in the place where, even if it does not exist, even if it is not – not yet or never – *present*, *there is* justice. Wherever one can replace, translate, determine the X of justice, one ought to say: deconstruction is possible, as impossible, to the extent that (where) *there is X* (undeconstructible), and therefore to the extent that (where) *there is* (the undeconstructible).[24]

This is a difficult passage (and not rendered particularly clearer by Derrida's revisions between the initial publication in *Cardozo Law Review* of the 1989 text and the book version in 1994). How does it sit with Hobson's description of singularities or 'strange attractors'? On the one hand, it looks a promising candidate for the twin features of negotiation (in Hobson's view, then, to do with an infinite approach or approximation) and interruption. But on the other, it illustrates the pitfalls of this understanding, and its affinities with the structure of the Kantian Idea as we have explicated it so far. It also has the advantage of relating this structure to the possible/impossible couple in a way which seems to precede the distinction Hobson makes between equation (possibility *is* impossibility) and imbrication (possibility *of* impossibility). The point of Derrida's description, in spite of some appearances, is not to accept a traditional (Kantian) distribution whereby what is here called 'right' would figure as the empirical and historical, and 'justice' as the object of an Idea of Reason, which we can *think*, and to which we are called to make an infinite asymptotic approach *through* or *via* that empirical and historical domain. Derrida makes this clearer a little later in his text, when he explicitly distinguishes the indeed infinite 'idea of justice' that deconstruction invokes from a Kantian type of construal, and indeed from any other construal that thinks of it on the model of a *horizon*.[25] And the reason for this is on the side of interruption rather than the continuous progressive approach: justice is always demanded *now*, in a moment of decision which stands a chance of being just only if it takes on the undecidable (it can never simply be the application of a pre-existing rule), only, therefore, if it escapes any horizon of knowledge such as still rules the Kantian formulation of the Idea. Escaping or exceeding the calculable domain of right in this way, with the incalculable demand of justice (which, however, demands that we calculate with the incalculable) justice-as-decision is never present, always come from the other, a sort of madness, an 'experience of the impossible', as Derrida now regularly says (FL, 57–8 [967–71]). And this means that there is no guarantee that justice is done in the decision: the 'madness' and irreducible alterity of the moment of decision[26] means that what Derrida tends to call 'the worst' is as close as can be to justice, and that the necessary possibility that the attempted just decision be the most unjust decision is written into the possibility of justice (whence the need to compromise, negotiate, with the most concrete detail of current arrangements of right: this is what defines deconstruction as radically political) – this is the concomitant impossibility of the possibility of justice, what is here, and elsewhere, called *aporia*.[27]

'Justice', then, does not function quite in the manner of the 'strange attractor' of Hobson's formulation, or at least only if we can give her sense of 'constant approximation' a reading which removes from it the reassuring teleological overtone it seems to inherit from the Kantian (or other) Idea. It is not so much that there is *on the one hand* an approximation and *on the other* an interruption or short-circuit of that approximation, on the one hand a negotiation and on the other an irruptive or disruptive moment of decision, as she tends to suggest, but that the 'il y a' of justice in the each-time-now of the inaugural decision that justice calls for is simultaneously (1) the approximation and the interruption, *and* (2) the necessary possibility of getting further rather than closer, *either* because the interruption is not an interruption, fails in fact to interrupt (falling back into mere bureaucracy or administration, nowhere near justice, simply the unfolding of a programme, without invention), *or* because the interruption is *too* interruptive, in the sense of being too dislocated from what it is calculated to interrupt, and so fails to interrupt (for example by being a merely pious invocation of the Idea of justice in the familiar way that used to be denounced as formalistic). The 'strange attractor' analogy here is unhelpful if, as we have seen Hobson saying, strange attractors name situations where 'prolongations of certain apparently chaotic series subside within the limits of a certain form': there is no *subsiding* here (nor, strictly speaking, 'limits' or 'form'). Oddly enough, the thought of singularity is much more helpful, if the justice here invoked comes each time singularly from the other, and if, therefore, 'justice' is another nickname ('lexeme') for the general alterity that the trace-structure, or *différance*, is already describing. So that when, summarising this chapter at the opening of the next, Hobson glosses the singularities by saying that 'They induce a pattern of negotiation, while imposing a relation of interruption – ' (p. 147), we might be inclined to agree (with some hesitation as to what logical operator is expressed by 'while'), while not accepting the second half of the same sentence, which seems to want to explain that situation by adding, ' – they attract but are out of reach' (*ibid.*), which seems to fall back into the structure of the Idea. The uncertainty here shows up in Hobson's wanting to make of negotiation and interruption 'two forms of relation to singularities' (*ibid.*), whereas I would want to say that they are *the same*, and that Derrida *says* this.

Hobson moves on to a difficult and very illuminating discussion of Derrida's use of some apparently negative formulations, or paradoxically double negative formulations inspired by Blanchot's use of 'X without X' structures. Again, she wants to say that Derrida's writing (syntax, micrologies) embodies these structures without quite saying them: ' ... the exercising of these negatives through the argument forms a kind of process which is only partially conceptualised there; it is nevertheless at work in the text. This process is a kind of moving on. It makes possible an extension to a formulation of a position without the elaboration being pointed out to the reader' (p. 147). Hobson shows wonderfully well how this structure is to be contrasted with Hegelian negativity, makes her habitual good use of analytic discussions, here of the logic of negation, and luminously lays out the 'pas sans pas' and limping gait of the reading of Freud in *The Post Card*. What is more important in our current perspective is her discussion of what Derrida calls *stricture* in *The Truth in Painting*, for in a passage she quotes (p. 162) Derrida explicitly makes of *stricture* a name (lexeme) of the type of negotiation-as-interruption we are trying to wrest clear of the pervasive Kantian Idea-structure:

The logic of detachment as cut leads to opposition, it is a logic or even a dialectic of opposition. I have shown elsewhere that it has the effect of sublating difference. And thus of suturing. The logic of detachment as stricture is *entirely other*. Deferring [*différante*]; it never sutures. Here it permits us to take account of this fact; that these shoes are neither attached nor detached, neither full nor empty. A double bind is here as though suspended and imposed simultaneously, a double bind which I shall not here attempt to attach strictly to another discourse on the double bind .... Any stricture is *simultaneously* stricturation and destricturation.

> (quoted Hobson, p. 162)

Oddly, though, Hobson does not pursue this logic through the explicit reading of Kant in *The Truth in Painting*, and more especially in the 'Without of the Pure Cut' section of 'Parergon', where Derrida finds *already in Kant* a curious logic of negativity in the analysis of the Aesthetic Judgement and its famous 'purposiveness without purpose' which leads to some of the most radical formulations of the sort of negativity Hobson is trying to pin down: the 'pas sans pas' is further explicated by a focus on the 'sans' [without] itself, a '*without* without negativity or meaning', which allows in 'Pas' the extreme formulation 'sans sans sans' [without without without], describing the logic of stricture which is the unity of negotiation and interruption we are trying to think together.[28]

Hobson's final chapter concentrates all these difficulties into the question of how we are to think of the possibility of coherence or consistency across Derrida's work, given its apparent questioning of such values. How are we to make sense of the intuition that in some deep sense Derrida is constantly saying *the same*, while constantly saying new and surprising things and thematically valorising the new and the surprising? Again, Hobson wants to insist that this version of coherence is not to be found in explicit statement by Derrida so much as in a manner or syntax of writing: 'This particular role of the style of exposition creates an effect which cannot be summarised merely by the explicit statements in Derrida's work ... it is derived from the patterns of the use of language, and goes beyond the words which are explicitly expressed' (p. 188). It is in this chapter that Hobson comes closest to formulating (with Derrida's usually explicit help: it is difficult in fact to find a single example of effects in Derrida's writing which are not *somewhere* described therein) the *single* (singular) logic of the same-as-different – but still she wants to insist, via the 'strange attractor' analogy, that there are 'entities which are out of the web of traces, which are unintuitable and unpresentable, but to which we can have some sort of access, paradoxically and imperfectly, by a process of negotiation and contamination' (p. 201). And this, I think, is just false. 'There is nothing outside the text' certainly claims that there are no such *entities* at all. Hobson's problem here stems no doubt in part from accepting too 'linguistic' a view of 'text' (although she is not entirely clear on this point). But 'text' in Derrida's displaced usage of that term is *already* a 'process of negotiation and contamination', so that 'paradoxical' and 'imperfect' *already* qualify our 'access' to all 'entities' in general. Hobson might of course accept this point and simply shift her vocabulary – but she clearly needs to maintain a distinction between two *sorts* of entities (those in the web and those not in the web), and this is what I believe to be mistaken – I take the whole point of the quasi-transcendental to be that instead of two realms of objects there is only one ('the same'), but that it is in *différance*, i.e. secreting or vomiting candidates for transcendental status, which always fall back down into the milieu from which they arose. Although Hobson certainly does not present the mistaken view in the more common terms with which it has become familiar,[29] she appears to be led into it by the 'strange attractor' *idea*, and wrongly comforted in it by Derrida's allusive remarks in a couple of places to a 'dissociation of thought and language'.

As Hobson recalls, Derrida's early piece on Foucault evokes this question, and in fact does so in just the context of the issue of negativity we have been tracking, and which it is worth resituating in its broader context to see the importance of the issue here:

> And if there is history only of rationality and meaning in general, that means that philosophical language, the moment it speaks, recuperates negativity – or forgets it, which is the same thing – even when it claims to avow or recognise it. Perhaps more securely in that case. The history of truth is thus the history of this *economy* of the negative. We must then return, perhaps it is time to return, to the ahistorical in a sense radically opposed to that of classical philosophy: not to misrecognise but this time to avow negativity – in silence. It is negativity and not positive truth that is the non-historical foundation [*fonds*, bottom, fund and fundament] of history. We would then be dealing with a negativity so negative that it could no longer even be given that name. Negativity has always been determined by dialectics – i.e. metaphysics – as *work* in the service of the constitution of meaning. To avow negativity in silence is to accede to a dissociation of a non-classical type between thought and language. And perhaps between thought and philosophy as discourse; knowing that this schism can only be said, effacing itself therein, in philosophy.[30]

So a non-negative (non-dialectical) thought of the negative, a without without without, leads to the thought of 'something' withdrawn from language, and suggests tentatively that 'thought' (but in a displaced, non-metaphysical sense, i.e. not thought of as *logos* or *dianoia* as against *lexis*) might be a name for that 'something'. In both cases that 'something' nonetheless *shows up* in a certain sense in the language from which it is said to withdraw – the 'something' in question is *said to be unsayable*. But this structure just is that of the trace, as it elaborates its logic as re-trace and re-trait. What escapes the web or the network is nonetheless still 'in' the web or network, which itself 'is' only in or through that re-trac(t)ing. Saying that there are entities to which we can only have imperfect access cannot fail to suggest the Idea of a *perfect* access to such entities, which would be a quite classical thought of God (which is the same thought as the classical thought of thought-without-language or of signified without signifier).[31] The sort of 'access' we might have to the type of negativity we are here discussing must be withdrawn from the alternative of perfect/imperfect if it is to avoid collapsing into just the classical distinctions it is supposed to precede or exceed.

It could be, of course, that nothing important hangs on Hobson's use of the term 'entity' in the passage I have quoted, and that she is expecting a charity on the part of the reader not to assume the implications I appear to have been assuming. She does, after all, go on to talk of the other of language being within language, and thereby, *contra* Wittgenstein, of our not necessarily being quite *silent* about that whereof we cannot speak (p. 212). Unfortunately, however, she is unable to make much progress with specifying the 'something' in question, though she takes the reader through some interesting and valuable reflections on the slightly different question of the plurality and historicity of natural languages in Derrida's work. But in our current perspective the issue will not be solved in this direction: the point is that Derrida is suggesting a thought of 'thought' whereby we can indeed think something beyond the 'bounds of sense' without being committed to construing that something after the fashion of the Kantian Idea. All we have said is that the supposed 'infinite' (let's keep calling it *différance* for the sake of simplicity) is affected by an 'interruption' (in scare-quotes because it does not come along to interrupt something that was there *before* interruption), an 'interruption' which folds back what classically always functions teleologically into the here and now of this singularity, which is thereby rendered as finite as it is infinite (i.e. neither). What Hobson comes preciously close to formulating is that this general structure simultaneously specifies and dislocates or exceeds the singularity, which will always need picking up again after the event which never quite achieved the identity of its happening in a present moment, just because of this same structure.[32] This set-up nowhere secretes entities outside its web (which is not especially linguistic), nor aims at or intends objects, ideas or resolutions in the future: the aim bends round, but the circle doesn't close – and that's thought (or life, or anything else we care to call it, here and now). Which is also why there is in fact no sustainable difference between lexemes and syntax (which is why Hobson ends up saying ' … stratifications, pushes and pulls in intellectual relationships, are syntactically embodied./ But, of course, they are also lexically expressed … ' (p. 226)), and why openings always, also, simultaneously, close.

NOTES

INTRODUCTION

1 Cf. G. W. F. Hegel, *Science of Logic*, II, 3, 2, B: 'The real possibility of something is therefore the existing multiplicity of circumstances which are connected with it ... When all the conditions of something are completely present, it enters into actuality ... its *immediate Existence*, the circle of conditions ... .'

2 GR, 233 [162]. (For abbreviations used in referring to Derrida's work, see above, p. xiii.) See my comments on this passage in 'Deconstruction and the Philosophers (The Very Idea)', in *Legislations: The Politics of Deconstruction* (London: Verso, 1994), 15–16.

3 See Derrida's piece 'Et cetera ... ', tr. Geoffrey Bennington, forthcoming in N. Royle (ed.), *Deconstructions* (London: Macmillan, 2000).

4 Cf. 'L'oreille de Heidegger: Philopolémologie (*Geschlecht* IV)', in PA, 341–419 [tr. J. Leavey in John Sallis (ed.), *Reading Heidegger – Commemorations* (Bloomington: Indiana University Press, 1993)].

5 Both reprinted in *Legislations*.

6 See *Sententiousness and the Novel* (Cambridge: Cambridge University Press, 1984), 168–71, *Dudding: des noms de Rousseau* (Paris: Galilée, 1991), 69–80, and *Legislations*, 1–5.

7 See *La frontière* (Paris: Galilée, 2000).

8 See my essay 'Lecture: de Georges Bataille', in Denis Hollier (ed.), *Georges Bataille – après tout* (Paris: Belin, 1995), 11–34. Cf. too Michel Lisse's *L'expérience de la lecture* (Paris: Galilée, 1998).

1   'JACQUES DERRIDA'

1 First published in Simon Critchley and William Schroeder (eds), *A Companion to Continental Philosophy* (Oxford: Blackwell, 1998), 549–58.

2 See the 'Avertissement' in GEN, and especially pp. vi–vii: 'This reading ... claims the authority of a sort of law the stability of which seems to me today all the more surprising for the fact that, *even in its literal formulation*, it has never ceased, *since then*, to rule everything I have attempted to demonstrate, as though a sort of idiosyncrasy were negotiating in its own way, already, a necessity that would always outstrip it and that would need to be interminably reappropriated. What necessity? Always to do with an originary complication of the origin, an initial contamination of the simple,

197

an inaugural discrepancy that no analysis could *present, make present* in its phenomenon or reduce to the instantaneous, self-identical punctuality of the element.'

2   DERRIDA AND POLITICS

1   'Mochlos, ou le conflit des facultés', in DP, 424 [23].

2   'Ponctuations: le temps de la thèse', in DP, 451 [42].

3   See for example Allan Bloom, *The Closing of the American Mind: How Higher Education has Failed Democracy and Impoverished the Souls of Today's Students* (New York: Simon and Schuster, 1987), 379–80. See too Derrida's notes and references in 'Les pupilles de l'Université: le principe de raison et l'idée de l'Université' (DP, 488 n. 1 [15 n. 8]), and in MEM, 34–6 n. 2 [41–3 n. 5].

4   See my analysis of this motif in 'Demanding History', in *Legislations: The Politics of Deconstruction* (London: Verso, 1994), 61–73. A notable exception to the schema I am analysing here is the work of Ernesto Laclau and Chantal Mouffe, which is arguably the only political theory as such to have engaged seriously with Derrida's work.

5   See for example Terry Eagleton, *Walter Benjamin, or Towards a Revolutionary Criticism* (London: New Left Books, 1981), 138, and Frank Lentricchia, *After the New Criticism* (Chicago: University of Chicago Press, 1980). Michael Ryan's *Marxism and Deconstruction: A Critical Articulation* (Baltimore and London: Johns Hopkins University Press, 1982) is a more interesting case: see my analysis of this book in 'Outside Story' (*Legislations*, 88–98).

6   There were enough discreet signals and reserves to give this description some plausibility, as for example in the piece on Nelson Mandela which comments on Mandela's admiration for Western parliamentary democracy ('Admiration de Nelson Mandela', in PSY, 453–75 [NM]. See too the objections put forward to 'Le dernier mot du racisme' (PSY, 353–62 [RLW]), by Ann McLintock and Rob Nixon in 'No Names Apart: The Separation of Word and History in Derrida's "Le dernier mot du racisme"', *Critical Inquiry* 13/1 (1986), 140–54, and Derrida's reply in 'But, Beyond … ', tr. P. Kamuf, *Ibid.*, 155–70; or see Terry Eagleton's review of SM in *Radical Philosophy* 73 (1995), 35–7. In this context, see too more generally Nancy Fraser's review of some 'Derridean' work on politics: 'The French Derrideans: Politicizing Deconstruction or Deconstructing Politics?', *New German Critique* 33 (1984), 127–54, and Simon Critchley, *The Ethics of Deconstruction* (Oxford: Blackwell, 1992), 200ff.

7   The Heidegger 'affair' began in France with the publication in France of Victor Farias's *Heidegger et le nazisme* (Paris: Verdier, 1987) [*Heidegger and Nazism*, tr. T. Rockmore and J. Margolis (Philadelphia: Temple University Press, 1987)], at almost exactly the same time as Derrida published DE, which explicitly analyses Heidegger's Nazi involvement. Numerous polemical pieces and books followed in France (by, among others, Bourdieu, Lyotard, Ferry and Renaut, Janicaud), with much discussion in the press. The American side of this 'affair' was concentrated around a book edited by Richard Wolin, *The Heidegger Controversy* (New York: Columbia University Press, 1991), and Derrida's disagreement with the publication of one of his interviews in it. The De Man affair began with the discovery by the Belgian scholar Otwin de Graef of a large number of newspaper articles (some of an apparently anti-Semitic nature) the young Paul de Man had written for the Nazi-controlled Belgian newspaper *Le Soir* during the occupation. See the two volumes devoted to these pieces: W. Hamacher, N. Hertz and T. Keenan (eds), *Paul de Man: Wartime Journalism 1939–45* (Lincoln and London:

University of Nebraska Press, 1988), and *Responses: On Paul de Man's Wartime Journalism* (Lincoln and London: University of Nebraska Press, 1989). See especially Derrida's piece 'Like the Sound of the Sea Deep in a Shell: Paul de Man's War', tr. P. Kamuf, *Critical Inquiry* 14 (1988), 590–652, repr. in *Responses*, 127–64, and the issue of *Critical Inquiry* 15 (1989) devoted in part to responses to this piece and Derrida's further reply, 'Biodegradables: Seven Diary Fragments' (812–73). What is striking about these two 'affairs' is on the one hand the alacrity with which supposedly serious scholars were often prepared to make gross and unsubstantiated accusations and assimilations, and on the other Derrida's patience and appetite for arguing with unworthy opponents, for reasons it is hard not to see as political. It is also worth noting that already in the late 1960s Jean-Pierre Faye had (incorrectly and indeed scurrilously) suggested that Derrida was urging an espousal of *mythos* over *logos*, as had been the case with Nazi philosophers. See the account in Elizabeth Roudinesco, *La bataille de cent ans: Histoire de la psychanalyse en France*, vol. 2 (Paris: Seuil, 1986), 542, and Derrida's comments in POS, 75–6 [55–6, and Alan Bass's helpful translator's note 28 on pp. 103–4].

8 See especially AC, SM and PA.

9 The confusion of levels of analysis that this involves is explicitly pointed out in 'Violence et Métaphysique': see ED, 189 n. 1 [129 n. 46].

10 For a fuller explanation of this pervasive structure of Derrida's thinking, first clearly brought out by Rodolphe Gasché in *The Tain of the Mirror: Derrida and the Philosophy of Reflection* (Cambridge, Mass.: Harvard University Press, 1986), see my 'Derridabase', in JD, 248–63 [267–84].

11 The history of Derrida's 'silence' about Marx would merit treatment in itself, starting with what is now quite a complex job of decoding the third of the interviews collected in POS (see especially 85ff. [62ff.], where Derrida famously suggests that his reading of Marx is 'still to come' (85 [62]). That *Spectres of Marx* always might be taken to maintain rather than dissipate Derrida's silence about Marx was illustrated at the 1995 'Applied Derrida' conference in Luton, where, in a general discussion with Derrida, an irritated participant demanded that Derrida say 'what he really thought' about Marx; when politely pointed by Derrida to *Spectres of Marx*, the now angry participant replied that he'd read that, but wanted to know what Derrida *really thought* about Marx ...

12 See my detailed discussion of this gesture with respect to Freud in 'Circanalysis (The thing itself)', Chapter 7, below.

13 One way of reading Derrida's work as a whole is as working through, not only the inheritance of the tradition, but the inheritance of the event of his own early thought: it could be argued, for example, that insights formulated in the early OG (and maybe even GEN) provide the matrix of which all the rest of Derrida's work is the (often surprising) reception.

14 In a companion piece to this, I try to take up some of these issues with respect to the traditional philosophical domain of 'ethics'. See 'Deconstruction and Ethics', Chapter 3 below.

15 A hint of this is given in an aside in the early text on Bataille: 'If the entire history of meaning is gathered and *represented*, at one point in the picture, by the figure of the slave, if Hegel's discourse, the Logic, the Book Kojève is speaking about are servile language or the language of the slave, i.e. working language or the language of the worker, they can be read from left to right or from right to left, as a reactionary

movement or a revolutionary movement, or both at once. It would be absurd for the transgression of the Book by writing to be read in a determinate sense. It would be both absurd, given the form of the *Aufhebung* which is maintained in transgression, and too full of meaning for a transgression of meaning. From right to left or from left to right: these two contradictory and over-meaningful propositions are equally lacking in pertinence. At a certain determined point.

A very determined point. An acknowledged impertinence the effects of which must be carefully watched. Nothing would have been understood of general strategy if one absolutely gave up on controlling the use of this acknowledgement. If one lent it, if one abandoned it, if one put it in either hand: left or right.' ('De l'économie restreinte à l'économie générale: un hégélianisme sans réserve', ED, 369–407 [251–77] (pp. 406–7 [276]); see too the remarks on 'left' and 'right' in 'Mochlos ou le conflit des facultés', DP, 434–7 [31–2].

16 See FL, in the course of which Derrida makes the startling claim that justice (always prior to its formulation as law) is the undeconstructible condition of deconstruction (35 [945]), or that deconstruction *is* justice.

17 I have elsewhere attempted to derive the necessity of this conceptual 'politics' from temporal finitude: see 'Contre (le) temps, pour (le) temps', at http:// www.sussex.ac.uk/Users/sffc4, and pursued the analysis of the appeal to urgency as a mark of the political in 'Emergencies', Chapter 12, below. Richard Beardsworth's important and challenging book *Derrida and the Political* (London: Routledge, 1996), reviewed in 'Emergencies', attempts more ambitiously to derive 'the political' in general from what he calls 'the aporia of time'.

18 PA, 99–100, [81].

19 This is still consistent with the closing sentence of VP, 'La chose même se dérobe toujours': 'the thing itself always escapes [steals away]'.

20 Derrida's 'early' work appeals to the notion of the undecidable (see for example D, 240, 248–9 [211, 219–20], or POS, 58 [42–3], where Derrida insists that this term is being used *analogically*). The explicit claim that undecidability is a positive condition of possibility of decision comes later: see, for example, in the Introduction to PAR, 15: 'But the event – encounter, decision, call, nomination, initial incision of a mark – can only come about from the experience of the undecidable. Not the undecidable which still belongs to the order of calculation, but the other, the one no calculation could anticipate'. It seems to me that Simon Critchley's criticisms of the 'political impasse' of deconstruction are based on a misunderstanding of this relation between undecidability and decision. See *The Ethics of Deconstruction*, ch. 5, in which Critchley finds himself suggesting on the one hand that Derrida is, in the name of the undecidable, reducing 'the factical, the empirical, the contingent, the ontic', and on the other that this condemns him to making decisions themselves 'contingent'. This contradiction in what is generally a helpful account stems from Critchley's desire, in the name of politics, to oppose the empirical to the transcendental in a context (the quasi-transcendental) which de-limits just that opposition.

21 [[Derrida's note:] See *De l'esprit, Heidegger et la question* (Paris: Galilée, 1987), 147 [tr. G. Bennington and R. Bowlby (Chicago: University of Chicago Press, 1989), 94 n. 5] and especially 'Nombre de Oui' in *Psyché* (Paris: Galilée, 1987), 644–50 [tr. B. Holmes, 'A Number of Yes', *Qui Parle* 2/2 (1988), 120–33]]. The analysis of the *Zusage* to which Derrida refers occurs in an enormously long footnote to *De l'esprit*,

which appears to have been added as something of an afterthought to the original text: see my discussion in 'Spirit's Spirit Spirits Spirit', in *Legislations*.

22 PA, 58–9 [38]. This analysis of the 'perhaps' (pursued more informally but more fully in a talk with Alexander García Düttmann at the ICA in London in May 1996 (see the transcript, 'Perhaps or Maybe', in *PLI (Warwick Journal of Philosophy)* 6 (1997), 1–17) appears to involve a shift or radicalisation of the earlier positions here mentioned. The pre-eminent dignity of the *question* appears accepted by Derrida in the 1966 essay 'Violence and Metaphysics', but is duly displaced in the late 1980s in the text on Heidegger to which he refers, as in texts on Joyce from the same period (see especially 'Ulysse gramophone: l'ouï-dire de Joyce' in UG [AL, 256–309]), and then pushed further here. See too my remarks in Chapter 8, below.

23 This sketch of a notion of self-interrupting structures is carried further in 'Le mot d'accueil', in AD, 38–211, esp. 95–8, 117, 146, and is implicit at least since 'Le sans de la coupure pure', in VEP, 95–135 [83–118]. See too Chapter 10, below.

24 See too AP, which also refers to this passage from PA, and, in AD, around a certain silence or non-response in Lévinas as to the rules that would allow the formulation of better mediations between ethics and politics: 'This non-response conditions my responsibility, where I am alone in the duty to respond. Without the silence, without the hiatus, which is not the absence of rules, but the necessity of a leap at the instant of the ethical, juridical or political decision, we would merely have to unroll knowledge into a programme of action. Nothing would be more deresponsibilising and totalitarian' (AD, 201).

25 GR, 69 [47].

26 The thematics of the ghost in SM (as in the earlier improvisations in Ken McMullan's film *Ghost Dance* (1983)) are a further ramification of this trace-structure of alterity, giving rise there to the proposition of a 'hauntology' prior to any ontology.

27 See too AP, 66ff. [33ff.], for an analysis of the figure of the *arrivant*.

28 GR, 149–202 [101–40], and esp. 164–5 [112–13].

29 See especially ED, 171ff. [114ff.]. It must be said that this is a misleading formulation if it implies a simple one-dimensional scale stretching between 'violence' and 'non-violence', and a relatively simple calculation as to where the 'lesser violence' lies. In the light of what we have said about the structure of decision, it follows that any decision made in the name of the 'lesser violence' *always might* be the most violent decision – this radical thought of violence necessarily implies that the violence inherent in decision cannot simply be accurately calculated in advance as more or less violent. That this still follows from the thought of the trace can be judged from the following: 'If one wishes as a last resort to determine violence as the necessity for the other to appear as what it is only, to be respected only in, for and through the same, to be dissimulated by the same in the very liberation of its phenomenon, then time is violence. This movement of liberation of absolute alterity in the absolute same is the movement of temporalisation in its most absolutely unconditioned universal form: the living present ... . Presence as violence is the meaning of finitude, the meaning of meaning as history' (ED, 195 [133]). See too the much later development of some of these themes in AD.

30 Again, this fundamentally archaeo-teleological structure of politics could be illustrated from Aristotle. To this extent, the concept of 'politics' follows a schema first identified by Derrida around the concept of the sign: 'But we cannot do away with the concept of the sign, we cannot give up this metaphysical complicity without

simultaneously giving up the critical work we are directing against it, without running the risk of erasing difference in the self-identity of a signified reducing to itself its signifier, or, what comes to the same thing, simply expelling it outside itself. For there are two heterogeneous ways of erasing the difference between the signifier and the signified: one, the classical way, consists in reducing or deriving the signifier, which is in the end to *subject* language to thought; the other, the one we are here directing against the first, consists in putting into question the system in which the first reduction functioned: and first of all the opposition of sensible and the intelligible. For the *paradox* is that the metaphysical reduction of the sign needed the opposition it was reducing. The opposition forms a system with the reduction. And what we are saying here can be extended to all the concepts and all the sentences of metaphysics ... ' (ED, 413 [281]); see too the remarks at the end of the same piece on 'two interpretations of interpretation', but also the comments on 'two deaths of metaphor' at the end of 'La mythologie blanche' (M, 247–73 [207–29]), and the rather schematic presentation of deconstruction at the end of 'Signature, événement, contexte' (M, 365–93 [307–30]). For a 'formalisation' of this paradoxical situation, see M, 251 [222], and the remarks about doubles and doubling in POS, 48, 56 and n. 4 [35, 41 and n. 8]. Carl Schmitt's claim on Derrida's interest in PA can be motivated not only by his attempt to think decision and the event of exception, but also because of the unusual twist he places on this archaeo-teleological structure: for Schmitt, politics is *regrettably* drawing to an end because of the loss of the ability to define enemies. See PA, ch. 5.

31 This affirmation of endlessness is not, as might appear, an affirmation of what Hegel would call a 'bad infinite', but grows very specifically from a non-Hegelian (and non-Husserlian) understanding of the Kantian notion of the Idea of Reason, which functions in Kant as a way of organising future progress towards something which may well be empirically unrealisable as such, but to which an asymptotic approach is obviously recommendable. Derrida's suspicion of this Kantian motif goes back to his earliest work: see for example OG, 150–55 [134–41]. This is rigorously consonant with the view of the event and the decision we have outlined, and with earlier formulations as to the 'monstrosity' or 'formlessness' of the future.

32 James Joyce, *Ulysses* (Harmondsworth: Penguin Books, 1968), 144.

33 See DP, 435 [31].

34 In SM, this will become the text's major motif, borrowed from Hamlet, that of the 'time out of joint' (see esp. 43ff. [18ff.]). See too PA, 126 [103], and AD, 200.

35 OTO, 23 [10].

36 See too the comment from one of Derrida's earliest papers: 'Ce que je ne peux jamais comprendre, dans une structure, c'est ce par quoi elle n'est pas close' [What I can never understand in a structure is that by virtue of which it is not closed] (ED, 238 [160]).

37 This non-negative status of something that looks like a failing or failure affects more generally all attempts to 'ground' something 'in' something, such as ethics-and-politics in ontology (this is one of the points of *Spectres de Marx*), or even politics itself in ethics, as suggested in Derrida's third essay on Lévinas: 'Let us suppose that one cannot *deduce* from Lévinas's ethical discourse on hospitality a right and a politics, a given right and a given politics in such or such a determined situation today, near us or far away ... . How then are we to interpret this impossibility of grounding, deducing or deriving? Does it signal a failing? Perhaps one ought to say the opposite.

Perhaps we would in truth be called to an other trial by the apparent negativity of this lacuna, by this hiatus between ethics (first philosophy or metaphysics, in the sense Lévinas gives these words, of course) on the one hand, and on the other, right and politics. If there is no lack there, does not such a hiatus require us in fact to think right and politics differently? And above all, does it not open, like a hiatus, precisely, both one's mouth and the possibility of an other speaking, of a decision and a responsibility (juridical and political, if you will) which must be *taken*, as we say of decision and responsibility, with no assurance of there being an ontological foundation? In this hypothesis, the absence of a right or a politics, in the narrow and determined sense of these terms, would be merely an illusion. Beyond this appearance or this convenience, a return would be necessary to the conditions of responsibility or decision. Between ethics, right and politics' (AD, 46–7).

38 The promise is an important motif in the third lecture in MEM, in DE, SM, AC and PA. The logic of the promise is that a promise is worth its name only if there is a necessary possibility that it be broken, so that a promise is partly defined – positively defined – by the *threat* (usually thought of as the opposite of a promise) of its non-fulfilment. 'Democracy' is the political name Derrida associates with this motif. See too Beardsworth's extensive analysis of the promise in *Derrida and the Political* (London: Routledge, 1996), and his reservations about it.

39 This formula, which can still be read as an elaboration of the remarks on the trace from GR, is first developed in DM in the context of a questioning of the distinction made by Kierkegaard between ethics and religion. David Wills comes to the inevitably compromising translation: 'Every other (one) is every (bit) other.'

40 See for example PAS, 42–3 [15].

41 I attempt to follow this logic of exemplarity a little further in 'Derrida's Mallarmé', Chapter 4, below.

3   DECONSTRUCTION AND ETHICS

1 GR, 68 [46].

2 See Derrida's comments on this prospect in PAS, 13–15 [12–14]. Quoted at some length by Simon Critchley in 'The Ethics of Deconstruction: An Attempt at Self-criticism', and by Robert Bernasconi in his remarkable article 'Justice without Ethics', p. 58. Critchley's book *The Ethics of Deconstruction* (Oxford: Blackwell, 1992) remains in many ways a helpful introduction to the issues.

3 FL, 35 [945].

4 Derrida's second text on Lévinas, 'En ce moment même ... ' makes much of instances in Lévinas's writing where he appeals to the present moment of writing or reading in the text itself, showing how such moments are dislocated repetitions of each other, where the text both interrupts itself and gathers up its interruptions into its texture. The inscrutability or indeterminability of deictic or indexical terms in written texts is one of Derrida's favourite features of writing, and the point from which the ambitions of phenomenology are systematically undone: VP already made the pronoun 'je' and the effects of its repeatability a crux of its analyses.

5 The following reflections on reading are summarised from the longer presentation at the beginning of my piece 'Lecture – de Georges Bataille'. Compare Critchley's somewhat different account of 'clôtural reading' in *The Ethics of Deconstruction*.

6   The 'ethics of reading' adumbrated here bears an obvious relation of respectful inheritance (and distance) to the description Heidegger gives in §35 of the *Kantbuch*, but could not quite accept Heidegger's justification of what he sees as the inevitable violence of interpretation by 'the force of an inspirational Idea'. I discuss this in relation to Kant in *La frontière* (Paris: Galilée, 2000). See too J. Hillis Miller, *The Ethics of Reading* (New York: Columbia University Press, 1987).

7   'Admiration de Nelson Mandela', 456 [17]; cf. too 471–2 [34–5], and DP, 82 and 449.

8   This is the point of some of Derrida's objections to Lévinas in 'Violence et Métaphysique': Lévinas opposes to Husserl's difficulties in the *Cartesian Meditations* with the problem of the other the sense that the other is *absolutely* other than me, and Derrida defends Husserl on the grounds that the alterity of the other has a chance of being registered only to the extent that that other is in some sense the *same* as me. The other is only really other to the extent that he, she, or it does not simply fall back into the status of the sort of alterity the objects of the external world can have: the alterity of the other in Lévinas's sense depends, according to this early analysis, on the fact that the other is presumed to be enough like me for its otherness (as 'another origin of the world' in phenomenological parlance) to become salient. Derrida here finds himself in a curious position: *La voix et le phénomène* suggested (without producing detailed analysis) that this issue of the analogical appresentation of the other was, along with the temporal issues attaching to terms in 're-' (repetition, representation, retention), one of the points at which Husserl's phenomenology was at its most vulnerable. In 'Violence and Metaphysics' he appears to be defending Husserl on just this issue, on the grounds that Husserl allows the real alterity of the other to emerge just because of the impenetrability to me of what is nonetheless manifestly an *alter ego*, the *same* as me. The possible coherence of these two gestures is no doubt given by Derrida's complex thinking about 'the same' as constitutively non-identical. Derrida does leave open the possibility of criticising Husserl on this point (ED, 194 n. 1 [316 n. 51]), as indeed he does in VP, and returns briefly to it in AD, 96.

9   I argue this in the particular context of the journal *French Studies* in a paper presented to that journal's 50th annual conference in 1997: 'Faire semblant', probably not forthcoming in *French Studies*. This text is available at http://www.sussex.ac.uk/Units/frenchthought/texts/semblant_frames.htm.

10   See for example Kant, *Critique of Practical Reason*, tr. Mary Gregor (Cambridge University Press, 1997), 69: 'The concept of duty, therefore, requires of the action *objective* accord with the law but requires of the maxim of the action *subjective* respect for the law, as the sole way of determining the will by the law. And on this rests the distinction between consciousness of having acted *in conformity with duty* and *from duty*, that is, respect for the law, the first of which (legality) is possible even if the inclinations alone have been the determining grounds of the will whereas the second (*morality*), moral worth, must be placed solely in this: that the action takes place from duty, that is, for the sake of the law alone.' The Derridean re-writing of this into an obligation to act inventively *out of* duty would position that for the sake of which we should so act not as the law, but as justice, in the sense appealed to in FL, where justice (beyond any formalisation of it as law or right or institution) is presented as the 'undeconstructible condition of deconstruction', or even as deconstruction itself (35 [945]). The apparent ethical pathos generated here needs to be tempered by the necessary possibility of the sort of aping Kant is concerned to exclude: my supposedly

deconstructive invocation of justice as that for the sake of which I act *always might* be a mere simulacrum, and indeed always will be in the absence of invention. Derrida's regular appeals to the need for invention in the fields of ethics or politics necessarily disappoint: we would obviously like to be told what to invent – at which point we would be released from the responsibility of invention …

11 I discuss this gesture in the specific context of Derrida's relation to Freud in 'Circanalysis (The thing itself)', Chapter 7 below.

12 'The quality and fecundity of a discourse are perhaps measured by the critical rigour with which this relation to the history of metaphysics and of inherited concepts is thought through' (ED, 414 [282]).

13 On the question of responding and responsibility, see Gasché's *Inventions of Difference* and my reservations in 'Genuine Gasché (perhaps)', Chapter 11 below. The displacement responsibility operates on ethics probably means that it is at least as compelling to call this a political situation, and one of the points of 'Le mot d'accueil' is to question the distinction between ethics and politics.

14 In 'Violence and Metaphysics', Derrida associates Husserl and Heidegger at least in that they share (1) a commitment to the essentially Greek source of philosophy; (2) a demand for a transgression or reduction of metaphysics, and (3) 'the category of the *ethical* is here not only dissociated from metaphysics, but related to something other than itself, an earlier and more radical instance. When it is not, when the law, the power of resolution and the relation to the other come back to the αρχη, they lose their ethical specificity there' [Derrida's footnote: 'Husserl: "Reason does not tolerate being distinguished into 'theoretical', 'practical' or aesthetic, etc." Heidegger: "Even such names as 'logic', 'ethics', and 'physics' flourish only when original thinking comes to an end": *Letter on Humanism*'] (ED, 121 n. 1 [312 n. 5]).

15 These are, equally spaced at intervals of 16 years: 'Violence et Métaphysique' (1964, in ED), 'En ce moment même dans cet ouvrage me voici' (1980, in PSY [ATM]), 'Le mot d'accueil' (1996, in AD).

16 Lévinas characterises the face at length in section III of *Totalité et infini: essai sur l'extériorité* (The Hague: Martinus Nijhoff, 1961) [tr. Alfonso Lingis, *Totality and Infinity* (The Hague: Martinus Nijhoff, 1969)].

17 See the important essay 'La signification et le sens', in *Humanisme de l'autre homme* (Fata Morgana, 1972; repr. Le Livre de Poche, 1987), [tr. Alphonso Lingis as 'Meaning and Sense', in *Collected Philosophical Papers* (Dordrecht: Martinus Nijhoff, 1987)]. The notions of orientation and disorientation appear insistently in this text: see for example 34, 36, 39, 40, 42, 43, 44 [91, 93, 97, 99]. It would be possible to show, in a parallel reading of Kant's short 1786 text 'What is Orientation in Thinking?' (tr. Barry Nisbet, in H. Reiss (ed.), *Kant's Political Writings*, 2nd, enlarged edn (Cambridge: Cambridge University Press, 1991), 237–49), that the appeal to orientation makes sense only in a prior context of disorientation, so that orientation always retains the trace of the very disorientation it is supposed to overcome. See too Derrida's reflections on the notion of a 'heading' in AC.

18 I use the masculine pronoun to recall the fact that Lévinas has a specific and complex thinking around sexual difference and the feminine. Derrida draws attention to this at the very end of 'Violence et Métaphysique' (ED, 228 n. 1 [320–1 n. 92]), and devotes a large part of 'En ce moment même … ' to discussion of it (PSY, 192–8 [ATM, 39–48]); see too AD, 71–85, on Lévinas's figuring of domestic space as feminine.

19 Lévinas himself introduces this notion of the 'Il', of *illeity* to describe the 'beyond being' from which the alterity of the other issues (cf. 'La signification et le sens', 65 [104], recalled in passing by Derrida in AD, 74 n. 1: Derrida also points out that this co-originarity of the third person is clear in Lévinas from *Totalité et infini* onwards (AD, 111–12)). It is this dimension that allows the transcendence of the other to provide an orientation and to be related to God, and it is crucial for Lévinas to conceive of a 'God not contaminated by being', as he puts it in the 'Preliminary Note' to *Autrement qu'être, ou au-delà de l'essence* (The Hague: Martinus Nijhoff, 1974) [tr. Alfonso Lingis, *Otherwise than Being* (The Hague: Martinus Nijhoff, 1981)]. But for Derrida, just this illeity is the principle of contamination, and just this will ensure that any 'orientation' it might be said to provide must be taken in the context of a greater and more encompassing disorientation. See the explicit commentary on the necessity of contamination in 'En ce moment même … ' (PSY, 182 [ATM, 26]).

20 This is a generalisable structure in deconstructive thought, perhaps most easily grasped in the arguments about life and death in the context of Freud: life is life only to the extent that it protects itself to some extent from itself (pure or unprotected life would be instant death) in an *economy of death* ('Freud et la scène de l'écriture', ED, 300–1 [202]). The same logic works the analysis of the relationship between plea-sure and reality principles in 'Spéculer – sur "Freud" ', CP, 303–11 [283–91].

21 Cf. 'Violence et métaphysique', ED, 136 n. 1, 172, 191 [313 n. 21, 117, 130]. These remarks should not be taken as implying that such a calculation is simple, nor even that we already know what violence is.

22 This 'necessary possibility' argument (that a promise is only a promise if it is neces-sarily possible that it be broken, only if there is the threat that the promise not be kept), suggests that the distinction between a promise and a threat is harder to grasp than might at first appear: the earliest hint of this thinking in Derrida's work appears to be in LI, 141–2 [74–5].

23 The quasi-transcendental argument (the transcendental pendant, as it were, to the quasi-logical argument about necessary possibility) which is *quasi*-transcendental just because of this complication of the levels of empirical/factical and transcendental is already put, rather discreetly it is true, in Derrida's first published work: see OG, 168–9 [150–1]. Cf. my attempt to formalise this situation in 'Derridabase', JD, 248–63 [267–84].

24 See Derrida's explicit appeal to a notion of chance in the context of Lévinas (and of reading) in 'En ce moment même … ', PSY, 175 [ATM, 24]; and more generally in MC, which develops something like an ethics of 'giving chance its chance'.

25 See the short paper 'Nombre de oui', dedicated to Michel de Certeau, which begins with the untranslatable sentence 'Oui, à l'étranger' ('Yes to the stranger' or, as the context goes on to suggest, 'Yes, abroad') (PSY, 639 [NY, 120]).

26 The figure of the *arrivant* arrives in AP as a name for the absolute unpredictability of the event to come. See too Derrida's more informal elaboration of this issue in discussion with Alexander García Düttmann, 'Perhaps or Maybe'.

27 This is the tension that marks Alasdair MacIntyre's influential *Short History of Ethics* (1966; 2nd edn London: Routledge, 1998). MacIntyre wants to associate a founding truth of ethics with a pre-philosophical (for example Homeric) moment at which ethical judgements were tied unproblematically with social function, and so writes a book devoted to lamenting ethics as the history of the loss of this (pre-) ethical truth. We might want to say against this that ethics only begins with the (primary) divorce

between function and action, and that this is just a version of the pre-ethical opening of ethics. Ethics on this view would be bound up with its necessary *impossibility*, which could not then reasonably be the object of the sort of nostalgic pathos given to it by MacIntyre.

28 Derrida discusses Schmitt at length in PA, and recalls that discussion in 'Le mot d'accueil' (AD, 52 n. 2).

29 Here too, ethics would involve a certain experience of the impossible, which Derrida is happy to associate with deconstruction as such. This is of a piece with the sense of an obligation to be inventive or creative. For a non-deconstructive view of the link between creativity and impossibility, see Margaret Boden, *The Creative Mind* (London: Weidenfeld and Nicolson, 1990). It seems to me that Simon Critchley miscontrues the logic of decision by associating it with a 'decided' use on his own part of the language of the tradition, and by insisting in the light of *that* decision on *opposing* the factical or the contingent to what he can then only understand as Derrida's transcendentalism (*The Ethics of Deconstruction*, 43 and ch. 5).

30 See Derrida's developments of this theme in work on Joyce (UG), and, in more autobiographical vein, MON. This theme of the constitutive other-in-me is, naturally enough, developed in Derrida's work on Freud: see especially MA, 124–5 [78–9], and the untranslatable formula 'L'un se garde de l'autre'.

31 Cf. 'La guerre des noms propres', in GR, 157–73 [107–18], and the distinguishing there of three levels of violence. On the 'opening' of ethics, see esp. 202 [140]: 'Archi-writing is the origin of morality and of immorality. Non-ethical opening of ethics. Violent opening.' On the paradoxical relationship of names and their bearers, see too 'L'aphorisme à contretemps' (PSY, 519–33 [AL, 414–433]).

32 See Chapter 1, above, p. 12.

33 It is curious that Derrida has nowhere published a detailed analysis of this moment in the *Greater Logic*, which he cites, apparently with approval, in 'Violence and Metaphysics' (ED, 227 n. 1), but which he evokes more critically in POS, 59–61 [43–4].

34 This is already the effect of the analysis of the trace in the *Grammatologie*, where the choice of that term is, interestingly enough, in part motivated by Lévinas's own usage (GR, 102–3 [70]). The trace is explicitly presented in the *Grammatologie* as opening up the areas of language, temporalisation, and the relation to the other (GR, 69 [47]).

35 'War does not merely line up – as the greatest of them – among the trials that morality lives on. It renders morality derisory. The art of foreseeing and winning war by any means – politics – then imposes itself as the very exercise of reason. Politics is opposed to morality as philosophy is opposed to naivety' (*Totalité et infini*, ix [21]).

36 See especially DM, 114–57 [82–115], PA, 259 [232], and MA, 123 [77].

4   DERRIDA'S MALLARMÉ

1 First published in Michael Temple (ed.), *Meetings with Mallarmé in Contemporary French Culture* (Exeter University Press, 1998), 126–42.

2 A note on the title-page of the article explains that in fact Derrida's text originally had no title, 'La double séance' being supplied by the review *Tel Quel*.

3 This distinction between the theoretical and the practical will not, naturally enough, survive the deconstructive process, but it is worth pointing out that Derrida's other text on Mallarmé ('Mallarmé', in *Tableau de la littérature française*, vol. 3 (Paris:

Gallimard, 1974), 369–78) stresses this value of the practical in a context where many other familiar terms are being placed in question: ' ... we are beginning to glimpse there has been some machination (...) to outplay the categories of history and of literary classifications, of literary criticism, of philosophies and hermeneutics of all sorts. We are beginning to glimpse that the upsetting of these categories was also the effect of what was, by Mallarmé, written.

We can no longer even speak of an *event* here, the event of such a text; we can no longer interrogate its *meaning* without falling back short of it, into the network of values it has *practically* placed in question; that of event (presence, singularity, singularity without possible repetition, temporality, historicity)' (369: all italics Derrida's); and again at the end, arguing that Mallarmé cannot be contained within the philosophical representation of rhetoric: 'His text escapes the control of the representation, it demonstrates *practically* its non-pertinence' (378).

4   In *Diderot: Thresholds of Representation* (Columbus: Ohio State University Press, 1986), James Creech takes issue with Derrida's claim in 'La double séance' (D, 216–17 n. 12 [190 n. 18]) that even Diderot does not escape this programme. In a 'postscript' entitled 'Idealism and Reversal: On a Note by Jacques Derrida' (172–4), Creech argues that something other than the reversal of Platonism Derrida attributes to Diderot is happening in the latter's texts. This is indubitably the case, but can be presented as *critique* of Derrida only if one fails to note the difference between the moment in Derrida at which an 'official' doctrine is being reconstructed, and the moment at which that official doctrine is shown necessarily to be untenable on its own terms. It is true that Derrida nowhere produces this second moment with respect to Diderot, nor indeed with respect to many other authors further commentators can then enjoy themselves defending.

5   Derrida discusses at some length the very considerable complexities of the text by Paul Margeritte that Mallarmé refers to, and summarises as follows: 'a mimodrama "takes place", unscripted gestural writing, a preface is projected then written *after* the "event" to precede a script written *after the fact*, reflecting the mimodrama instead of commanding it' (226 [199]).

6   This structure of what it is tempting to call 'reflexivity' is often the source of misapprehension: cf. Descombes's complaints about a similar moment in Foucault, which I discuss in 'Outside Language', *Oxford Literary Review* 11 (1989), 89–112. Rodolphe Gasché devastatingly pointed out the error of some 'deconstructive criticism' in identifying deconstruction with reflexivity: cf. 'Deconstruction as Criticism', in *Inventions of Difference: On Jacques Derrida* (Cambridge, Mass.: Harvard University Press, 1994).

7   I discuss this structure in the context of deixis more generally in 'Index', *Legislations: The Politics of Deconstruction* (London: Verso Books, 1994), 274–95.

8   In 'Psyché: invention de l'autre' (in *Psyché: inventions de l'autre* (Paris: Galilée, 1987), 11–61), Derrida develops a similar argument around Francis Ponge's 'Fable', which begins 'Par le mot *par* commence donc ce texte/ Dont la première ligne dit la vérité' [With the word *with* begins then this text/ Whose first line tells the truth']: 'Dans le corps d'un seul vers, sur la même ligne divisée, l'événement d'un énoncé confond deux fonctions absolument hétérogènes, "usage" et "mention", mais aussi hétéro-référence et auto-référence, allégorie et tautégorie' (23). [In the body of a single line, on the same divided line, the event of a statement confuses two absolutely heterogeneous functions, 'use' and 'mention', but also hetero-reference and self-reference, allegory and tautegory.] The undecidability about use and mention Derrida exploits

here and elsewhere (cf. for example ESP, 52 [29–30]) can in fact be extended to the seminal Fregean distinction between *Sinn* and *Bedeutung*, as I try to show in forthcoming work. The principle of these arguments can be given by Derrida's simple claim in *Limited Inc.* that 'la différance est la référence'. [*Différance* is reference.]

9 I use 'official' here to refer to the doctrine most obviously put forward by Plato's text, the reading most obviously encouraged by it. It is axiomatic in deconstructive thinking that such a reading always co-exists more or less uneasily with other textual resources it cannot by definition control.

10 Cf. 248 [219] : 'The Mime *plays* from the moment he bases himself on no real action, and tends to no verisimilitude. Play always plays difference without reference, or rather without referent, without absolute exteriority, i.e. just as well without interiority.'

11 D, 239 [211]: 'Le référent étant levé, la référence demeurant.' [The referent lifted, reference remaining.]

12 To this extent, all the remarks about ghosts in 'La double séance' anticipate the 'hauntology' developed much later by Derrida in SM.

13 This involves Derrida's acceptance of a famous Hegelian argument from the *Greater Logic*. Absolute difference collapses back into absolute identity. Cf. G. W. F. Hegel, *The Science of Logic*, Book II, Section I, ch. 2, and Derrida's comments in POS, 59–60 and n. 6 [43–4 and 101 n. 13], and at the end of 'Violence et Métaphysique', ED, 117–228 (p. 227 n. 1) [79–153 (p. 320 n. 91)].

14 Cf. the remarks in *Positions* on a 'strategy without finality'. It is important not to read this concept of strategy as leading to a political voluntarism, where readings would be dictated by desired political outcomes determined in advance of the reading. This was the mistake which inspired a certain sort of 'left' deconstruction, as recommended and variously practised by Tony Bennett and Terry Eagleton among others. See my remarks in 'Inter', in McQuillan, MacDonald, Purves and Thomson (eds), *Post-Theory: New Directions in Criticism* (Edinburgh: Edinburgh University Press, 1999), 103–19.

15 Cf. 282 [250]: 'S'il y a un système textuel, un thème n'existe pas' [If there is a textual system, a theme does not exist].

16 'Excès irréductible du syntaxique sur le sémantique' [Irreducible excess of the syntactic over the semantic] (250 [221]), 'excès de la syntaxe sur le sens' [excess of syntax over meaning] (261 [231]). Syntax here refers to the fact that meaning is not to be understood as atomically specifiable, but, in the wake of the Saussurean view of language and differences-without-positive-terms, as relational or 'lateral'. It would be interesting to compare this notion of syntax to the notion of 'grammar' developed by Wittgenstein.

17 Cf. 204, 291, 293, 312 [178, 259, 261, 279–80].

18 Cf. the discussion of 'entre', leading to 'We are no longer even justified in saying that "between" is a purely syntactic element. Apart from its syntactic function, by the remark of its semantic emptiness, it begins to signify.* Its semantic emptiness *signifies*, but it signifies spacing and articulation; its meaning is the possibility of syntax and it orders the play of meaning. *Neither purely syntactic, nor purely semantic*, it marks the articulated opening of that opposition. [*Derrida's note: 'Given this, the syncategoreme "between" has as its meaning-content a semantic quasi-emptiness, it signifies the relation of spacing, articulation, the interval, etc. It can allow itself to be nominalised, become a quasi-categoreme, receive a definite article, or even the mark of the

plural. We said "between(s)" and this plural is in some sense "first". One "between" does not exist.'] (251–2 and n. 27 [222 and n. 36]).

19 Cf. 267ff. [237ff.] on the letter *i*.

20 Cf. for example the very prudent progression in *La voix et le phénomène* from a reasonably traditional use of 'commentaire' and 'interprétation' to a reading '*A travers* le texte de Husserl, c'est-à-dire dans une lecture qui ne peut être simplement ni celle du commentaire ni celle de l'interprétation' VP, 98 [88]. On the concept of analysis, see esp. 'Résistances' (in RP, 13–53 [1–38], and esp. 41ff. [25ff.] on the complex relation of deconstruction to analysis: let us say provisionally that deconstruction is the *hyperbolic exasperation* of analysis.

5   R.I.P.

1 This previously unpublished paper was presented to the 'Futures, for Jacques Derrida' conference at the University of Alabama, Tuscaloosa, in September 1995.

2 *The Rhetoric of Romanticism* (New York: Columbia University Press, 1984), 81.

3 64a–b; tr. Hugh Tredennick: cf. too 67d–e: 'If a man has trained himself throughout his life to live in a state as close as possible to death, would it not be ridiculous for him to be distressed when death comes to him? ... Then it is a fact Simmias, that true philosophers make dying their profession [αποθνηισκειν μελετωσι: practise dying] and that to them of all men death is least alarming.'

4 *Phaedo*, 68c. The argument is that goodness is to be had not in an economic system of exchanges of emotions (so the non-philosophical version of courage exchanges one fear for another, and that of temperance one pleasure for another), but in the absolute measure of wisdom, which is to be approached only through philosophy as the sort of living death we have seen. Cf. too 82b–d. The application of a 'logical' criterion to ethical questions might provide a further link to our later discussion of Kant.

5 79c–d, for example, makes very clear the link between death and transcendence that Derrida insists on in, for example, 'Signature, Event, Context' (M, 375 [316]): 'Did we not say some time ago that when the soul uses the instrumentality of the body for any inquiry, whether through sight or hearing or any other sense – because using the body implies using the senses – it is drawn away by the body into the realm of the variable, and loses its way and becomes confused and dizzy, as though it were fuddled, through contact with things of a similar nature?

[...]

But when it investigates by itself, it passes into the realm of the pure and everlasting and immortal and changeless, and being of a kindred nature, when it is once independent and free from interference, consorts with it always and strays no longer, but remains, in that realm of the absolute, constant and invariable, through contact with beings of a similar nature. And this condition of the soul we call wisdom.'

The earlier section I have been quoting has made it clear that this condition of the soul called wisdom is in fact attained only in death: 'If [true philosophers] are thoroughly dissatisfied with the body, and long to have their souls independent of it, when this happens would it not be entirely unreasonable to be frightened and distressed? Would they not naturally be glad to set out for the place where there is a prospect of attaining the object of their lifelong desire – which is wisdom [φρονεσις] – and of

escaping from an unwelcome association? Surely there are many who have chosen of
their own free will to follow dead lovers and wives and sons to the next world, in the
hope of seeing and meeting there the persons whom they loved. If this is so, will a
true lover of wisdom who has firmly grasped this same conviction – that he will never
attain to wisdom worthy of the name elsewhere than in the next world – will he be
grieved at dying? Will he not be glad to make that journey? We must suppose so, my
dear boy, that is, if he is a real philosopher, because then he will be of the firm belief
that he will never find wisdom in all its purity in any other place. If this is so, would it
not be quite unreasonable, as I said just now, for such a man to be afraid of death?'
(67e–68b).

6 *Phenomenology of Spirit*, tr. Miller (Oxford: Oxford University Press, 1977) §32. That
Socrates is proposing a general dialectics is clear from the development which aims to
establish that the soul must have been alive before the body and must survive the
body's death, beginning at 70d: 'Let us see whether it is a necessary law that everything which has an opposite is generated from that opposite and from no other
source.'

7 This is a tempting reading, which would centre on the moment of Socrates's past
enunciation as reported in the 'current' discourse by Phaedo to Echecrates, that enunciation stretching through the time of *arrêt de mort* between the dawn and dusk of the
day of execution, which itself of course occurs only after the much longer *arrêt de
mort* provoked by the coincidence of the date of the pronunciation of Socrates's death-
sentence, his *arrêt de mort* in the usual sense, and the departure of the ritually
garlanded Athenian ship for Delos.

8 This possibility (what I earlier called the 'half-life' of philosophy) returns explicitly in
Socrates's reconstruction of Cebes's objection to the doctrine of the immortality of
the soul: 'Indeed [the soul's] very entrance into the human body was, like a disease,
the beginning of its destruction; it lives this life in increasing weariness, and finally
perishes in what we call death' (95d). Socrates's long refutation of this view, however
it may convince Cebes, leads, precisely via the supposedly established immortality of
the soul, to the intractable problem that that very immortality brings with it the risk
that the soul will carry evil (i.e. bodily contamination) with it into the next world,
the existence of which has nonetheless been proven by appeal to the soul's essential
purity with respect to just such bodily contamination. The subsequent fable of the
souls of the dead being led to Hades by a guardian spirit provides us with another link
to Kant via the motif of *guiding* which it entails (107e–108a). The fact that according
to this fable souls cannot easily find their *own* way into the underworld spawns further
aporias I cannot detail here.

9 See my detailed discussion of this motif in Kant in *La frontière* (Paris: Galilée, 2000).

10 Derrida is often thought of as generating paradoxical formulations, as though the
discovery of paradox were the end of deconstruction. But it seems to me he is still a
traditional enough philosopher to see in paradox a challenge to thinking which must
be taken up, rather than held up for admiration. The 'I am dead' deduction in VP, for
example, is less concerned merely to be striking and shocking than to show up an
insuperable problem (or an uneradicable dogmatism) in the concept of the transcendental ego insofar as that concept allows and indeed entails that deduction.

11 See 'Circumfession', in JD, 18 [16].

12 I cannot here attempt to do justice to Lyotard's development of the figure of child-hood in texts from the mid-1980s onwards. See esp. *Lectures d'enfance* (Paris: Galilée, 1991), and my analyses in 'Before' and 'Childish Things' (forthcoming).

13 ' ... the wandering of a thought faithful and attentive to the world irreducibly to come announcing itself [*qui s'annonce*: English words like 'looming' or 'brewing' might catch this better in some ways, but would lose the allusion to the annunciation] in the present, beyond the closure of knowledge. The future can only be anticipated in the form of absolute danger. It is what breaks absolutely with constituted normality and can therefore announce itself [*s'annoncer* again], *present* itself, only in the form of monstrosity' (GR, 14 [4–5]). Derrida has of course reflected on these formulations and the apocalyptic impression they make in TA, in the context of a reading of Kant very germane to what I shall be attempting to argue shortly, and in 'Comment ne pas parler' (in PSY [HAS]). At the time of first writing this chapter, I had not been able to read 'Résistances', where there is an explicit link of birth and death to the concept of 'analysis': 'for what here doubles the *archeological* motif of analysis, is here an *eschato-logical* movement, as if analysis carried extreme death and the last word, just as the archeological motif in view of the originary would be turned towards birth' (RES, 33 [20]).

14 See my essay 'De la fiction transcendantale', in Michel Lisse (ed.), *Passions de la littéra-ture: pour Jacques Derrida* (Paris: Galilée, 1996), 141–60.

15 Emmanuel Kant, *Prolegomena to any Future Metaphysics that Will be Able to Come Forward as Science*, tr. James W. Ellington, rev. Paul Carus (Indianapolis: Hackett, 1977), 94.

16 Cf. too 'Is it time?', Chapter 9 below.

17 In AP, Jacques Derrida reminds us, in the context of a discussion of death, of Cicero's reflexion on the Latin translation of the Greek *telos*, and the suggestion that it might advantageously be translated by the Latin *finis*. The whole of what I will be suggesting here might be summarised in the phrase 'the end is the end'.

18 See especially SM. The analysis of Kant that follows is a slightly earlier version of what appears in French as the beginning of Chapter 6 of *La Frontière*.

19 Cf. too *Anthropology from a Pragmatic Point of View*, §42.

20 This attempt has at the very least many affinities with what Peter Fenves exposes around the notion of 'tone' in Kant, and especially about how only attention to tone allows philosophy to avoid the twin deaths of peace on the one hand and *Schwarmerei* on the other. See Peter Fenves (ed.), *Raising the Tone of Philosophy* (Baltimore and London: The Johns Hopkins University Press, 1993).

21 At Dartford, to the east of London, north-bound vehicles cross the Thames through a tunnel, whereas south-bound vehicles cross using a bridge over the same spot. This gives a working image of the relationships in Kant between theory and the practical.

22 *Being*-law of law is of course already too ontological a formulation of this situation, but the fact that there is no satisfactory non-ontologising alternative – 'law of law' being perhaps not ontological *enough* – tends to confirm Kant's point about the origi-nality of the practical realm. Cf. Derrida's point against Lévinas's proposal of an 'Ethique de l'Ethique', in 'Violence et métaphysique', ED, 164 [111], in its complex relation with the Law.

23 With the same proviso as in the previous note, we might say that this pre-prescription shows up as a sort of prior 'Obey me!' which forms the being(?)-prescription of the prescription.

24 As Peter Fenves has so brilliantly insisted: cf. *A Peculiar Fate: Metaphysics and World-History in Kant* (Ithaca and London: Cornell University Press, 1991).

25 Cf. too §64, which argues that the contingency of certain natural objects in terms of any mechanical explanation calls for a teleological explanation, and §67, which extends this logic to the whole of nature considered as a system. This antinomy of judgement between mechanical and teleological explanation is complicated by the fact that its *apparent* resolution (according to which one or other type of explanation is adopted as appropriate or convenient by a judgement appealing to each only as a subjective maxim) tends to conceal another 'resolution' whereby nature as a whole, considered as a totality, cannot be thought of as subject to the mechanical causal laws which are to be preferred for intra-natural explanation. This leaves the curious situation in which teleological explanations are *necessary for necessity*.

26 In the third *Critique* Kant describes an object as monstrous 'if by its magnitude it nullifies the purpose that constitutes its concept' (§26), in the immediate context of the remarks about the colossal that form the object of the fourth section of the 'Parergon' section of VEP.

27 Cf. my very preliminary discussion of this relationship in *Dudding: des noms de Rousseau* (Paris: Galilée, 1991), 143–8.

28 This would be the point at which, sometime in the future, to append an analysis of Heidegger's analysis of Kant's analysis of reading from §35 of the *Kantbuch*.

6   X

1 This paper was presented to the 'Applied Derrida' conference, University of Luton, 1995, and published in John Brannigan, Ruth Robbins and Julian Wolfreys (eds), *Applying: To Derrida* (London: Macmillan, 1996), 1–20.

2 By 'common view', I mean less something to do with the currency of the view in question than something to do with the fact that it is not based on a *reading* of the text in question, but on a received version of its content.

3 This is an extremely gross summary of Hegel's argument in the *Greater Logic*, I, 2, B, β, tr. A. V. Miller (Atlantic Highlands: Humanities Press, 1969), 131–6. Cf. Gillian Rose's helpful commentary in *Hegel Contra Sociology* (London: Athlone Press, 1981), 187–92. I take issue with Rose's version of Hegel's version of Kant in work in progress.

4 Elsewhere, and indeed just a little earlier in the text, Kant tends to identify the X and the *noumenon* so long as this latter is thought *negatively*, as indeed, he suggests he thinks it. Cf. A255/B310–11: 'The concept of a noumenon is thus a merely *limiting concept*, the function of which is to curb the pretensions of sensibility; and it is therefore only of negative employment. At the same time it is no arbitrary invention; it is bound up with the limitation of sensibility, though it cannot affirm anything positive beyond the field of sensibility.'

5 *Kant and the Problem of Metaphysics*, §5. Heidegger reserves his discussion of the X 'itself' until a much later section of his book (§25), after the detailed – and controversial – reading of the schematism. Heidegger reads the X as the 'term of prior orientation' or the 'horizon', the object of 'ontological knowledge', and proceeds to interpret this in his own terms from *Being and Time*. This is not the place to discuss in detail Heidegger's reading, which moves on a little later to discuss the place of logic, and particularly transcendental logic, in the first *Critique*: on the one hand, he

recognises the importance of *application* in transcendental logic, which confirms a certain dignity of the 'intuition' side of knowledge; but on the other, he suggests that Kant is obliged to borrow from scholastic structures of logic in order to organise his account, but that this is more a question of external exposition than internal dynamic. Heidegger's own reading moves in a direction we might call phenomeno-logical: in *La Frontière* (forthcoming), I propose a different sort of reading which tracks Kant's ana-logics rather than his phenomeno-logics.

6   In *Contemporary Literature* 36/1 (1995), 173–200.

7   I discuss at length Kant's remarks about reading Plato and Leibniz, and Heidegger's reading of some of those remarks, in *La Frontière*.

7   CIRCANALYSIS (THE THING ITSELF)

1   This is a translation (and slight enlargement) of a paper written in French and deliv-ered to the 1996 Colloque de Cerisy *Depuis Lacan*, forthcoming in P. Guyomard (ed.), *Depuis Lacan* (Paris: Flammarion, 2000).

2   JD, 87 [69–70], quoting CP, 273 [256]: 'I will ask myself what, from my birth – or more or less – onwards "turning around" has meant.'

3   Which does not prevent many allusions to psychoanalysis, and a direct reference to Melanie Klein (132 [138]). And cf. 217 [233]: 'comme le don la confession doit être de l'inconscient, je ne connais pas d'autre définition de l'inconscient' [like a gift confession must be from the unconscious, I know no other definition of the uncon-scious].

4   Serge Leclaire, *Psychanalyser* (Paris: Seuil, 1968), 25.

5   *Ibid.*, 26.

6   We should have to follow, for example, what each says of 'flair' (Leclaire, 26; GR, 223 [162]).

7   *Psychanalyser*, 69.

8   I refer here to the polemic launched by Alain Badiou around the 'Lacan avec les philosophes' conference, especially aimed at the title announced by René Major for his own paper: 'Depuis Lacan: y a-t-il une psychanalyse derridienne?'. See the docu-ments presented in the Appendix of the volume *Lacan avec les philosophes* (Paris: Albin Michel, 1991), 423–52. It goes without saying that at many points my paper will intersect with Major's.

9   This is the lecture reprinted as 'Reason from the Unconscious', tr. Geoffrey Bennington and Rachel Bowlby, *Oxford Literary Review* 12 (1990), 9–29.

10 In the case of Lévinas, indeed, Derrida is famously on record as saying he never has any objections, which might be taken as a declaration that he subscribes to *all* Lévinas's propositions … (Jacques Derrida and Pierre-Jean Labarrière, *Altérités* (Paris: Editions Osiris, 1986)).

11 And we know about Derrida's reservations with respect to the classical concept of fraternity: see PA.

12 This (often misused) pair of expressions might be translated as 'Nothing less than' and 'Anything but' respectively.

13 Cf. just before: '*There is no out-text*. And this not because Jean-Jacques's life does not interest us in the first place, nor the existence or Maman or Thérèse *themselves*, nor because we only have access to their so-called "real" existence in the text and have no means of doing otherwise, and no right to neglect this limitation. All reasons of this

type would already suffice, naturally, but there are more radical ones … ' (GR, 228 [158]).

14 Robert Castel, *Le psychanalysme* (Paris: Minuit, 1976).

15 ED, 314 [212].

16 This motif of the call would be worth following throughout Derrida's work, from the early OG, 155 and 156 n. 2 [141 and 142 n. 170], where hearing is played off against seeing, at least to the 'Viens' of TA, *passim*, and the texts on Blanchot in PAR: see especially 204–18, and beyond to the very recent work on responsibility.

17 Pelican Freud Library, 15 vols, 1973–86, vol. 11: *On Metapsychology*, ed. Angela Richards (Harmondsworth: Penguin, 1984), 334.

18 'The Rhetoric of Blindness: Jacques Derrida's Reading of Rousseau', in *Blindness and Insight: Essays in the Rhetoric of Contemporary Criticism* (Minneapolis: University of Minnesota Press, 1983).

19 This schema informs, for example, Barbara Johnson's reading of the Derrida–Lacan issue, in 'The Frame of Reference: Poe, Lacan, Derrida', in R. Young (ed.), *Untying the Text* (London: Routledge, 1981); Shoshana Felman's account of Derrida and Austin, in *The Literary Speech Act: Don Juan with J. L. Austin or Seduction in Two Languages* (Cornell University Press, 1983); and all of Gillian Rose's remarks on Derrida, notably in *Dialectic of Nihilism* (Oxford: Blackwell, 1984). On Zizek, see my remarks in *Legislations*, 6 n. 8.

20 See Derrida's remarks in 'As if I Were Dead', in John Brannigan, Ruth Robbins and Julian Wolfreys (eds), *Applying: To Derrida* (London: Macmillan, 1996), 212–16.

21 See too a reference to 'the thing itself' in PA, 100 [82].

22 In RES, 93–146 [70–118].

8   FOREVER FRIENDS

1 This previously unpublished paper was first delivered to a conference devoted to *The Politics of Friendship* at the Institute of Contemporary Arts, London, November 1997.

2 See my *Dudding: des noms de Rousseau* (Paris: Galilée, 1991).

3 In 'Derridabase' (JD).

4 This view of love receives one of its definitive formulations in Benjamin Constant's *Adolphe*. See for example: 'Malheur à l'homme qui, dans les premiers moments d'une liaison d'amour, ne croit pas que cette liaison doit être éternelle …

L'amour supplée aux longs souvenirs, par une sorte de magie. Toutes les autres affections ont besoin du passé. L'amour crée, comme par enchantement, un passé dont il nous entoure. Il nous donne, pour ainsi dire, la conscience d'avoir vécu, durant des années, avec un être qui naguère nous était presque étranger. L'amour n'est qu'un point lumineux, et néanmoins il semble s'emparer du temps. Il y a peu de jours qu'il n'existait pas. Bientôt il n'existera plus. Mais tant qu'il existe, il répand sa clarté sur l'époque qui l'a précédé, comme sur celle qui doit le suivre.'

[Unhappy the man who, in the first moments of a liaison of love, does not believe that liaison to be eternal.

Love supplies the want of long memories by a sort of magic. All other affections have need of the past. Love creates, as though by enchantment, a past with which it surrounds us. It gives us, so to speak, the sense of having lived for years with a being who was only recently almost foreign to us. Love is but a point of light, and yet it seems to take hold of time. A few days ago it did not exist. Soon it will exist no longer. But while it exists, it spreads its light over the time preceding it, and that to come.] (Benjamin Constant, *Adolphe* [1816] (Paris: Flammarion, 1989), 81, 77–8. My translation.)

5 J.-L. Nancy, *La communauté désoeuvrée* (Paris: Bourgois, 1986), tr. P. Conner, *The Inoperative Community* (Minneapolis: University of Minnesota Press, 1991).

6 On this motif, see FS, 40.

7 See ESP, 147–54 n. 1 [129–36 n. 5].

8 Cf. my commentary in 'Spirit's Spirit Spirits Spirit', in *Legislations*.

9 On the death of Lyotard, six months after this paper was delivered, see Derrida's piece ' "Amitié-à-tout-rompre" ', in *Libération*, 22/4/98, in which he says, 'Jean-François Lyotard remains one of my closest friends … '.

10 *Libération*, 7/11/95, 37–8.

9   IS IT TIME?

1 Lewis Carroll, *Through the Looking-Glass: And What Alice Found There* (London: The Folio Society, 1962), 47.

2 Jacques Derrida, *Spectres de Marx*, 60 [31].

3 Revelation, 1:3.

4 This paper was delivered to a conference on 'The Moment', University of Warwick, November 1998, and subsequently at the Unversity of Sussex and the State University of New York, Albany.

5 According to Diogenes Laertes, the notion of seizing or grasping time goes back to Pittacos of Mitylene, one of the so-called seven sages.

6 Agamben, Badiou, Lyotard and Derrida all have recent work on St Paul, for example. See Agamben's seminar series at the Collège International de Philosophie, Paris, 1998–9; Alain Badiou, *Saint Paul, la fondation de l'universalisme* (Paris: PUF, 1997); Jean-François Lyotard, *D'un trait d'union* (Sainte-Foy (Quebec): Les presses du griffon d'argile and Presses Universitaires de Grenoble, 1993) [tr. Pascale-Anne Brault and Michael Naas, with other texts by Lyotard and Eberhard Gruber as *The Hyphen: Between Judaism and Christianity* (Amherst, N.Y.: Humanity Books, 1999)]; Derrida, VS. This nexus, and the very different versions of Paul that emerge from it, would merit a separate discussion.

7 'This meditation too is untimely, because I am here attempting to look afresh at something of which our time is rightly proud – its cultivation of history – as being injurious to it, a defect and a deficiency in it; because I believe that we are all suffering from a consuming fever of history and ought at least to recognise that we are suffering from it … it is only to the extent that I am a pupil of earlier times, especially the Hellenic, that though a child of the present time I was able to acquire such untimely experiences. That much, however, I must concede to myself on account of my profession as a classicist: for I do not know what meaning classical studies could have for our time if they were not untimely – that is to say, acting counter to our time and thereby acting on our time and, let us hope, for the benefit of time to come.', tr. R. J. Hollingdale, in D. Breazeale (ed.), *Untimely Meditations* (Cambridge: Cambridge University Press, 1997), 60.

8 *Theses on the Philosophy of History*, tr. Harry Zohn, in *Illuminations* (London: Fontana, 1992) XVIII B, p. 255. Derrida quotes from this in SM, 95–6 n. 1 [180–1 n. 2].

9 A properly careful typology of thoughts of 'the moment' would of course need to be much more differentiated than I can attempt to be here: for example, it would have to distinguish this interruptive moment from the sort of totalising or epiphanic moments found in, for example, Woolf and Joyce.

10 And also, of course, inheriting something of his eschatology from a Judaic tradition. See for example W. D. Davies, *Paul and Rabbinic Judaism*, 2nd edn (London: SPCK, 1955).

11 In context: 'For he saith, I have heard thee in a time accepted [*kairos dektos*], and in the day of salvation have I succoured thee: behold, now *is* the accepted time; behold, now *is* the day of salvation'. Naturally enough, if the thematics of the *kairos* are inseparable from the language of fruition, pregnancy and childbirth, it is not surprising that the birth of Christ should be the best example of the *kairos*: 'when the fulness of the time [*pleroma kronos*] was come, God sent forth his Son, made of a woman, made under the law.' (Galatians 4:4) Cf. too Ephesians 1:9–10: 'Having made known unto us the mystery of his will, according to his good pleasure which he hath purposed in himself: / That in the dispensation of the fulness of times [*ekonomian tou pleromatos ton kairon*] he might gather together in one all things in Christ, both which are in heaven and which are on earth.' Also I Timothy 2:6 and 6: 14–15, where the expression *kairois idiois*, the proper time or its own time, can, according to Herman Ridderbos, be taken as synonymous with the expressions for 'fullness of time [*pleroma tou chronou*]' or just 'the moment [*ton kairon*]'. See H. Ridderbos, *Paul: An Outline of his Theology* [1966], tr. J. R. de Witt (Grand Rapids, Mich.: Eerdmans, 1975), 47 n. 12. It is striking that there is always a moment of repetition in this thought of the moment: in separating the Old from the New, the *kairos* always makes the New into some form of repetition of the Old, and the Old some form of anticipation of the New. (See Hebrews 8 and 9, and of course the whole thematic of re-birth in e.g. John 3:3–8, where Jesus is answering Nicodemus: 'Jesus answered and said unto him, Verily, verily, I say unto thee, Except a man be born again, he cannot see the kingdom of God. (4) Nicodemus saith unto him, How can a man be born when he is old? can he enter the second time into his mother's womb, and be born? (5) Jesus answered, Verily, verily, I say unto thee, Except a man be born of water and *of* the Spirit, he cannot enter into the kingdom of God. (6) That which is born of the flesh is flesh; and that which is born of the Spirit is spirit. (7) Marvel not that I said unto thee, Ye must be born again.'). And of course if the presence of the *kairos* is determined as always-going-to-have-been, then it is in some sense *already* a repetition ... We would need to explore carefully the relationship of this thinking with that of Benjamin, for whom the *Jeztzeit* emerges from a sort of non-linear superimposition (a 'constellation' (*Theses*, XVIII A)) of past and present, a nonidentical repetition, and in which the figure of redemption is difficult to separate from this thematic of rebirth. We should also point out a further ambivalence in Paul's thought of the moment, which is also often the 'now' of worldly existence as opposed to the 'now' of salvation: see Ridderbos, 52: 'It is this remarkable ambivalence of the "now", which can have the sense of the "*already* now" of the time of salvation that has been entered upon as well as of the "*even now*" of the world time that still continues, which imparts to Paul's eschatology its wholly distinctive character'; and cf. *ibid.*, 487 ff. on the future this opens up: the first coming is the moment of fulfilment of time, but it opens up the perspective of the need for a second coming to fully achieve that fulfilment. This complication of the now is increased if we take into account more than does Ridderbos the reflexive or

auto-graphical 'now' through which the text refers to its own enunciation or inscription – this *textual* now that contaminates any other nows and opens the text to its own future reading is something we shall pursue a little later. It is perhaps worth pointing out that these temporal expressions occur much more frequently in the epistles of Paul than in other parts of the Bible.

12 Cf. II Thessalonians 2:6–8: 'And now [*nun*] ye know what witholdeth that he might be revealed in his time [*en tou autou kairo*]. / For the mystery of iniquity doth already work: only he who now letteth *will let*, until he be taken out of the way. / And then shall that Wicked be revealed, whom the Lord shall consume with the spirit of his mouth, and shall destroy with the brightness of his coming [*epiphaneia tes parousias autou*].' It is this feature of the *kairos* that justifies the appeal to the prophetic character of the Old Testament, and the thought that this is the prepared fulfilment of God's promise made 'before the world began' (Titus 1:2).

13 The choice of Hegel here is of course overdetermined, but we might attempt to summarise that overdetermination by saying that the specifically Hegelian concept of 'moment' as a specific stage in a dialectical process has *already* gathered up the more interruptive sense we are also trying to understand. It goes without saying that the 'Hegel' presented here is the Hegel of the 'official' version, and makes no attempt to do more than posit as inevitable that another, more interruptive thought of the moment could also be found inhabiting his text. For some sense of that other thought, see Catherine Malabou, *L'Avenir de Hegel: Plasticité, temporalité, dialectique* (Paris: Vrin, 1996), and Derrida's remarks in 'Le temps des Adieux: Heidegger (lu par) Hegel (lu par) Malabou', *Revue philosophique* 1 (1998), 3–47.

14 This would then be the taking up again of the gage or wager laid down ten years ago in 'Deconstruction and the Philosophers', where I propose to 'argue against anybody that deconstruction really is a thinking of and for the present, for now, *en ce moment même*' (*Legislations: The Politics of Deconstruction* (London: Verso, 1994), 44). Cf. on the same page the argument that the 'old names' deconstruction uses 'are not provisional stand-ins in view of a perfected language to come: the necessary imperfection of these words means they are just fine as they are, nothing could do better *this time* … '.

15 G. W. F. Hegel, *Introduction to the Philosophy of History*, tr. J. Sibree [1899] (New York: Dover Books, 1956).

16 See, among many references, the remark to §146 of the *Encyclopedia*, where Hegel says straightforwardly enough, 'The problem of science, and especially of philosophy, undoubtedly consists in eliciting the necessity concealed under the semblance of contingency.' The fact that contingency in Hegel is *sublated* rather than simply denied or abolished again suggests the necessity of a more complex account of their relation than the 'official' words of Hegelianism might suggest. Cf. J.-M. Lardic, *La contingence chez Hegel* (Arles: Actes Sud, 1989); Malabou, *op. cit.*; and Bernard Mabille, *Hegel: l'épreuve de la contingence* (Paris: Aubier, 1999).

17 Whence Hegel's persistent illustrative use of the figures of seed and plant to expound the movement of spirit, in, for one example among many, the *Lectures on the History of Philosophy*: 'The seed is simple, almost a point; even the microscope cannot discover much in it; but this simplicity is large with all the qualities of the tree … This evolution comprises a succession. The root, the trunk, the branches, the leaves and flowers … all these determinations, all these moments are absolutely necessary and have as their aim the fruit, the product of all these moments and the new seed.'

18 This motif of tying together past, present and future would be worth pursuing as a rhetorical figure, often in surprising places. See, for example, the very end of the *Traumdeutung*, or the passage from Nietzsche quoted above, note 7. See too Revelation 1:8, 'I am Alpha and Omega, the beginning and the ending, saith the Lord, which is, and which was, and which is to come, the Almighty'; cf. also 1:18–19: 'I am he that liveth, and was dead; and, behold, I am alive for evermore, Amen; and have the keys of hell and death;/ Write the things which thou hast seen, and the things which are, and the things which shall be hereafter.'

19 Cf. the return of this verb in the review of Malabou, *art. cit.*, 10.

20 See my discussion of this passage in a different context in 'R.I.P', Chapter 5, above.

21 The place for this explicit development is none the less already given by the earlier identification in VP of Husserl's determination of being as presence as an 'ethico-theo-retical' act or decision (VP, 59 [53]; cf. too VP, 6 [7]).

22 Cf. Benjamin, 'Theses on the Philosophy of History', XIV: 'Fashion has a flair for the topical, no matter where it stirs in the thickets of long ago; it is a tiger's leap into the past. This jump, however, takes place in an arena where the ruling class gives the commands. The same leap in the open air of history is a dialectical one, which is how Marx understood the revolution'. Compare Derrida's remarks about fashion at the beginning of 'Force and Signification' (ED, 10 [4]).

23 Derrida quotes this text in *Spectres de Marx*, 95–6 n. 1 [180–1 n. 2], and elsewhere in the book is prepared to claim that deconstruction only ever made sense to him as a radicalisation of Marxism (SM, 151 [92]), and see 152 n. 1 [184 n. 9] for a thematisa-tion of the word 'radicalise' and its insufficiencies (tied to the motif of the 'root' which inhabits it, and the tendency of that motif to assume a root that is, at root, unified and singular).

24 SM, 102 [59].

25 GL, 258a–260a [231a–233a].

26 Cf. the reflexions on 'inventive' reading in the Malabou review, *art. cit.*, 14.

10   ALMOST THE END

1 A shorter version of this paper was delivered to the 1998 Centre for Modern French Thought conference on 'Critique and Deconstruction'. Fuller versions were subse-quently presented at the Universities of Nottingham, Memphis and Vanderbilt.

2 It is this tendency that gives rise to the persistent assimilation of deconstruction and negative theology: see 'La différance' (M, 6 [6]); TA; 'Comment ne pas parler' (in PSY [HAS]); SN.

3 See the analysis of this persistent Derridean motif in Céline Surprenant, 'In Spite of Appearances', *Fragmente* 'Psychoanalysis and Poetics', ed. D. Marriott and V. Lebeau, 8 (Summer 1998), 39–53.

4 And this 'topology' is also true of the relation of deconstruction more generally to metaphysics: deconstruction can reasonably claim to be the least metaphysical of discourses to the extent that it is also as close as can be to metaphysics, *right up against it.*

5 RES, 33 [19–20].

6 We should of course be careful about making too neat a pairing here of analysis with the archaeological and critique with the teleological: in 'Résistances', Derrida finds a teleological or eschatological character in the second constitutive motif of analysis:

'decomposition, unbinding, unknotting, deliverance, solution, dissolution or absolution, and by the same token final completion; for what doubles the *archeological* motif of analysis is here an *eschatological* movement, as though analysis carried with it extreme death and the final word, just as the archeological motif in view of the originary would be turned towards birth' (RES, 33 [20]). The same text goes on to distinguish deconstruction both from 'the Kantian analytic and its dialectical [Hegelian] critique', where the motif of analysis would come under the general Kantian sense of critique, and a different ('general') sense of critique invoked against it. Part of our problem and our task is to recognise this complexity in the sense of 'critique'. It is also true that many of Derrida's earlier texts are concerned to bring out a solidarity of the archaeological and the teleological, as for example towards the end of 'Ousia and Grammè', discussing the figure of the circle in Aristotle's account of time (M, 68–70 [59–61]).

7   AD, 96–7; cf. too 117, 146, 201. It is no accident that this interruptive moment is associated with the ethical (and in fact more strictly political) moment, as we shall see.

8   'Teleology: The Meaning of History and the History of Meaning', GEN, 245–83.

9   You will remember how Kant uses the notion (concept, Idea) of 'Idea': concepts have objects which are possible objects of experience; Ideas have 'objects' which lie beyond the bounds of any possible experience. The 'transcendental illusion' consists in taking the objects of Ideas as though they were the objects of concepts, i.e. as though they could give rise to *knowledge*.

10 Cf. 156 n. 2: 'L'Idée peut seulement s'*entendre*'. This motif of the call will, of course, as is often the case in Derrida later be the object of fuller and more explicit treatment: see especially the essay 'Of an Apocalyptic Tone Recently Adopted in Philosophy', which is of course largely devoted to Kant.

11 See HOS.

12 Much more attention has been devoted to the 'Critique of Aesthetic Judgement'. Kant himself describes the Aesthetic Judgement as the essential part of the third *Critique*, on the grounds that it is the 'pure' part of Judgement, providing the transcendental principle of the formal purposiveness of nature for our cognitive abilities: the teleological judgement relies on this to go on to postulate (always problematically) an *objective* purposiveness in nature, which can never be *proved*, but can only be *assumed* in the interests both of our ability to cognise nature, and of our sense of our practical destination. The teleological judgement functions 'impurely' in the theoretical domain, but just that impurity gives it its interest for us, once we develop the general sense of a constitutive impurity of the transcendental itself. (The following pages are a condensed summary of a much longer reading of the Teleological Judgement in Chapter 5 of *La Frontière*. All quotations are taken from the translation by Werner S. Pluhar (Indianapolis: Hackett, 1987); but I often use the word 'end' to translate Kant's *Zweck*, traditionally translated as 'purpose': this allows some resources (more easily suggested by the French term *fin*) to be brought into play.) It might be added that the teleological judgement fell into some disrepute on more scientific grounds: Darwinism is widely thought to provide a non-teleological view of just those items of nature that Kant thought could *only* be understood teleologically. It would not be difficult to show that the current fortune of a popular science writer such as Richard Dawkins (and in fact the cultural authority of much 'science' more generally) draws its polemical authority and attraction from a Darwinian appeal to the power of

mechanical explanations over teleological ones; but also that Dawkins's view are, in spite of themselves, and in spite of his persistently aggressive remarks about philosophy more generally, teleological through and through (his fundamental thought, that of the 'selfish gene', cannot not be teleological). Dawkins's apparently intransigent and even heroic denunciation of religious illusion can simply enough be read as the uncontrolled symptomatic return of that repressed element in his own thought.

13 'Once we adopt the principle that there is an objective purposiveness in the diverse species of creatures on earth and in their extrinsic relation[s] to one another as purposively structured beings, it is reasonable to think of the[se] relation[s] as having a certain organization in turn, and forming a system, of all the natural kingdoms, in terms of final causes. And yet it seems that experience flatly contradicts such a maxim of reason, especially [the implication] that there is an ultimate purpose of nature. An ultimate purpose of nature is certainly required for such a system to be possible, and we cannot posit it anywhere but in man: But man too is one of the many animal species, and nature has in no way exempted him from its destructive forces any more than from its productive forces, but has subjected everything to a natural mechanism without a purpose' (§82).

14 It seems that this structure is exactly congruent with the one Derrida attributes to Gödel's concept of undecidability, as it is read by Husserl: 'Thus undecidability has a revolutionary and disconcerting sense, is *itself* only to the extent that it remains essentially and intrinsically haunted in its original meaning by the *telos* of decidability whose disruption it marks' (OG, 40 n. 1 [53 n. 48]).

11   GENUINE GASCHÉ (PERHAPS)

1   Reviewing Rodolphe Gasché, *Inventions of Difference: On Jacques Derrida* (Cambridge, Mass.: Harvard University Press, 1994). First published in *Imprimatur* 1/2–3 (1996), 252–7. Gasché's earlier *The Tain of the Mirror: Derrida and the Philosophy of Reflection* (Cambridge, Mass.: Harvard University Press, 1986) is the object of extensive discussion in 'Deconstruction and the Philosophers (The Very Idea)', in my *Legislations: The Politics of Deconstruction* (London: Verso, 1994), 11–60.

2   This is confirmed rather than challenged by the remarkable frequency in these essays of the rhetorical gesture which consists in saying things like, 'I must here *limit* myself to … '. See for example pages 181, 183, 185, 195, 206.

3   I make this argument in 'Deconstruction and the Philosophers (The Very Idea)', 26–7, and urge the superiority of 'quasi-transcendental', which has the advantage of marking its nonpropriety from the start. Gasché in his Introduction 'recalls' that his earlier use of 'infrastructure' was 'strategic', 'Other terms would have served equally well, "undecidables," or "the law of the law," for example' (p. 5), and refers the reader to Derrida's own comments on the use of the term in *Acts of Literature*, ed. Derek Attridge (New York and London: Routledge, 1992), 70–2, where Derrida says, however, that the term 'troubles me a bit', and 'I think it has to be avoided.'

4   Cf. p. 231, 'Although "Ulysses Gramophone" certainly performs what it establishes through its argumentative procedures and thus has "literary" features, there is also ample evidence that this text belongs to philosophy', and p. 234, 'A genuine philosophical question is at the center of "Ulysses Gramophone".'

5   E.g. pp. 83 and 144.

6   Note 14 to Chapter 8 shows how Zizek's rather feeble attempt at a Hegelian refutation of Derrida relies on a misreading of the structure of the *Greater Logic*.

7   'For what mode of relating do [these texts] most properly call?' (p. 1).

8   'Any genuine response ... a genuine response ... the *yes* of the genuine response ... any genuine response ... any genuine response ... the essential risk of failing to genuinely respond ... a genuine response ... a genuine response ... ' (pp. 199–204).

9   'Truly achieve an adequate encounter ... Any adequate response' (pp. 153, 228).

10 *Eigen*, proper, one's own; *Eigenheit*, particularity, property; *eigentlich*, proper, true, genuine, etc. Derrida has of course drawn attention to these terms and their implications in Heidegger, around the latter's *Eigentlichkeit* (authenticity); M, 154–5 n. 16 [129 n. 25].

11 Cf. Heidegger's link of the question of truth and the question of the proper and the genuine at the beginning of 'On the Essence of Truth', tr. John Sallis, in D. F. Krell (ed.), *Martin Heidegger: BasicWritings* (London and Henley: Routledge and Kegan Paul, 1978), 117–42 (p. 119).

12 As one example among many, cf. Kant, *Critique of Pure Reason*, A235–6/B294–5: 'We have now not merely explored the territory of pure understanding, and carefully surveyed every part of it, but have also measured its extent, and assigned to everything in it its rightful place. This domain is an island, enclosed by nature itself within unalterable limits. It is the land of truth – enchanting name! – surrounded by a wide and stormy ocean, the native home of illusion, where many a fog bank and many a swiftly melting iceberg give the deceptive appearance of farther shores, deluding the adventurous seafarer ever anew with empty hopes, and engaging him in enterprises which he can never abandon and yet is unable to carry to completion. Before we venture on this sea, to explore it in all directions and to obtain assurance whether there be any ground for such hopes, it will be well to begin by casting a glance upon the map of the land which we are about to leave, and to enquire, first, whether we cannot in any case be satisfied, inasmuch as there may be no other territory upon which we can settle; and secondly, by what title we possess even this domain, and can consider ourselves as secured against all opposing claims.'

13 Cf. most recently FS, 39 ff. In a complex argument, Derrida tries to show how this structure 'mechanically' generates God and religion, which would thus have the same root as reason and techno-science – and I unpack this more fully in a discussion of recent work by Richard Beardsworth and Bernard Stiegler, Chapter 12, below.

14 In fact, as Derrida's work since *Of Spirit* has shown, the time or place of responsibility, and the nexus of 'concepts' accompanying it (pledge, promise, faith, hope, affirmation, etc.) precedes that of the question. To that extent, making responsibility into a *question* already guarantees an *irresponsible* response.

15 This 'perhaps' just is what is marked in the 'quasi-' of the quasi-transcendental, and is exposed more explicitly in PA, 46 ff. [26 ff.], where Derrida also invokes an essay by Gasché not included in the present volume, and goes on to show how the *question* is secondary to the 'perhaps'. See too Chapter 8, above.

16 Even this, which is part of Gasché's critique of Mark Taylor, is probably too rapid. It is, for example, tempting to seek something 'opaque' and singular in what we might naively call Gasché's *style*, with its discreet but insistent marks of linguistic alterity. Although the book is thus *signed* on every page, Gasché's own text nowhere provides for such an approach to his work.

17 Gasché's new attempt to correct his earlier presentation, however, is still historicist through and through: although he is quite correct to insist on the naivety of trying to present Derrida's work as an absolute break with the tradition (he has no difficulty in showing in dialectical style that this is in fact the most traditional presentation (pp. 59–60)), he nowhere elaborates on the curious (ancient and unprecedented) structure whereby 'Derrida' as the othering of tradition is everywhere *in* the tradition. What we might call for shorthand the non-historical becoming-Derrida of Plato is both funnier and spookier than Gasché's account allows for.

18 This is why, shockingly enough, none of Derrida's arguments really depends on the historical accuracy of any of his comments on the authors he reads. It is at least sometimes a salutary exercise to read Derrida as though Plato, Hegel and the rest were his inventions, and wonder what difference it would make. See too Chapter 7, above.

12   EMERGENCIES

1   Martin Heidegger, 'Vom Wesen und Begriff der φυσις: Aristoteles, Physik B, 1' (1939), in *Wegmarken* (*Gesamtausgabe*, vol. 9; Frankfurt am Main: Vittorio Klostermann, 1976), 257. My translations from this text are guided by the French version by François Fédier in *Questions I et II* (Paris: Gallimard, 1968), 471–582 (here, pp. 511–12), and the English version by Thomas Sheehan, in *Man and World* 9 (1976), 219–70 (p. 235).

2   Reviewing Bernard Stiegler, *La technique et le temps, 1. La faute d'Epiméthée* (Paris: Galilée, 1994), and Richard Beardsworth, *Derrida and the Political* (London: Routledge, 1996). This is a shortened version of an article first published in the *Oxford Literary Review* 18 (1997), 205–46. For reasons of space, and given the focus of this volume, I have cut developments about Kant and Heidegger from the section about Stiegler's book.

3   Immanuel Kant, 'Preface' to *Critique of Judgement*, tr. Werner S. Pluhar (Indianapolis: Hackett, 1987), 8.

4   Cf. Plato, *Theatetus*, 155d, and Aristotle, *Metaphysics*, A, 982b, 12, for a start.

5   Cf. Georges Bataille, pushing the logic of this philosophical precipitation to a certain limit, in *Theory of Religion*: 'the response of the philosopher is necessarily given before philosophical elaboration and if it changes in the elaboration, even because of the results, *it cannot in principle be subordinated to them*. The response of philosophy cannot be an effect of philosophical work, and if it cannot be arbitrary, this assumes that from the start are given scorn for the position of the individual and the extreme mobility of thought open to all earlier or *future* movements; and, linked from the start to the response, or better, consubstantial with the response, the lack of satisfaction and unfinished nature of thought' (*Oeuvres complètes*, vol. 7 (Paris: Gallimard, 1976), 287–8). Deconstruction is the most rigorous attempt to think in the thought of the irreducibility of precipitation: cf. Derrida's recent 'there is always too little time left' (RES, 39 [25]), or the reflections on lateness at the beginning of VS.

6   I argue this point in a talk given for the launch of the journal *Le Contretemps* in February 1995. The text is available for downloading via http://www. sussex.ac.uk/Users/sffc4.

7   *Hegel's Science of Logic*, tr. A. V. Miller (Atlantic Highlands: Humanities Press, 1969), 34 and 42.

8 So, for example, Aristotle says, in a passage referred to by Hegel in his preface, that metaphysics is the freest and therefore highest science (*Metaphysics* A, 982b, 4 ff.), but in the *Nicomachean Ethics* (I, 1094a, 24 ff.) that Politics is that science ('the supreme and architectonic science *par excellence*'). The articulation of philosophy and political freedom in Hegel (cf. the opening of the *Lectures on the History of Philosophy*) is still caught up in this undecidability. This confusion or uncertainty at the highest point of philosophy is, arguably, primarily a confusion in the concept of *law*, out of which the distinction between descriptive law and prescriptive law, knowledge and ethics emerges more or less violently.

9 Beardsworth, co-translator with George Collins of Stiegler's book, also has a long review article urging its importance: 'From a Genealogy of Matter to a Politics of Memory: Stiegler's Thinking of Technics', *Tekhnema* 2 (1995), 85–115. Beardsworth is prepared to go so far as to claim that Stiegler's book 'is a work the importance of which can be compared, in the continental tradition at least, with Heidegger's *Being and Time* [and this is a comparison Stiegler's title clearly invites] and Derrida's *Of Grammatology*' (p. 87). The present discussion will try to indicate why, despite the very considerable merits of Stiegler's book, that assessment may be a little exaggerated.

10 The second volume, subtitled *La désorientation*, appeared in 1996, and involves lengthy and fascinating analyses of, especially, memory and its 'industrialisation': I cannot here elaborate on the questions these analyses call for.

11 A little later this reaction of 'stupefaction' returns when Stiegler, drawing on Jean-Pierre Vernant, shows how in Greek thought the irreducibility of *eris* (discord) in human affairs flows directly from the *eris* introduced between mankind and Zeus by Prometheus's theft: 'It is stupefying ... to note the fundamental *negligence*, the *forgetting* of this Promethean origin which is almost constitutive of modern and contemporary philosophical analyses of Greek religion and politics ... ' (p. 199 [192]).

12 Many other Derrida texts could be taken to illustrate this bizarre 'logic', which Stiegler is not wrong to think is that of *différance* 'itself'. One of the more interesting in this context would be '*No Apocalypse – Not Now (à toute vitesse, sept missiles, sept missives)*', in PSY [NA].

13 Page 30 [17]. Cf. p. 40 [26]. On p. 91 [77] Stiegler suggests that technical objects form a third term which is not answerable to the metaphysical determinations of *physis* or *tekhnè*.

14 For a very different exploitation of this motif, see David Wills's remarkable *Prosthesis* (Stanford University Press, 1995).

15 'The zootechnological relation of man to matter is a special case of the relation of the living creature to its *milieu*, a relation of man to *milieu* that goes via an organised inert matter, the technical object. The singularity is that the inert but organised matter that the technical object is *itself evolves in its organisation*: so it is not *simply* an inert matter, and yet no more is it a living matter. *It is an organised inorganic matter which transforms itself in time like living matter transforms itself in its interaction with its milieu.* What is more, it becomes the interface through which the living matter that man is enters into a relation with the milieu.' (p. 63 [49]).

16 In the passage to this effect that Stiegler quotes from the *Grammatology*, Derrida immediately qualifies this 'appearing as such' by calling it 'a new structure of non-presence'. As an earlier and dense deduction in the *Grammatology* has shown, the trace is such that its 'appearing as such' entails the hiding or effacing of its 'as such'.

17 Cf. the formally identical reproach in *La désorientation*, p. 43, on the specificity of phonetic writing.

18 I am here explicitly at issue with Richard Beardsworth's presentation of these same passages in his review article, pp. 110 ff.

19 'The twenty-first century approaches, and it is clear that our political concepts, and, therefore, the fields in which these concepts are discursively organized, acquire meaning and operate, need to be reinvented' (p. xii); 'the reinvention of politics for the next century' (p. 48); 'political imagination in the next century will be limited' (p. 96).

20 'Perhaps there is no "vulgar concept of time". The concept of time belongs through and through to metaphysics and it names the dominance of presence. We must then conclude that the whole system of metaphysical concepts, throughout their history, develops that 'vulgarity' of this concept (what Heidegger would no doubt not contest), but also that one cannot oppose to it an *other* concept of time, since time in general belongs to metaphysical conceptuality. If one tried to produce this other concept, one would rapidly see that one was constructing it with other metaphysical or onto-theological predicates' (M, 73 [63]).

21 Cf. the drawing reproduced in '+R', in VEP, 179 [158].

22 Contrary to Stiegler, Beardsworth talks well and at length about Kant, but again this is a Kant who could well respond differently if read more patiently, especially perhaps on the problem of insurrection and revolution, where it is possible to show that Kant, perhaps in spite of himself, has a much more 'revolutionary' understanding of revolution than most revolutionaries. To put it bluntly, revolution is revolutionary only to the extent that it is always a crime carried out in the name of justice.

23 Beardsworth himself would no doubt retort that I am the one doing the singularising, because he in fact sets up a *double* aporetics, of time *and* law. But however important law quite rightly is in Beardsworth's book, and however illuminating his analyses of it, he states unequivocally at the beginning of Chapter 3, '*the aporia of law is an aporia of time*', and, a little later, 'The unsurpassable violence of law (its aporia) is predicated on the *delay of time*. Any act of legislation always arrives too early and/or too late ... the need to justify the law – to give it meaning, to conceal its violence and make it effective – is only derivatively a question of ideology or of power. It is, firstly, a question of disavowing time' (pp. 99–100).

24 The two texts in question are the 'Exergue' to *De la grammatologie* (the one Beardsworth quotes), and the end of the famous 1966 essay 'La structure, le signe et le jeu dans le discours des sciences humaines'. See too Chapter 5.

25 This 'speculation' is worth quoting in full:

'Let me conclude with a loose speculation, imagining for one moment two possible futures of Derrida's philosophy.

The first would be what one may call within classical concepts of the political a "left-wing" "Derrideanism". It would foreground Derrida's analyses of originary technicity, "avoiding" the risk of freezing quasi-transcendental logic by developing the trace in terms of the mediations between human and the technical (the very process of hominization). In order to think future "spectralisation" and establish a dialogue between philosophy, the human sciences, the arts and the technosciences, this future of Derrida's philosophy would return to the earlier texts of Derrida which read metaphysical logic in terms of the disavowal of *techne*.

The second could be called, similarly, a "right-wing" "Derrideanism". It would pursue Derrida's untying of the aporia of time from both logic and technics, maintaining that even if there is only access to time through technics, what must be thought, articulated and witnessed is the passage of time. To do so, this Derrideanism would mobilise religious discourse and prioritise, for example, the radically "passive" nature of the arts, following up on more recent work of Derrida on the absolute originarity of the promise and of his reorganisation of religious discourse to think and describe it' (p. 156).

Beardsworth's gesture in proposing this scenario only immediately to refuse it really might be described by the operator of disavowal.

26 'Foi et savoir', *op. cit.*; J. Derrida and B. Stiegler, *Echographies: de la télévision* (Paris: Galilée, 1996). Cf. the following footnote from the first of these: 'In a digitalised "cyberspace", prosthesis on prosthesis, a heavenly, monstrous, bestial or divine eye, something like a CNN eye keeps permanent watch: on Jerusalem and its three monotheisms, on the unprecedented number, speed and scope of the journeys of a Pope now versed in televisual rhetoric (whose last encyclical, *Evangelium vitae*, against abortion and euthanasia, for the sacredness or holiness of the healthy and safe life – intact, *heilig*, holy – for its reproduction in conjugal love – supposed to be the only *immunity*, along with the celibacy of the priesthood, against the human immuno-deficiency virus (HIV) – is immediately distributed, massively marketed and available on CD-ROM; they ceedeeromise even the signs of presence in the eucharistic mystery); on pilgrimages by aeroplane to Mecca; on so many miracles live (usually healings, i.e. returns to the intact, *heilig*, holy, indemnisations) followed by ads in front of 10,000 people on an American television show; on the international and televisual diplomacy of the Dalaï-Lama, etc.

So remarkably fitting in with the scale and evolutions of world demography, so tuned to the technoscientific, economic and media power of our time, the *witnessing* power of all these phenomena is thus massively increased as it is gathered in digitalised space, by supersonic aeroplane or audiovisual antennae. The ether of religion will always have been hospitable to a certain spectral virtuality. Today, like the sublimity of the starry sky within our hearts, ceedeeromised, cyberspaced religion is also the accelerated and hypercapitalised relaunch of the founding spectres. On CD-ROM, celestial trajectories of satellites, jet, TV, e-mail or Internet networks. Actually or virtually universalisable, ultra-internationalisable, embodies by new "corporations" more and more freed from State powers (democratic or not, basically it matters little, all that is up for revision, like the "mondialatinity" of international right in its current state, that is on the threshold of a process of accelerated and unforeseeable transformation).'

27 Cf. Pascal's *Pensée* 5 (Lafuma), my translation: 'A letter of exhortation to a friend to encourage him to seek. And he will reply: but what use will seeking be, nothing appears. And reply to him: do not despair. And he would reply that he would be happy to find some light. But that according to this religion even if he were to believe in this way it would do him no good. And that this being the case he may as well not seek. And at this point reply to him: The Machine.', and, again from Derrida's 'Foi et Savoir': 'Presupposed at the origin of every address, come from the other itself *addressed to it*, the wager of some promise under oath can not, immediately taking God as its witness, cannot not have already, if we can put it like this, engendered God quasi-mechanically. Ineluctable *a priori*, a descent of God *ex machina* would put on stage a transcendental machine of the address' (*op. cit.*, 39), or: ' … perhaps we could

try to "understand" how the imperturbable and interminable development of critical and technoscientific reason, far from being opposed to religion, carries it, supports it and supposes it. We would have to demonstrate – it won't be easy – that religion and reason have the same source. (We are here associating reason to philosophy and to science *qua* technoscience, *qua* critical history of the production of knowledge, of knowledge *as* production, know-how and intervention at a distance, tele-techno-science always by essence high-performance and performative, etc.) Religion and reason develop together, from this common resource: the testimonial gage of every performative, which engages one to reply as much *before* the other as *for* the high-performing performativity of technoscience. The same single source divides mechanically, automatically, and reactively opposes itself to itself: whence the two sources in one' (*ibid.*, 41). And *passim*.

13   AN IDEA OF SYNTAX

1   Reviewing Marian Hobson, *Jacques Derrida: Opening Lines* (London and New York: Routledge, 1998). A short portion of this chapter appeared as part of a more general review in *Paragraph* Vol. 22, No. 3 (1999), 319–31.

2   See for example POS, 77–8 [57], or M, 392–3 [329–30].

3   See Derrida's remarks on expressivism in POS, 45–6 [33–4].

4   But see my 'Derridabase', in JD, 122–3 [128].

5   Hobson pursues the issue of metaphor in her final chapter, which is working closer to the surface of Derrida's interest in language and the plurality of languages as a sort of transcendental *factum* for philosophy.

6   *Marges: de la philosophie* (Paris: Minuit, 1972), 304 [254–5]. This refers back to an earlier barbed reference to Foucault and the need for 'a new delimitation of corpuses and a new problematic of signatures' (*ibid.*, 275 [231]).

7   Derrida explicitly refers this gesture to his discussion of J.-P. Richard in 'The Double Session' (D, 199–317 [172–286]), the other text in which the notion of syntax is most clearly foregrounded. See my discussion in 'Derrida's Mallarmé', Chapter 4, above.

8   This usage of the term 'grammar' is unusual in Derrida, but encourages the thought that the sense of 'syntax' being developed here could interestingly be compared with Wittgenstein's notion of 'Philosophical Grammar', a comparison that Hobson does not explicitly entertain, in spite of several references to Wittgenstein.

9   For a generalisation of the structure of 'is and is not' here, see Derrida's paper 'Et cetera', forthcoming in N. Royle (ed.), *Deconstructions* (London: Macmillan, 2000).

10 See especially GEN, for example p. 7: 'there is no genesis without an absolute origin … but … every genetic product is produced by something other than itself'.

11 For example, 'In the beginning was the telephone' (UG, 80 [AL, 270]), or 'In the beginning was the pardon' (DM, 209: this part of the text is not included in the English translation).

12 GR, 88 [60]; quoted by Hobson, p. 28.

13 This essential 'escaping' of the thing itself, which Derrida works to generalise in VP, is probably what motivates Lévinas's rather laconic description of Derrida's achievement as involving a demonstration that *all* concepts (in the Kantian sense) are really Ideas (in the Kantian sense), just because the validating, fully present intuition is, supposedly, shown *always* to be postponed to infinity in Derridean *différance*.

(Emmanuel Lévinas, 'Jacques Derrida: Tout Autrement', in *Noms Propres* (Montpellier: Fata Morgana, 1976; rpt. Paris: Le Livre de Poche, 1987), 65–75.)

14 Hobson in this context explicitly signals a disagreement with my 1988 paper 'Deconstruction and the Philosophers (The Very Idea)': she quotes me as claiming that '*différance* just is the postponement to infinity of the Kantian Idea'. But in fact that is the (Lévinasian) construal I am there explicitly contesting – the phrase she quotes appears in the following context: 'put bluntly, a very common misconception of what Derrida is about, which Lévinas's comment runs the risk of reinforcing, could lead to a version of deconstruction which assumes that *différance* just is the postponement to infinity of the Kantian Idea. This misconception would be encouraged by the insistence on finitude we have so far been inclined to accept.' (*Legislations: the Politics of Deconstruction* (London: Verso Books, 1994), 40.) So it looks as though we really agree …

15 See for example M, 375 [316].

16 See especially AP.

17 This being already the point of the infamous slogan 'infinite différance is finite' at the end of VP.

18 This apparent tension between logic and history is constant, and explicit in Derrida. Is it by accident that one of the texts in which it is explicit is 'The White Mythology', where a logical argument is followed by a long historical excursus? See too ESP, 24 [8–9] and especially FL, 48 [957–9]: 'In general, deconstruction is practised in two styles, that most often are grafted one onto the other. The one has the demonstrative and apparently non-historical look of logico-formal paradoxes. The other, more historical or more amnesiac, seems to proceed by textual readings, minute interpretations and genealogies. Allow me to indulge successively in these two exercises' (48). In 'Derridabase' (JD, 122–3 [127–9]) I try to suggest that the coexistence of these two 'styles' just is constitutive of deconstruction.

19 This is of course already the question in the opening of 'La structure, le signe et le jeu dans le discours des sciences humaines', in ED, 409–36 [278–293]. See especially the remark on p. 409 [279]: 'And still today a structure deprived of any centre represents the unthinkable itself.'

20 For an accessible account, see James Gleick, *Chaos: Making a New Science* (London: Heinemann, 1988). 'Attracteurs étranges' appears to be the 'normal' French translation of the expression 'strange attractors'.

21 SCH, esp. ch. 2. For example: 'These coded marks [i.e. dates in the standard calendrical sense] have a common resource but also a potential that is dramatic, fatal, fatally equivocal. Assigning or consigning absolute singularity, they must simultaneously, *at once* and of themselves, un-mark themselves by the possibility of commemoration. For they indeed mark only to the extent that their legibility announces the possibility of a return. Not the absolute return of the very thing that cannot return: a birth or a circumcision take place only once, that's obvious. But the spectral returning of the very thing that, as a once-off in the world [*unique fois au monde*], will never return. A date is a spectre' (SCH, 37 [317]).

22 This new insistence on the suffix '-bility' suggests the need to read the terms 'possibility' and 'impossibility' along the same lines: 'impossibility' would then already bespeak 'necessary possibility', the 'always perhaps not', as Hobson helpfully glosses it.

23 See the comments in POS, 55 [40].

24 FL, 35–6 [943–5].

25 See FL, 56–7 [965–7]: 'I would hesitate to assimilate too rapidly this to a regulative idea in the Kantian sense, to any content of a messianic promise (I say *content* and not form, for all messianic form, all messianicity is never absent from a promise, whatever it be) or to other horizons of the same *type*. And I am speaking only of a *type*, of this type of horizon of which there may be many concurrent species. Concurrent, i.e. quite similar and always claiming absolute privilege and irreducible singularity. The singularity of the historical situation – perhaps ours, in any case the one I'm obscurely referring to here – allows us to glimpse the type itself, as the origin, condition, possibility or promise of all its exemplifications (messianism or determined messianic figures of jewish, Christian or islamic type, Idea in the Kantian sense, eschatoteleology of neo-Hegelian, Marxist or post-Marxist type, etc.). It also allows to perceive and conceive a law of irreducible concurrence, but from an edge where vertigo is awaiting us at the moment when we can see only examples and when some of us no longer feel engaged in the concurrence: another way of saying that we always run the risk, henceforth (I'm talking for myself) of no longer being, as we say in French, "in the race". But not being "in the race", in a lane, does not permit one to stay at the starting line or simply be a spectator, far from it, on the contrary. Maybe just that is what, as we also say in French, "makes you run" more strongly and rapidly, for example deconstruction.'

26 See too the analyses of the decision as always decision of the other (in me) in PA, 86–8 [67–9].

27 See FL, 37–8 [947]: 'An experience is a crossing, as its name indicates, it crosses and journeys towards a destination toward which it finds the passage. Experience finds its passage, it is possible. Now in this sense, there can be no full experience of the aporia, i.e. of what does not let one through [*ne laisse pas le passage*]. *Aporia* is a non-path. Justice would from this point of view be the experience of that of which we cannot have an experience ... / 2. But I believe that there is no justice without this experience, impossible though it be, of the aporia. Justice is an experience of the impossible.' See too the much longer exposition of aporia in AP, 32 ff. [12 ff.]. We might wonder whether it is by chance that, if we looked for an earlier *analogon* of this position of the aporia in Derrida's later work, we would no doubt find none other than the Idea, at least as it appears in Husserl. See especially OG, 151–2 [138]: 'It is no accident if there is no phenomenology of the Idea. The Idea cannot be given in person, it cannot be determined in a self-evidence, for it is merely the possibility of evidence and the opening of the 'seeing' itself; it is merely *determinability* as horizon of every intuition in general, invisible *milieu* of seeing ... ', and 'The Idea is that on the basis of which a phenomenology is instigated to accomplish the final intention of philosophy [remember this expression 'final intention']. That a phenomenological determination of the Idea itself be, thereafter, radically impossible, signifies perhaps that phenomenology cannot reflect itself in a phenomenology of phenomenology, and that its *Logos* can never appear as such, never give itself to a philosophy of seeing, but only, like all Speech, give itself to be heard through the visible' (155 [141]). Derrida also identifies here 'the ethico-teleological prescription of the infinite task', and, in a note, claims that this Idea 'is the common root of the theoretical and the ethical' (149 n. 1 [136 n. 162]). The motif of the *call* can also be found here (155 [141]), as in FL (38 [949]). See my further discussion of these issues in Chapter 10, above.

28 VEP, 95–135 [83–118], and especially 108 [95]. 'Pas' in PAR, 9–116. The 'sans sans sans' formulation can be found on p. 92.

29 See, for a refutation of the common misconception, the 'Beyond' section of 'Derridabase' (JD, 95–100 [98–104]).

30 ED, 55 n. [308 n. 4]. The passage in PAR, commenting a usage of the 'expression' 'Come' at the end of *L'arrêt de mort*, is arguing that 'Come' here is not to be understood as a modification of the verb 'To come', but rather as withdrawing 'something' from any thetic positing, and goes on: '*Come* gives no order, it proceeds here from no authority, no law, no hierarchy. I stress *here*. And to recall the fact that it is only on the condition of a context, here Blanchot's story, that a "word", ceasing to be quite a word, disobeys the grammatical or linguistic, or semantic prescription that would assign it to be – here – imperative, present, in such and such a person, etc. Here is a writing, the riskiest there is, withdrawing something from the order of language that it bends in return to that something with a most gentle and inflexible rigour. But what can be withdrawn in this way? "Thought"? A thought "outside language"? That would be something to scandalise a certain modernity. That's a risk to be run, the price to pay for thinking otherwise the "outside language" of thought' (26, partially quoted by Hobson, p. 212, who gives 'dense and inflexible', misreading 'douce' as 'dense').

31 See, for example, GR, 25 [13].

32 This is what allows Derrida to write in 'Circumfession', 'it's enough to recount the "present" to throw G.'s theologic programme off course, by the present you are making him, *Everybody's Autobiography*, yours which tells *you* so well … you are unrecognizable … ' (JD, 288–9 [311–12]).

INDEX

undecidable 7, 15, 16, 25, 27, 29, 49, 51,
    56, 108, 110, 123, 172, 175, 192, 200,
    208, 221, 224
urgency 24, 32, 79, 131, 136, 162–9, 172,
    176, 178, 179, 200

Valéry, P. 13, 14
Vattimo, G. 156
violence 28–30, 40, 42, 118–19, 122, 147,
    201, 204, 206, 207, 225

Wills, D. 45, 203, 224
Wittgenstein, L. 61, 68, 90, 196, 209, 227
Wolfreys, J. 77, 213, 215
worst, the 26, 40, 42–3, 161, 192
writing 8–11, 13, 15–6, 28, 29, 34–5,
    49–51, 55, 63, 77, 92, 115, 138, 168,
    180, 188, 200, 203, 207, 208, 225, 230
writing: archi-writing 10, 188

Zizek, S. 106, 107, 156, 215, 222